Things were not going according to plan for Hightower. Once again he had been thwarted. Ernie should have died instantly. Chris, when playing the scene in his mind, had envisioned a nice, clean one-shot attack with a minimum of blood and only a few seconds between pulling the trigger and the death of his enemy. Clean. Neat. Instead Ernie refused to roll over and die like he was supposed to. The man was stuck full of arrows, bleeding profusely, and still challenged the authority of Chris Hightower, mocking him! He would not tolerate that! Not today, not ever again. Ernie was supposed to die, and die he would!

Hightower dropped the crossbow and reached into his pocket, his fingers closing around the cold steel of the claw-tipped pry bar. He pulled it free and stepped between the two cars. Ernie had managed to wrest open the door of the Toyota and was half inside when Hightower overtook him with a combination bear hug and football tackle. Ernie tried to struggle but was too weak from the loss of blood, which was spraying around the car like a crimson fountain as his heart pumped madly. Chris raised the pry bar and struck heavily on Ernie's head as he crawled on top of him. The arm went up and he delivered a second blow, and a third, a fourth. . . .

Death of an Angel

DON DAVIS

For Artice and Oden

Acknowledgments

This book is the result of many voices. More than a hundred people were interviewed in three states, and hundreds of relevant documents and microfilm records were examined, in addition to attending an eight-week trial.

Still, the reader will find a few gray areas, for the deeper one goes into this event, the more complicated it becomes. The only person who knows everything is currently serving two life terms without parole and had absolutely no input into this project.

I have changed the names of a few individuals who became involved with Christopher Hightower through no fault of their own. Names that have been changed include Ellen Crown and her daughters, Debra and Donna, Hightower's two sons, John and William, and Susanne Henderson, Daniel Wagner, John DeSistine, James Romano, Jerry Molina, Rollo Caffarelli and Steve Bracchi. Facts concerning them are as stated. Also, the scenes in the garage and basement of 51 Middle Highway were compiled through the theories of many investigators, available forensic evidence, and the testimony of witnesses. No one will ever know for certain what happened on that horrible weekend.

I owe a great debt to many people in bringing this story to print. Ken Franckling, a friend of two decades and a fine writer himself, furnished extraordinary assistance over a period of months. Mike Stone and Pat Youngs were generous with their guidance, and Bob George made time for me throughout the trial. Their level of cooperation is as unusual as it is valuable. Ted Salad of the CIA provided significant insight. Major thanks to Doug Badger, Mike Quinn, and Jim Lynch of the Rhode Island State Police, and to John Lazzaro, Gary Palumbo, and Ken Schauble of the Barrington Police Department. Equally helpful were the friends and relatives of the Brendel family, particularly Arthur and Fred Bobb in Florida. Mary Lou Slicker and the White Church Sewing Circle shared information and Girl Scout cookies.

The residents of Barrington, Rhode Island, who welcomed me into their homes and lives, deserve special recognition for helping sort out details of this dreadful crime. Without their kindness, the book could not have been written.

Finally, I would like to thank Robin, my wife and editor, who makes all things possible.

Book One

1

Vikings

They materialized from the chill fog like ghosts from an ancient past. The *Gaia*, *Saga Siglar*, and *Oseberg*, their dark sails bellied out before a northwesterly twenty-knot wind, were shadows against a dreary morning sky. Pointed bows knifed effortlessly through rolling four-foot seas, and low hulls lunged forward, hunting shelter from the stinging rain that lashed the Rhode Island coast. The Vikings were coming.

Captain Ragnar Thorseth had nursed the *Gaia* from Norway to Greenland to Canada, retracing the sea route that Viking explorers such as Leif Ericsson may have traveled a thousand years before. The other ships joined him along the way and they rode the heavy swells left over from Hurricane Bob to arrive off Brenton Point right on schedule.

As they swung into East Passage, the Newport Artillery Company slammed out a thirteen-gun salute from its antique Paul Revere cannon. The retort rolled over the water along with the cheers of six hundred people lining the shore at 10:00 A.M. on that wet Friday, September 20, 1991.

Up on the bluff of Brenton Point State Park was a yellow school bus, its windows foggy from the breath of about sixty excited children squirming inside. Each year the Alternate Learning Program class at Primrose Hill School in Barrington, twenty-five miles from Newport, chose a foreign land to study. Last year it was England, with tales of castles and dragons. This year Scandinavia had been picked, and the red and blue flag of Norway was tacked to a classroom wall. When the Norse ships planned to call in Newport as part of a program dreamed up by a Norwegian cruise line, there was no doubt the ALP class would have a field trip.

The three ALP teachers put together a package of information. In addition to the permission slips the parents had to sign, there was a newspaper clipping about the event, pictures of Viking ships, information on lunch, and advice on how the kids should dress. It also explained that students would get out of school later than usual on Friday because of the travel.

Early on that Friday morning, eight-year-old Emily Brendel bounded from bed in her second floor room at the rear of a broad white house located at 51 Middle Highway. While her mom made a point of neatness elsewhere in the house, Emily's room remained in comfortable chaos, the lair of a young child. She pushed aside her favorite white blanket, which she called "Blankie" because it was more of a friend than a piece of cloth, and pulled together her outfit for the day: size eight white panties with little red hearts, light blue jeans with zippers at the ankles, a pink turtleneck sweatshirt, and a white sweater emblazoned with the cartoon characters Minnie and Mickey Mouse. On her feet were white socks and a pair of L.A. Gear white sneakers with sparkling laces. She would put on a pale green jacket before leaving the house. Emily brushed her teeth, gave her short brown hair a quick brushing, and satisfied, smiled at her reflection in the mirror with her hazel eyes.

At eight her father loaded his excited daughter into the red Toyota sedan parked beside the front porch and drove the few hundred yards down Middle Highway to the brick school. The bus was waiting, and Emily piled aboard with her ALP friends. A sticker with her name printed on it was pasted to her jacket. With teachers and chaperons, the bus set off for Newport.

It was the stuff of dreams for the energetic little girl whose name was shortened by her friends, who called her Em. Not only was she off to see real Vikings, but there was Newport itself, with its chic red-brick waterfront shopping district and the huge mansions that hid behind iron gates and generous sloping lawns, giant places as big as a child's imagination.

But today belonged to the Vikings, who were about to drop anchor near the place where unknown souls in a distant age had built the Old Stone Mill, a round tower on eight pillars of weathered rock. Historians say it was constructed by Vikings in the twelfth century for their Norse gods. As the low ships drew near, the parked school bus rocked on its wheels and tilted as the kids all surged to one side, noses pressed to frosty, closed windows.

When the three boats faded from view, the children reluctantly returned to their seats and the bus took them down to the wharf, where the ships tied up. Under the watchful eyes of their escorts, the ALP students walked around, took photographs, and asked a barrage of questions of Norsemen wearing furs, sailors from warships, men dressed in American Colonial Militia uniforms, and people posing as Native Americans. The hodge podge mixture of music, cultures, and dress worked because it was fun. By 2:00 P.M., when it was time to head back to Barrington, the ALP troop was a tired bunch of kittens. A photograph shows Emily sitting on the grass beside the old fort, surrounded by classmates in various forms of foul-weather gear. She is in the front row, eyes squinting to her left. Her thick hair, parted in the middle, is disheveled, a slight smile brightens her face, and she clutches a wad of tissue.

Back in Barrington, Primrose Principal Elizabeth Durfee was out in the parking lot to watch the other Primrose students leave classes for the day, departing with parents, boarding school buses, or heading for day care centers until their families could pick them up. The school had a specific list of who could meet a child, and

Durfee was adamant that every kid be watched until they were safely away. A slight problem had emerged. Although Emily's parents approved the class trip, her father had telephoned a secretary at the school about 1:00 P.M. to authorize Durfee to let Emily walk home today. Without further confirmation, Durfee decided to keep Emily on the preapproved schedule.

The bus from Newport pulled into the lot at 3:00 P.M. and the ALP kids came off in a rush, to be parceled out to their respective destinations. Durfee picked the little girl she was looking for out of the jostling crowd. "Emily, your dad called and said he wanted you to walk right straight home." A teacher standing on the school property could have watched Emily walk all the way to the front door of her two-story white colonial home.

The child scrunched her eyebrows, looked puzzled at the unexpected rearrangement of schedule. Her father was a lawyer, her mother a librarian. Plans and schedules in the family were firm. "That can't be right, Mrs. Durfee. I know I'm supposed to go to the Y because it's gymnastics day."

"Let's call him." The principal smiled to put the little girl at ease. Inside Durfee's office, Emily took the telephone and punched in 246-1666, her home number, listened with a frown, then hung up. "He's not home, Mrs. Durfee. I only get the answering machine."

The school was emptying rapidly and the YMCA van pulled into the parking lot, making a late trip to Primrose to gather the ALP students who had gone to see the Vikings. Durfee made a choice. "I'll tell you what, Emily. You go on to the Y, and I'll leave a message on the answering machine that you're there."

The principal explained to Pam Poirier, the Y program director driving the van, that there seemed to be some confusion. Poirier told the principal not to worry. Emily would call home once she got to the Y.

Barrington is not a big place, and open roads have few signals to impede traffic. The van went straight down Middle Highway, turned left at Volpe Pond onto Maple

Avenue, then right onto West Street. Less than ten minutes after leaving the school, the van reached the sprawling YMCA building on the flank of Brickyard Pond. The kids hurried past the carved wooden double statue of an Indian brave with his hand on the shoulder of a child, burst through two sets of doors and turned to the big gymnasium, where others were already playing noisily in the School's Out program.

Emily, however, paused long enough in Poirier's office to call her home again. She again heard the answering machine message. Her father's brusque recorded voice said, "Hello, you have reached 246-1666. We're out right now. If you wish to leave a message, please wait for the beep."

When the tone sounded, she spoke. "Hi, Dad. It's me. I'm at the Y. What?" Nearby, Poirier whispered for Emily to say what time it was. "It's 3:25, and you called the school for me to walk home, but I came here." She hung up and ran toward the sounds of the gym.

Only a few minutes later the Brendels' red Toyota pulled into the lot and Christopher Hightower, a close friend of the family, strolled into the Y. He went directly into the day care room and found a counselor, then walked over to where Emily was playing with other children at a table. "Hi, Emily. Remember me? I'm Mr. Hightower." The muffled sounds of balls bouncing on hardwood courts and children's shouts provided an undercurrent of noise and he had to raise his voice to be heard.

Poirier, the program director, took Hightower to her office and pulled the cards listing who was authorized to pick up the children. She had sent several reminders for Emily's parents to update the list, but they had not replied. The last completed form was from 1989, two years before, and showed that Alice and Ernest Brendel, and Christopher Hightower, were the only people who could collect Emily from the after-school program. Hightower explained that Ernie was wrapped up in some important business work today and could not get away, then showed

Poirier the keys to the car that Brendel had loaned him for the errand. Still, Poirier was concerned. She would not allow Emily to leave, because Hightower did not have current authorization.

Hightower, a Sunday school teacher whose own family were longtime YMCA members, politely nodded, said he understood the dilemma, and left. Poirier notified her supervisor of the situation, then returned to work.

At ten minutes to four the telephone rang at the Y reception desk and was answered by Nancy Paiva. A male voice spoke. "This is Mr. Brendel. May I speak to Pam?" Paiva had frequently seen Ernie Brendel come into the Y, usually right at 5:10 P.M., but had never met him. She put the caller on hold, walked into the room where the kids were playing, but did not see the program director. Returning to the telephone, she said Pam could not be located. The caller seemed piqued. "Tell Pam that Mr. Hightower will be picking up my daughter Emily. He will have my license for ID."

Fifteen minutes later the Toyota rolled up again and Hightower walked inside, where Poirier asked how things had worked out. He smiled and displayed Ernest Brendel's driving license along with a handwritten note that said Emily could be released to his care. Poirier thanked Hightower for his patience, then called to Emily to leave her seat. On the signout sheet, beside the typewritten name of *Brendel, Emily*, is the autograph of Chris Hightower as the parent or guardian picking her up. Poirier also wrote her initials, PP. The time of departure was exactly 4:00 P.M.

Emily had known Hightower for much of her young life, and gave him a toothy grin. She had seen him working with her father, and they had even vacationed with the Hightower family in New Hampshire. Anyway, after the long day in Newport and exercising at the gym, she was ready to call it a day. That soft bed upstairs, her "Blankie," her pet turtle, her stuffed animals, dinner, and the twenty books she had recently checked out of the library were all calling to her. She left the YMCA hand in hand with Christopher Hightower.

Emily Brendel could not know that the kind man who was joking with her had already tortured and murdered her father and, within hours, would horribly strangle both her and her mother, and dump all of their bodies into shallow graves.

2

Rockets and Roundball

The path that led Christopher Jemire Hightower to those oblong graves hidden in the soggy brush of Barrington, Rhode Island, began more than four decades earlier on the hardscrabble east coast of central Florida.

He was born on the twentieth day of August in the year of 1949, one of those years that delights modern historians. The United States was on the cusp of change at the end of a decade that had been stamped forever as the time of World War II. Even with that holocaust over, the world still teetered on the edge of global chaos. Mao Tse-tung's Communists had taken control of China, Russia tested its first atomic bomb, and the United Nations set up shop in New York to watch a troubled world.

Change was everywhere. Women had become part of the work force during the war and were reluctant to return to the kitchen. They still wore modest calf-length skirts, but skimpy new bathing suits, called bikinis, were showing up on beaches. Radio was giving way to the excitement of television, where male viewers ogled the girls of Roller Derby and women tuned in a wavy-haired piano impresario named Liberace. *South Pacific* started a four-year run on Broadway.

Three major works of literature were published that year, two of them popular: *Death of a Salesman* and *Gentlemen Prefer Blondes*. The third piece was primarily aimed at an arcane scientific audience. *Space Flight—A Program for*

International Scientific Research, was written by Werner von Braun, one of the brainy German scientists who built the V-2 rockets for his Nazi masters. After the war, the U.S. brought over one hundred captured members of von Braun's team, listing the technically elite Germans as government employees instead of prisoners of war, settled them in strategic locations and let them resume their rocketry work.

Von Braun's dream of breaching the heavens was about to come true in a place where alligators, not people, reigned.

The scent of wild oranges had wafted out from the sun-drenched Florida coast in 1547, as Spanish explorer Ponce de Leon sailed north, toward establishing a colony at St. Augustine. He charted one particular outcropping, but didn't stop because the place had a decidedly swampy look about it. It became Cape Canaveral. The king in Madrid gave his court physician in 1818 the vast central coast of Florida, and the United States purchased it all in 1821.

Shielded by the cape from the angry Atlantic Ocean storms, a little village took root beside the Indian River after the Civil War, as Colonel Henry Titus established a settlement with a few hundred sturdy pioneers. People from the North might ride to Miami on the Florida East Coast Railway, but few would stop in the hot and dusty little town in central Florida.

Even as late as 1945, only 2,600 people had settled in the isolated place that was part tropical paradise and part devilish existence. Alligators snored in subtropical heat, snakes were everywhere, wild pigs grumped about in the underbrush, and mosquitoes swarmed in great clouds. Staying at the Hotel Dixie could be a survival adventure. Parboiled aviators at the only military base in the area, the Banana River Naval Air Station, christened their post the Bug Capital of the World.

Two months after Christopher Hightower was born in nearby Winter Haven, President Harry Truman activated the Joint Long Range Missile Proving Ground, putting the focus of rocket testing on the Florida coast, where scientists could aim over the entire Atlantic Ocean, and the earth's rotation added speed to a rocket going up on the easterly course.

Concrete pads were poured beside the old lighthouse, and on July 24, 1950, the countdown began for the Cape's first rocket, a Wac Corporal missile stuck atop an old German V-2. Fifteen seconds before launch, an alligator waddled into one of the shelters where the rocketeers were awaiting blast-off. But the count went on, and at 9:29 A.M. people around Cape Canaveral got their first glimpse of the future when a white rocket with big fins rode a needle of incandescent fire into the sky.

On the ground, civilians in Titusville and distant villages watched in awe as that first clumsy rocket roared away. Science had arrived on their doorstep, and their children were going to be swept along by the excitement of the newest frontier. Titusville doubled in size in eight years because of the space boom, but the scientists among its five thousand residents still derided the place as "a constipated village."

Nevertheless, government money poured in, while in Winter Haven, one hundred miles away, things were stagnant. One young couple, Margaret Lonell Weeks and her husband, James Robert Hightower, a printer, heard what was going on at the Cape and that money seemed more plentiful than orange trees. It was an attractive lure.

They had four children—Christopher Jemire, Paul Robert, Judy Gail, and Clara Lugene—little money, and a lot of anger. For the oldest boy, called Jemire at home and Jerry by his classmates at Elmwood Elementary and later at Westwood Junior High, friends were few. His home life, never the best, worsened when he discovered the man who was married to his mother, the man whose last name he bore, was not his real father. His real last name was Barber, not Hightower, and his mother never married the man by whom she had her first baby at the tender age of seventeen. She never had the chance to, for the man abandoned his pregnant girlfriend. To his everlasting shame, Christopher Hightower learned he was a bastard. The knowledge drove a wedge between him and the rest of the family.

Efforts by the strict stepfather to discipline the only one of Margaret's children who was not a true Hightower came with the lash of a leather dog leash. The punishment stoked a quiet anger within the youngster, who went along with the strict regime at home, tried to be the well-behaved child and stay out of trouble, and hated every minute of it. For the rest of his life Christopher Hightower would rebel against any rules that confined his actions. His home life bred an overwhelming determination to be better than his stepfather, to excel beyond the family's wildest imagination. He dreamed of being everything his absent father and punitive stepfather were not—reliable, industrious, respected, and rich.

By 1965 the lure of space work finally drew the interest of the out-of-work James Hightower to Titusville, and his stepson, Jemire, was more than ready to get out of Winter Haven, eager for a fresh start where nobody knew anything about him.

They moved into one of the many tracts springing up around the Cape, houses of stacked concrete blocks painted white or a bright pastel color. The Hightowers' new home was the color of the sand on which it stood and was located just west of Titusville, inland and away from the more expensive land near the water. It covered about 1100 square feet, had an open car port, and slick terrazzo floors in the two bedrooms, living room, and small kitchen. It soon would reek of cigarette smoke. The following year Margaret gave birth to her fifth child, another boy, Leroy Dale.

"The count is at T-minus-ten." The voice on the loudspeaker at Titusville High School was followed by a clanging of bells. "This is a fire drill." Doors banged open and students put down their books as excitement gripped everyone in the Spanish-style building. They gathered on the broad lawn and the dirt athletic field or hurried up the steps of the tall bell tower. Some just moved from their desks to the big windows on the second floor.

Everyone knew there was not really a fire. In fact, there was a scheduled launch of an American spacecraft from the Cape, and the kids at Titusville High had some of the best seats in the nation.

"The Apollo shots were spectacular and not something you would miss if you were right on the oceanside," one teacher recalled years later. You could look out over the red roof tiles of a restaurant across the road, over the brown-green waters of the Indian River, and see the giant Vehicle Assembly Building, where gantry cranes nursed the waiting rockets. By the time the students were in position, the countdown would reach its critical moment, and with a flash of brilliant light and a roar that set herons aflight, the rocket would ride a tail of fire into the bright Florida skies. "We could see it from the moment it came off the pad," a former student remembered.

The kids would watch the rocket soar out of sight, then return to class. In the 1960s there was no better science lesson anywhere than the launches the National Aeronautics and Space Administration conducted just across the river from Titusville High.

By 1966 the population of the little city blossomed to 27,493 people, most involved with the program at the Cape. As Titusville High expanded to meet the growth, student laziness became a thing of the past. The United States was in a Space Race with the Soviet Union, and NASA needed engineers. Where better to groom them than a place where they could study by the rockets' red glare?

"I came in from another school district, where I had been in an advanced math class," one former student recalled of those dizzy days. "When I got here, I was surprised to find that I was several lessons behind their normal class. They were writing the book as they went along, using mimeographed copies instead of a text."

The school system was hiring more science teachers, the curriculum was upgraded, and a full calculus course was offered. This was a time of opportunity, when someone with a bent for science could look forward to lucrative employment at the Cape.

Jerry Hightower was among the students who would dash outside to watch the launches, but while he was in the Science Club, his mind was not really on math and science. He had discovered something he enjoyed better, a place where a boy with a secretive background was *somebody*! He became an athlete, and the polished basketball courts and dirt baseball diamond attracted him far more than schoolwork. Rockets were nice, but roundball was better.

In his freshman year of 1965, the lanky boy joined the track team and began his love affair with basketball, actually making the varsity as only a skinny tenth grader wearing dark-rimmed glasses and a dour expression. Hightower, sturdy number 35 on the Titusville Terriers, is pictured in the *Oklawena*, the school yearbook, crouched low, as if guarding an opponent, his arms flung wide, feet ready to move. It was a good year and the team went 17–8 under the guidance of Coach Art Tolis, who would go on to gain a reputation at higher levels of basketball. Hightower appeared in the yearbook as both Jerry and Jemire, as if he did not know who he really was. A picture of him in an industrial arts class showed a youngster at a drafting board, hair slicked back and wearing a tie and sport coat. On the pocket was the school crest, in the middle of which is a rocket.

As a junior, Hightower stood five feet ten inches, wore the number 12 and enjoyed more time on the court and fewer minutes on the bench. He is shown in the *Oklawena* soaring into the air, guiding a basketball with his left hand. "He wasn't a scoring threat, but he was a good, scrappy hustler," recalled a teammate. While he might never light up the scoreboard, Jerry Hightower was becoming a reliable player who helped move the team. And move they did. Their record in his junior season was 20–5 and the following year they lost only a single game in the regular season. Hightower, a hustling, aggressive kid with the flat-top haircut and the black headband holding his big glasses in place, was accepted as a *player* if not as a star.

By 1967 Jerry Hightower was a senior and the yearbook photos show a young man brimming with new ability. In his formal senior picture he looks somewhat uncomfortable in a tuxedo jacket with a bow tie and button-down shirt. His hair, already showing a broad forehead, is combed back, parted on the left, and plastered in place with oil. It is his photograph among the varsity basketball team where one really sees the change. He has grown another inch, to five-eleven, and is pictured making a jump shot.

Although he still had not made the starting lineup, he was a terror coming off the bench for a team that was almost a dynasty in prep basketball, sometimes scoring more than a hundred points in a game. "Jerry was a raving wild man when he went onto the floor. He might foul out, but the guy he was assigned to guard would go back to the bench wondering who that damn guy was," said a teammate. "He could run like a damn fox and would dive through a set of bleachers for the ball. I hated to go against him, because I knew I wouldn't get anything done. Then he would come up to me and grin and say, 'I busted your ass out there today.' "

Jerry Hightower just could not be intimidated and would not accept defeat. Coach Tolis designed a special practice for his hot-shooting stars. They had to go one-on-one against Jerry Hightower, who regularly beat the hell out of them until Tolis called him off, fearful that one of his stars might suffer a broken bone while battling the kid with the big glasses.

Still, there was the iciness of the loner about Hightower. Success as a jock was not accompanied by popularity in a school where bubbling personalities seemed to flourish. One classmate was the effervescent Dennis Mahan, and another the smooth Bobby Davis. Both would change their names in later years, Mahan becoming Dennis Terio and making a hit of the television show *Dance Fever*. Bobby Davis became Brad Davis, a Hollywood movie star.

When the gang would cruise over to the Whataburger drive-in or hang out at the Dog and Suds, Jerry Hightower normally would not be present. He dated occasionally, but did not go steady. When someone would drive him home from a ball game, they never got inside the front door. It seemed that once he disappeared inside his home, he vanished.

"He wasn't unpopular ... but he was very stiff and rigid. You didn't really want to go out and extend yourself to become his friend," said a fellow student. Another commented, "Jerry was always pleasant and courteous, one of those clean-cut good ol' boys with a sense of humor. He could come to my house anytime."

That double image, like a view through a faulty mirror, would follow him through life. On the outside Hightower was calm and polite and easily liked. Inside, a private inferno raged.

His class graduated on Thursday, June 8, 1967, in ceremonies at Draa Field. The class flower was the Peace Rose, the colors were sky-blue and white, and the motto was, "Each step in life leads to a greater one." Exiting Titusville High School, Hightower owned a solid yearbook résumé: Interact Club 10; Track 10; Basketball 10, 11, 12; Science Club vice president 12; Lettermen's Club 12.

He had a reputation as a sharp student. "Not an El Braino and not a nerd, but he was definitely at a different level of education than most of us," said a classmate.

Another lifelong pattern was developing. Unknown to those who thought him to be among the best and the brightest, Jerry Hightower had almost flunked out. He made the graduation ceremonies by the skin of his teeth.

Despite his recognized athletic ability, his studious demeanor and his officer's role in the Science Club, Hightower had only gotten around to taking his final required mathematics course in his senior year. While others were pushing through calculus, he struggled mightily with basic algebra. Part of the problem was that he cut class so much, and logged fourteen absences that year from his required math class. He squeaked through with a D, the lowest passing grade, just enough to graduate. But the important thing was that he made it, and was able to smile to himself as he listened to class vocalist Rebecca Johnson sing "Born Free."

Six days later after the Class of 1967 graduated, *Mariner 5* blasted off from the Cape, en route to the planet Venus. There were no cheers from the bell tower. School was out. So was Jerry Hightower. High school done, he wanted to get the hell away from home.

3

Moving On

Art Tolis, the basketball coach at Titusville High School, was big, talented, and ambitious. After carving a winning tradition for the Titusville Terriers, he and his wife Julie launched a coaching career that would eventually find him work at such schools as Alabama, Tennessee, and Louisiana State University. It began with a first step, and that was leaving Titusville for a crack at college ball.

His target was just an hour down Interstate 95, in Fort Pierce, where the brand new Indian River Junior College had been bulldozed from the scrub brush at the corner of Virginia Avenue and Thirty-fifth Street. At IRJC, Tolis could hone his shoot-out-the-lights style of basketball.

The college conferred its first two-year degrees in 1962 and was still in its early phase of growth when it was decided in 1965 to field a basketball team. Since the average student at IRJC at the time was thirty-two years old and female, pickings were slim for players. The first intercollegiate team was made up of eleven older guys, many carrying extra weight around their chins and waists.

That kind of athlete went out the door as soon as Tolis from Titusville arrived in time for the 1966–67 season with his plan to jack the Indian River Pioneers into the junior college elite. His first squad went 19–10 and gained national ranking, but Tolis was unsatisfied. He already knew what major universities would discover a de-

cade later—that Florida's sunshine allowed young men
to play ball outside almost year-round, giving them a
competitive edge over boys from the cold weather states.
Tolis found promotional money for brochures and pa-
pered the Sunshine State in a talent hunt that paid bigger dividends every year. His 1969 team featured five
players who had earned all-state rankings in high school,
and at one point IRJC led the nation with a blistering
scoring average of 141.9 points per game.

That was yet to come, but Tolis lost no time laying his
foundation. He demanded *players* in his program, not
wannabes.

When Jerry Hightower graduated from Titusville High
in 1967, he knew what Tolis was building just down I-95.
The college wasn't much, but it seemed to offer him everything he wanted—a chance to play ball, an opportunity for some decent studying at a reasonable price, and
most of all, an escape from Titusville and the house on
Overlook Place. He picked up the telephone and called
his old coach. Tolis remembered the kid's determination
and told him to come on down to Fort Pierce and give
things a try. Some minor financial help was arranged.

The decision had the added attraction of a 2S draft
status, meaning that while he stayed in school, he would
not be swept into the Selective Service maw that was
sending young men to Vietnam.

In the fall of 1968 Hightower paid $275 for two semes-
ters and became a student in the premed program at Indian River Junior College. He moved into a dorm, got a
part-time job to help pay expenses, and began classes on
August 21, one day after he turned eighteen.

Pre-Med was little different than any other specialty
that year, as the freshmen students buckled down to general education courses, such as English, history, and biol-
ogy. But his course of study allowed him to speak grandly
about becoming a physician, and was a respectable facade behind which he could hide. In reality it was just a
dodge. Hightower was discovering that he had the ability

to charm people, to make them believe whatever he wanted, and he loved to argue with, persuade, and fool them.

He had come to IRJC to play ball for Tolis, although the coach had not actually recruited him. But when Jerry Hightower laced up his sneakers and ran onto the polished IRJC gymnasium floor, he discovered that aggressiveness and desire were not enough. Instead of facing high school kids, he was in a mirthless pit with older, tougher athletes. Now when he pushed, he got pushed back. Hard. "He was in over his head among some far superior athletes," recalled one player. "He didn't make the team."

Hightower's dream of playing college ball fizzled on that polished gym floor. He did not have a shooter's eye and could not stop taller, more talented players from running up the numbers on him, almost at will. Eventually he was cut from the brotherhood of jocks, a severe setback for someone who could not bear to lose at anything.

With his basketball career in ashes, he saw no reason to stay at IRJC. When final exams were over on Tuesday, April 23, 1968, Jerry Hightower quit, with transfer credits for only two courses—zoology and a freshman math elective. When the young man who liked to brag that he was studying to be a physician dropped out of school, he was already on academic probation.

Back in Titusville, Hightower got a job working in construction, helping build around the Cape area and hating it. His entire being was focused on what to do next. He damn sure wasn't going to stay where he was! A fresh, new start somewhere could set things right, he would think while wrestling a steel beam into place. A muscular guy, almost six feet tall, he would be able to work construction anywhere. It was a movable job.

A former IRJC roommate lived up in the Washington, D.C., area and urged him to come there, so in the summer of 1968 Hightower headed north, determined to put as many miles as possible between himself and his Florida failures. He never saw his stepfather alive again.

Hightower wound up living with a roommate in Arlington, Virginia, both of them working construction jobs around the nation's capital. He had money, freedom, and, for the first time, a busy social agenda on the D.C.-area nightlife scene. Best of all were the bull sessions, when Hightower could really fly. Those listening readily believed that this was a guy on his way to the top. They heard about his future, not his past.

There was a war going on, however, and no longer being in school had wiped out Hightower's draft exemption. His old IRJC roomie, Tommy, had been a Marine sergeant in Vietnam, and a new friend, Michael, served in Vietnam as a Navy corpsman. As an eligible single man, Hightower could see Vietnam looming ahead and knew it was better to *talk* about Vietnam than to *be* there. The bloody battles of Tet, in February of that year, had blown the glory right out of overseas duty. No thanks, said Jerry Hightower.

There were ways to solve his ripe-for-the-picking military status without becoming cannon fodder. Over and over in the discussions that filled long summer nights, he insisted to his buddies that his goal was to return to the classroom, not to tromp through rice paddies on the other side of the world.

The military services, hungry for volunteers as the Vietnam mess cycled higher, were offering attractive side benefits, such as money for a college education in trade for a few years in uniform. Why not enlist, his friends said, take advantage of the educational promises and choose which service to join? Why remain as draft bait and become an Army infantry grunt when, by enlisting, you could sleep on clean sheets and have stateside duty with the Navy? Why not, indeed, thought Hightower. It might provide that fresh start that had always seemed just beyond his fingertips.

In October 1968, as antiwar demonstrations wracked college campuses and the U.S. committed more than

500,000 men to the Vietnam grinder, Hightower enlisted in the Navy and penciled in the boxes that indicated that the trim recruit wanted to be a doctor.

For sixteen weeks, during the worst of winter, the boy from Florida, never so cold in his life, endured boot camp in Great Lakes Naval Training Center in Illinois. When he emerged as a full-fledged sailor able to tie knots and heave lines, the Navy assigned him to another sixteen weeks of training at Hospital Corpsman School. Completing that, in early 1969, Hightower received his Navy assignment. Not Vietnam. Not even on a ship. He was on his way to the sprawling Bethesda Medical Center in Maryland, back to the District of Columbia social swirl. He worked all over that huge hospital, where some of the most serious Navy and Marine casualties of Vietnam were brought for treatment. In the urology ward, on the neurology floor, and in the intensive care unit, Hightower saw the spectrum of severe wounds and understood fully that Vietnam simply was not good for one's health. Later in the year, he became an operating room technician and was assigned to assist surgeons in the operating theater at the Newport Naval Hospital in Rhode Island.

He was an anonymous and rather meek-looking sailor when he stepped from the bus on a fall day in 1969, just one of thousands of men at that big base. But twenty-two years later everyone in Rhode Island would know the name of Christopher Hightower.

4

Wedding Bells

Several periods in the life of Christopher Jemire Hightower remain unclear even today, after police have gathered every scrap of available information. The only person who knows the entire story is Christopher Jemire Hightower.

So it is with his first marriage. While he was stationed in Bethesda, Maryland, he courted an Asian girl, a petite woman-child with flowing black hair. Hightower bought her a diamond ring and married her, but the short relationship ended tragically when his young wife died while on a trip alone to visit her family in Malaysia.

For some reason never explained, the diamond ring that proclaimed their love was left behind in Maryland with the husband. Authorities looked into the mysterious disappearance, but no charges of wrongdoing were ever filed. While he told his family that he had wed the girl, Hightower never changed the marital status in his Navy records.

About the time he assumed his duties at Newport, Ellen Janet Crown, an attractive young woman who had been raised on New York's Long Island, took a nursing degree from Salve Regina College, a Catholic school in Rhode Island. She immediately enlisted in the Navy, was given an officer's commission and assigned as an obstetrics nurse at the naval hospital complex at Newport.

The excitement of her new duties, the work among

the new babies, and the role of being a naval officer
suited her well. An extra benefit for the young nurse was
the number of available men. Vietnam was still cooking
away, and that meant a steady stream of officers and
sailors passed through Newport.

Oddly, it wasn't any of the big-shot commanders and
admirals or foreign officers attending the Naval War
College who caught her attention. Instead she noticed a
quiet, mannered corpsman who worked in the operating
room. She did not like him at first, but his smooth talk
soon changed her mind. Although naval regulations pro-
hibit fraternization between officers and enlisted personnel, Ellen began to date the charming Chris Hightower.
Sharing hopes and dreams, she was fascinated by his apparent intelligence and his determination to improve
himself. He convinced Ellen that he planned to become
a physician, and, because of his own unhappy childhood,
that he desperately wanted to be a wonderful father.

Ellen, the product of a loving and supportive family,
was enchanted. Chris was about six feet tall, trim and
athletic, not bad-looking, and so what if he wasn't allowed in the Officers' Club, he was a good person. They
began to plan a future together after their military ca-
reers. Things would be good, he promised, real good. All
he needed was to get out of the service and start a professional life that could match his new personal happi-
ness.

Time passed quickly as the couple worked in the hospital
by day and spent as many off-duty hours together as
possible, not as officer and sailor, but as girlfriend-
boyfriend. By the time his enlistment was up in October
1972, their plans were firm.

Ever practical, they decided Chris would remain in the
Navy another three months to get one more promotion
and an increase in pay. When he was discharged in January 1973, he held the salary rank of E-5 and had spent
four years and three months in the Navy.

He no longer had to worry about that embarrassing

situation of Ellen being a superior officer. She stayed in
the Navy, but he was a civilian again, the equal of anybody! It was not long before they were sharing an apartment off base.

With his GI Bill, a woman working to support him, his
seven transfer credits from Indian River Junior College,
and seventeen educational credits from Navy schools,
Hightower was again ready to attack the academic world
and take that important first step toward becoming a
doctor. In the spring of 1973 he enrolled as a twenty-
three-year-old freshman at the University of Rhode Island in Kingston, choosing to major in zoology. The first
quarter was a snap, as he sailed through literature and
chemistry with A grades, and logged a B in botany. Math
still gave him trouble, and he made a D in that course.

Wanting to get through school as soon as possible,
Hightower loaded on more subjects in the URI summer
program, and earned A's in three subjects, one B, one C,
and a cumulative grade-point average after three quar-
ters of 3.14 on a scale that measures 4.0 as perfect.
There was no doubt that things were going his way, although he was having to study, hold down part-time jobs
to bring in money, and keep his fiancée, Lieutenant
Ellen Crown, happy. Time had become a precious commodity.

In August 1973 Chris and Ellen were married in the
base chapel at Newport. On the third finger of her left
hand blazed a diamond ring, the same stone her husband had once given to the mysterious Malaysian bride
who vanished into thin air. For Ellen, the diamond she
wore so proudly proclaimed that she was not only a naval
officer, but also the wife of an aspiring medical student,
a man who was rising above his dirt-poor beginnings and
was on his way to becoming a doctor!

The happy couple moved into an apartment on Meikle
Avenue, and Chris returned to school the next month
and almost immediately began a strange metamorpho-
sis.

Now that he was in school, now that he was wed—two

things that he insisted were the highest goals in his life—he felt tied down by stupid academic rules and by Ellen's demands at home. There was very little spare time, and despite the occasional outings and the bike rides to the lake, Ellen began to notice how her husband was irritable and not above complaining about the way she did things. Yes, he knew she loved him and had married him, but did she *accept* him, unconditionally, just as he was? He remembered the family in Florida. They were supposed to love him too, and look what happened. Ellen would just have to understand that he was not like everyone else. Chris Hightower had a destiny. He needed room to move.

Ellen, a college graduate and a successful naval officer, played down her own accomplishments before her husband, who was still beginning his college career. She didn't have to say a word. Chris was more than aware of his shortcomings.

His grades began a steep slide, and the fall semester of 1973 brought two A's, a single B, and three C's. The couple, trying to live only on her salary, surrendered the apartment and moved into Navy housing, where they could get a break in rent because she was still in uniform. The move to 327 Davis Street didn't help and in the spring semester of 1974, Hightower's grades collapsed into a pair of C's and a pair of D's. He could see his dream of becoming a doctor fading beyond his limited educational abilities.

With the resilience of the young, they stuck it out. Chris stayed in school while Ellen continued nursing for the Navy. His grades slipped further, and he now brought home the baggage of the bad student—C's, D's, incompletes, audits, and excuses.

Still, they looked ahead. Things would get better, they believed, for at least they were together. In November of his final year at school, the Hightowers bought a home at 9 Bedlow Place in Newport. In that fall semester of 1975, his last, Hightower failed his first course, Intermediate German.

On December 27, two days after Christmas, he graduated with a bachelor's of science degree in zoology. He
had exited URI with a cumulative grade point average of
2.44, slightly better than average, and had crammed four
years of work into two years of study.

There was little time to rejoice. Chris Hightower
seemed to be on a treadmill, running faster and faster.
Getting out of school should have been a time for relax-
ation and fun, but such was not the case.

Ellen was pregnant and ready to resign her commission, which meant an end to her Navy paycheck. It was
time for her husband, the man she had put through college, to support his family. It was time for Chris
Hightower to get a job.

And it worked! Beyond all expectation, Hightower's
charm in a one-on-one interview, his service record as a
medical specialist working in of some of the Navy's most
prestigious hospitals, his college degree in science, and
his outspoken desire to become a doctor, paid off hand-
somely.

Hightower began work as a drug salesman for Riker
Laboratories, a leading pharmaceutical company. Things
were finally looking good. Ellen was making the transi-
tion from starched Navy officer to homemaker, and their
first daughter, Debra Leigh, was born.

Being a "field representative" seemed perfect. After
all, he had always looked up to doctors, and in recent
years told everyone who would listen that he would become a physician himself. Now, peddling prescription
drugs, he would be in hospitals, drugstores, and the offices of doctors in his region, seeing his dream world
work from the inside. The salary was $12,000 a year, plus
bonuses, commissions, and an expense account. Riker
even provided a company car. There was only one
problem—he hated the job. Cooling his heals in waiting
rooms was not his idea of a career.

Doctors can have few social graces for someone trying
to sell products. For Hightower it was mental torture to
scrape and bow before these people just because they

had that degree and he had encountered some problems in his own university career. He would show them!

For two years he made his rounds with decreasing interest. At home, education was also a topic, because Ellen was entering a program that would earn her a master's degree—which would once again put the wife a step ahead of the husband.

By 1978 he was fed up with Riker Labs. How dare they expect him to spin gold out of this pig's ear of a territory. He had more important things on his mind, and the salary wasn't all that good anyway. Ellen was pregnant again and giving him grief at home. She was particularly critical when he quit the sales job that spring, surrendering their medical benefits with another baby on the way.

About the time he became a father again, to another daughter, Donna Helene, Hightower heard about a management program being offered by the Newport Creamery, a restaurant chain in Rhode Island. By working there, one could pile up credits for a scholarship, which could again get him away from the daily grind and back into the world of academics.

He went to work for the company, which specializes in ice cream dishes and has the odd symbol of a Golden Cow as a logo. As a management trainee, Chris Hightower may have only been a glorified soda jerk, but he could dream of grander things.

He had a new idea, and began to paper the globe with applications for medical schools in such faraway places as Poland and Lebanon. If only he could get accepted somewhere, he would prove he could do the work, even if Ellen was openly skeptical about his grades being good enough for *any* medical school.

Meanwhile, the Newport Creamery was somewhat taken by the meticulous young man. He always seemed to run a good shift, although somewhat of a martinet with young employees, making them keep the knives and forks straight on the napkins, and insisting the restaurant be kept as clean as an operating room. They rotated him through several locations, from the main store in Middletown, to the North Dartmouth Mall, to the store just over the Rhode Island line in Swansea, Massachusetts.

Hightower had no more than started his new career when good fortune struck. A letter drifted back from one of those exotic medical schools—Christopher Jemire Hightower had been accepted into the medical program at the American University of the Caribbean.

The breakthrough! Medical school beckoned! Unfortunately, he had not been at Newport Creamery long enough to qualify for a scholarship, so he would have to come up with the cash. Chris had to convince Ellen they should sell the home and persuade her family or the stepfather whom he had not seen for years to kick in some cash. And he wanted to attend school down in the Caribbean alone. It came as a shock when Ellen said she was not enthralled by the idea of selling her home and moving into an apartment again with their two young children, but without him. His father-in-law flatly rejected the idea of a $12,000 loan, and he learned there would be no money coming from Titusville.

Almost as fast as his dream bloomed, it began to wither. It soon became plain that attending medical school beside the sandy beaches of the Caribbean was not going to happen, and his anger focused on Ellen's stubbornness. He began spending more and more hours at work, away from home, charming the young girls who waitressed for him at the Newport Creamery. His wife didn't understand his dreams and nagged him about money and living in a world of reality.

But the lithe young girls, particularly one beautiful dark-haired coed home from college for the summer, did. Maybe there could be a fresh start after all.

5

Slick

They fell in love beneath the sign of the Golden Cow.

Never in her eighteen years of life had Susan Slicker met anyone like Christopher Hightower. Mature, charming, intelligent, polite, smiling, well-groomed, educated, ambitious and exciting Chris. Married, family man, forbidden Chris. Her boss.

She was home in Barrington for summer vacation after her freshman year at Wittenberg University in Ohio and had taken a waitress job at the Creamery to fill the hours and earn a few dollars. She did not know when she walked into the little roadside restaurant in Swansea, just a few miles from her home, that her life was about to change forever.

Chris Hightower was in charge and she immediately liked him. He was direct and forceful, a man who knew what he wanted and went out and got it. She had dated boys before, but Chris was a man! He was thirty years old, and his sandy beard and eyeglasses, the conservative way he dressed, the methodical way he went about things, reminded her of men like her father, Clyde, who exhibited admirable control in the Slicker family's successful lives.

Hightower and Susan spent hours chatting away over coffee, sometimes long after the restaurant closed, and soon the two of them realized that something special was happening. She was entranced by his tales of derring-do, like driving those race cars and being in underwater warfare teams in Vietnam. She felt sorry for him when he recounted the horrible things he had experienced in his Navy career, and his air of quiet bravery and sensitivity impressed her beyond words. He did not smoke, drink alcohol, or do drugs, things that were all high priorities for the boys her own age. His courtly manners and soft, southern drawl told her that he was a gentleman.

Of course, Chris was still married, but he sheepishly confided to Susan, over the Formica table where they had coffee, that his wife didn't understand him. He loved his little girls, but his wife was just driving him crazy. Ellen was stubborn and selfish and stood in the way of him becoming a doctor. As weeks went by, Chris looked into Susan's dark eyes, told her there was no love left in his marriage and that the person he really, truly loved was sitting across the table from him at that very moment. She was dazzled.

Hightower was dazzled too, but from a more practical standpoint. For the girl with whom he was flirting was not just a teenybopper filling a summer job. Susan Elizabeth Slicker was one of the best catches in Barrington! He felt as if a pot of gold had been placed before him at the Newport Creamery, and he intended to grab on with both hands. Talk about Fresh Start potential!

It did not hurt that she was beautiful, with long black hair that fell below her shoulders, a slender figure, flashing eyes, and a smile that could break a heart. Called "Slick" by her friends, she had graduated the year before from Barrington High School, where she was a member of the National Honor Society on the scholastic side and Tri-M, the music honor society. She played the flute in the marching band, appeared in the International Thespian Society drama festival, and was so popular that the gang loved to party down over at Slick's house. Her 1979 senior yearbook, the *Arrow*, carried a line of description about her that read, "All can hear, but only the sensitive can understand."

Hightower's interest went beyond the girl's beauty and proper sense of fashion, to the standing her family enjoyed in the tight-knit Barrington community. The Slickers had everything in Barrington that the Hightowers never achieved in Titusville. There was plenty of money, a neat home on Chantilly Lane, and a sense of *belonging*. Clyde Slicker was a well-respected educator, the type of mild-mannered person that Hightower wished he could have had as a father. Susan's mother, Mary Lou, was a state official of the Girl Scouts and secretary of the Barrington Congregational Church, while at the same time lavishing love on her husband and daughters, Susan and Kathy.

As Chris drove home each night, back to that meager existence with Ellen and the kids, he would think about Susan, the entire Slicker family, the cordiality of moneyed Barrington. Just imagine being part of that. It was enough to make his head swim. He made up his mind that Susan was his ticket to respectability.

Ellen was patently suspicious about her husband's long absences and surly attitude. There was more to this constant bickering than just long hours at work and the usual marital disagreements. He was always chatting up the teenage girls at the restaurant, but had no male friends. Ellen suspected her husband was involved with another woman, and thought she knew who it was.

When Chris hosted a summer beach party for the Creamery crew in Newport, he had paid particular attention to a stunning, dark-haired girl named Susan. Chris denied anything improper and said the girl was just one of the many employees who worked for him. It was with a sense of satisfaction that Ellen learned that with the end of summer, the girl went back to school in Ohio, far away from her husband.

Still, things went from bad to worse in their relationship. After seven years of marriage she was aware of her husband's mercurial temperament, his willingness to find the easy way out of things, his refusal to take re-

sponsibilities seriously. Ellen considered Sue to be only a
peripheral issue in the crumbling marriage, and silently
yearned for a simple, normal life.

Chris was sullen and they argued frequently. Ellen actually began to fear for the safety of herself and the girls
one day when Christopher did something that was totally unlike him. The quiet man suddenly exploded.

They had two female dogs. A neighbor's male dog,
which had impregnated one of the females the previous
year, came sniffing around again. Chris erupted in anger,
grabbed a shovel and attacked it. He bashed its head
and rained blows along its body, the dog crying out in
pain but unable to escape. It was horribly crippled, man-
gled, and finally, dead. Chris, breathing heavily from his
labors and clicking his jaws in anger, stuffed the corpse
into a box and threw it away. Horrified, Ellen wondered
if what happened to the dog might happen to her.

Beyond their house, her husband remained busy at
pursuits other than his job. Susan made frequent visits
from Ohio, visits that meant hours of stolen, forbidden
magic between them. His dreams were no longer of his
wife and family, but of the lure of Barrington respectability.

The Christmas holidays of 1980 were the end of the
line as far as Ellen was concerned. She had told him in
November to make up his mind whether he would be a
father and husband or go off to live as a bachelor in the
Caribbean. She did not demand the divorce herself, for
fear of how he would react. While not outwardly violent,
Ellen knew that when Chris became icy cold and quiet,
as he was when discussing their marriage, danger lurked
not far below the surface. Despite the emotional abuse,
she would not back him into a corner. Let the decision
be his.

In January 1981 she got her answer. Chris said he was
heading off to medical school, so Ellen initiated divorce
proceedings, citing irreconcilable differences. Hightower
was ordered by the court to make child support payments, and was allowed to visit Debbie and Donna. To

his chagrin, the proceeds from the house went to support his family. To her chagrin, Chris swore to the court that he was broke, then went out and bought a new car.

The divorce became final in April. Ellen and the girls moved back to Long Island, while Hightower, instead of going to medical school in the balmy Caribbean, moved in temporarily with Susan and her family in Barrington. By June he and Susan relocated to a little apartment in Fairborn, Ohio, as she continued her studies and Chris prepared to reenter academia. Ironically, he would be studying again around the edges of the space program, because they would both attend Wright State University, only a stone's throw from the sprawling Wright-Patterson Air Force Base, a training arena for astronauts and test pilots. Lacing through the community was a main highway named in honor of Marine Colonel John Glenn, one of the original Mercury astronauts launched from those concrete pads near Titusville.

For Susan and Chris, their living arrangement was perfect in that gritty Dayton suburb. As she finished her junior year at Wittenberg University, she planned a wedding while he set about getting admitted to school. Transcripts were needed, and glowing letters of recommendations, if he had any hope of winning a slot in the combined program that could win him a master's degree and a doctorate at Wright State. After graduation, Susan would work at Wright State and study psychology while her husband would attack the biomedical sciences. They would live together, go to school together, make love together, visit her family in Barrington together.

It was Christopher Hightower's dream. He could set aside past failures and get on with the bright prospects in his life. In Florida he had been held back by his family, in the Navy by the system, in his professional life by stupid bosses, in his first marriage by Ellen. Now he could focus. He would dote upon the lovely Susan and earn those elusive academic honors that would admit him to the world of science. He would not be a physician, but upon finishing the Ph.D. program, he would be addressed as "Doctor Hightower." That would be just as good. He could be a skilled researcher and bow to no man. Christopher Hightower felt part of a special intelligentsia, for while his abilities had stumbled, it was not through any fault of his own. That was something others had inflicted upon him, and now he was free to soar to his rightful position, a lofty place from which he could look down with disdain on everyone else.

On July 10, 1982, when he waited at the altar and watched his beautiful young bride-to-be, twenty years old and a vision in white, walk slowly up to him at the Barrington Congregational Church, Hightower felt his heart surge. Clyde Slicker proudly gave the hand of his daughter to the impressive thirty-two-year-old man who had already become like a son to him. Some 150 persons packed the White Church, as the historic house of worship was known, and summer sunlight streamed through narrow windows of stained glass. Barrington was offering total acceptance to Chris Hightower, who had been born dirt poor. By becoming part of the Slicker family, he would be part of this unique community. The outsider became an insider, something that all of the guests that day eventually would regret.

There was a silent warning that things were not as they seemed. On the bride's third finger, left hand, glittered a diamond ring, its stone well-traveled. After his divorce from Ellen, Christopher Hightower had stolen her wedding ring, popped the gem free and again had it reset. Susan was the third Hightower wife to wear the same rock.

6

Ratsicles

No sooner had Christopher Hightower gotten the just-exactly-perfectly-right things he wanted, than life would immediately go to hell in a hand basket.

Susan was bubbling with excitement as the newlyweds arrived back in Ohio, ready to resume their studies. Even as a child she enjoyed being right in the thick of things, but soon after her wedding, she noticed that it was Chris, not her, who had to be the center of attention. She didn't mind, because she was head over heels in love with the guy. And he was in love too. She mistakenly assumed that it was with her.

Hightower actually was in love with his work at Wright State, where he could don a white laboratory apron and play with his experiments or listen to lectures from erudite professors. At that level of education, teachers and the students mingled rather freely, each accepting, as fact, that the other had paid the educational dues to be where they were. Hightower would spend long, long days and nights in the dark brick building that housed the Department of Biomedical Sciences. He actually wanted to be next door, in the soft-carpeted School of Medicine, with the bronze bust of Hippocrates in the courtyard, but the workmanlike spaces of the biomed center were a terrific alternative.

He charmed his fellow students and his professors and totally immersed himself in the laboratory work, where he chose to examine the water weight of baby rats as his master's degree project. Some of his little subjects, after being dissected, were wrapped in plastic bags and placed in the lab freezers for later examination. Their tails, exposed, froze stiff, and Hightower told visitors the little corpses were his "ratsicles."

But despite his bravado and hard work, the man who considered himself brilliant was having difficulty with the scholastic work. The hours he spent at school were directly subtracted from the hours he could spend at the side of his latest wife. Even after they bought a modest home at 1812 Elsemere Avenue in July 1983, Christopher did not lighten his work load. He could not afford to! He had to keep the grades up to be a success. Home had to take second place for now, while he achieved his life's ambition. Susan would just have to understand.

Atop the other pressures he was feeling came a totally unexpected shock. His stepfather was dying of cancer in Florida. Christopher had not seen the man for more than a decade and was surprised to find himself upset by the news. He had never had a chance to sit down with the stepfather whose name he bore and resolve the many issues that separated them. He wanted to be able to say, "Look at me, Dad. Look at my pretty wife and beautiful kids. Look at my position as a graduate student in a fine university. Look at what I've accomplished!" And Hightower wanted his stepfather to acknowledge it all, give him pats on the back, and to say, "You did good for yourself, Jemire. You did your family proud." Most of all, he wanted his stepfather to say, "I'm sorry, boy. I love you." It didn't happen.

But the sorrow of death was replaced by the joy of a new life. On April 4, 1984, less than a year after Susan and Chris moved into the Elsemere Avenue home in zip code 45406, they became the proud parents of a son, and named him John. Susan felt that the boy would reel Christopher away from the test tubes and statistics in the laboratory and restore normalcy to their home. She was wrong.

When Christopher was home, he enjoyed sitting in front of the TV set, doing nothing. When he wasn't hitting the books or dashing out the door again to feed and weigh those damned rats, his behavior was rigid. Those endearing little traits she first enjoyed during their Newport Creamery romance days, when Chris made waitresses keep the silverware squared with the napkin edges, were now hated jibes. It seemed that nothing she did was right. He found fault with the way the house was cleaned, the way the baby looked, the way she dressed. Calm and polite to outsiders, at home he might shout at her, accuse her of marital infidelity and all sorts of things. He would later say that he had to keep Susan on "a tight rein" during this portion of their marriage. This was not the way love was supposed to be, she confided to friends and family. How had things gone so wrong, so quickly. Where did my Chris go? Who *is* this man?

His superiors at school were wondering somewhat the same thing. He was obviously having to throw his whole life into the wringer just to keep up. And he showed extraordinary lapses of judgment, like bringing his baby son into the lab and placing the infant's carrier on a table while experiments were conducted. They began to doubt that Hightower could meet the requirements to continue in the program.

Things boiled over early in 1985. Hightower published his master's thesis, a word-choked, forty-eight-page document entitled "Body Water and its Distribution in Neonatal Rats: The Effects of Adrenalectomy and Adrenalectomy with Aldosterone and/or Corticosterone Replacement." It was dedicated "To my mother for her support and belief in higher education. Also to my wife Susan for encouraging me to return to school and for providing the support and understanding necessary to complete my studies. Finally, to our children . . . for they have had to do without while I succeed." His name was stamped in gold on the glossy black cover.

He didn't exactly succeed. The data, the long bibliography, and the declaration of how his study could be the

first to show "corticosterone may have biological activity
in fluid volume regulation in the 12-day-old neonatal rat,"
might have impressed a layman, but it was nothing special to the faculty. The thesis was accepted and he passed
the written exam by a slight margin to get the valued
master's of science degree. But now he faced the major
hurdle, oral and written examinations to continue in the
Ph.D. program. This was something that he could not
charm his way through, and all the dead rats in the world
couldn't help him. Knowledge alone would get him to the
next level. If he wanted to become *Doctor* Hightower, he
had to pass those exams looming in the fall. Nobody
knew more than Christopher Hightower that he wasn't
up to the challenge. Then the darndest thing happened.

On the morning of March 5, Susan, pregnant with her
second child, took little Johnny off to day care as usual,
shortly after seven o'clock, then went on to school herself. Chris was at home, alone, when she left. While in
class, she was called to the telephone and a neighbor
told her their house was on fire. Susan dashed across the
WSU campus to find her husband, but he was not in his
office, so she quickly drove away to pick up the child.
When she called from the day care center, Chris had
reached his office and they went home, to find clouds of
heavy, oily smoke rising into the sky. Fire department investigators figured the flames started in the basement as
a result of spontaneous combustion between a bag of fer-
tilizer and an open can of motor oil. When Susan and
Chris finally entered the house, they had to slosh
through several inches of standing water. The combined
damage from the fire, smoke, and water had left the
place a shambles. But they were lucky. Despite a few
structural problems, the insurance adjustor said it could
all be repaired. They still had their home, and he wrote
them out a check.

Not only that, but Hightower would convince the biomed faculty at Wright State to postpone the dreaded
oral examination. How could someone facing such a personal crisis deal with the stressful academic exam? It

would be unfair, a committee decided. He would be given more time to prepare.

Money had been extremely scarce around the Hightower household for some time, and the dollars from student loans, the GI Bill, and a graduate fellowship would not make ends meet. The couple even had to borrow money from Susan's sister to pay the hospital bills when Johnny was born, and that fire insurance check from Allstate was most welcome.

So, two weeks later, the darndest thing happened. Again.

The family had moved into an apartment while the house was being repaired. Before moving out, Chris had stacked all of their remaining belongings in the middle of the living room. It was safer that way, he said. In the middle of the night they received a telephone call from the fire department. Fire had again struck the house on Elsemere Avenue, this time causing even more substantial damage. Arson investigators sifted through the ashes and declared that the flames had been deliberately set at four different places in the cellar. Gasoline cans bearing the fingerprints of Chris Hightower were found nearby. This time the Hightowers arrived to find not only a ruined house, but that everything they'd stacked in the living room had been stolen.

Later that night, the two were escorted down to the police station for questioning. Skeptical investigators wanted Hightower to take a lie detector test. He refused, saying he had been asleep in the apartment when the fire started, his wife would vouch for him, and that was proof enough that he had done nothing wrong. Arson investigators considered him a suspect and would still question the origin of those flames years later, but no charges were filed. Allstate wrote out a bigger check.

At Wright State his professors began to wonder about the bad luck that was suddenly plaguing Christopher Hightower, who reported losing all of his notes, books, and research material in the second blaze. Without those, how could he possibly prepare for the examination? Like the cops, arson investigators, and insurance adjustors, the professors began to have suspicions of their own.

That really didn't matter. Christopher Hightower decided he was through with those jerks at the university anyway. He was smarter than they were, so he was going to quit playing their silly classroom and laboratory games and put his brilliance to work making money. Real money too, just like so many other people in the 1980s were doing.

On July 3, 1985, Susan Slicker Hightower gave birth to their second son, Robert. She delighted in her children, but her marriage wasn't turning out like the fairy tales at all.

Spending fifteen hundred of their precious dollars, Christopher went away to Chicago and attended a get-rich-quick course in the strange business of commodity and futures trading. Excited, he returned to Dayton and told Susan that their worries were over. School was leading nowhere in a hurry, he had the master's degree and didn't want to waste any more time letting stuffy professors thwart his ambitions. He was going into business for himself.

Christopher Hightower, never so enthused about anything in his life, was once again ready to make a brand new start.

7

Semper Augustus

Christopher Hightower chose to set up shop not as a tailor or an accountant or even in some trade remotely related to his scientific training in zoology and physiology. After all, that's what the Fresh Start was all about. Instead he picked the risky business of trading in commodities and futures, where almost everyone who invests loses money, as he would prove repeatedly in a checkered financial career.

In such a financial arena, an investor pegs his money to the future. It is a stroll along the razor's edge, with the promise of fortunes on one side, disaster on the other, and an uncomfortable area in between. It is not rocket science, and almost anyone can become a commodities broker. Shysters operate alongside serious business types and it is almost impossible to tell the difference. The common link is money.

For Hightower the lure was pure and simple. As a successful broker he could achieve status in life and never worry about money again. Instead of being a doctor, he could invest their money. His companions would be money-makers, people like himself who could spin gold out of straw. Of course, that seldom happened in the world of commodities and futures. It was a system that had been created to stabilize Japanese rice prices, but was corrupted over the years to become one of the quickest methods ever devised to help an investor lose every cent he had.

Man's folly in placing an outrageous value on things hit a peak of stupidity in Holland during the seventeenth century, when speculators determined the tulip was much too valuable to be a mere flower. No true member of Amsterdam aristocracy could be considered actually wealthy without possessing the rarest bulbs.

A Dutch sailor mistook one bulb for an onion and added a few slices to his herring sandwich. The owner of that Semper Augustus varietal specimen was not pleased, since the tulip was worth more than the man who ate it. The sailor served jail time for the offense. Tulips were traded in financial markets from London to Paris and prices reached maniacal proportion. Suddenly, the speculative bubble burst, as all such bubbles do, and the tulip lost its glamour status almost overnight. Investors whose fortunes were wrapped up in a warehouse filled with rare bulbs now owned only a bunch of pretty flowers.

The tulip experience proved that markets can be made in anything where one person wants to sell and another wants to buy. Such frantic markets today have evolved in almost every known commodity, from frozen orange juice to fresh fish, bars of gold to sides of beef. Rice, Eurodollars, potatoes, wheat, U.S. Treasury bills, oats, yen, soybeans, platinum, stocks and bonds, eggs, silver and chickens are all traded daily in the exchange houses that dot the globe.

The need for such markets began in ancient Japan when rice merchants came together to solve a puzzle. Rice was plentiful and cheap at harvest, but expensive and hard to get before the shoots were planted. To stabilize the madly fluctuating prices, the merchants invented a contract in which a person would agree to buy or sell a certain amount of rice, at a set price and on a set date in the future. That would guarantee the farmer a particular price, while ensuring that the buyer would not be forced to pay some outrageous fee for a wagon load of rice in December. Because it was based on selling a commodity, such as rice, on a date in the future, the deals became known as commodity futures contracts.

Once the system began, prices stabilized and the contracts themselves, at a set value, became valuable items and were traded as financial instruments.

The heart and soul of such trading is the New York Mercantile Exchange, the Chicago Board of Trade, and the Chicago Mercantile Exchange, but the practice is spread all over the world. Gold is centered in London, and fish prices are set at the New Bedford Seafood Exchange. Other markets are handled in frantic sessions at the Minneapolis Grain Exchange, the Kansas City Board of Trade, the bustling market houses in Tokyo, Sydney, Paris, and almost every other major city. They all set a price today for something they will buy or sell at a future time. The result is a vast, interlocking web of money.

The money is in the paper, not the actual frozen pork bellies and blocks of silver, for no one wants to store a few tons of orange juice concentrate in their garage.

No matter what the language or the commodity, the players are professionals. It is not a place for a novice, and even knowledgeable traders shy away from the sheer speculation, for the Golden Rule of investment is that no one can forecast a market.

Modern communications enabled capital centers to span the globe, and a clerk with a cellular phone in Dallas could talk to a broker in Madrid. Computer screens could throw up charts, graphs, and calculations in the blink of an eye. It is the fastest game in town, the ultimate high for people who measure themselves in money. So it attracted the white collar thieves in the heyday of the eighties, when greed was a socially acceptable vice. A lot of them spent time in jail, leaving billions of dollars in bad debts, scandals, and shattered investor confidence behind them.

Peter Lynch, the investment guru who guided the

famed Fidelity Magellan mutual fund, wrote in his book, *One Up on Wall Street*: "Reports out of Chicago and New York, the twin capitals of futures and options, suggest that between 80 and 95 percent of the amateur players lose. Those odds are worse than the worst odds at the casino or at the racetrack, and yet the fiction persists that these are 'sensible investment alternatives.' If this is sensible investing, then the *Titanic* was a tight ship."

None of that deterred Christopher Hightower. All he needed were a few customers and the business would fly. He put the fires, the worries about a wobbly marriage, the dead-end studies at Wright State, behind him and set out to make some hard cash. At the age of thirty-six it was time to get serious about life.

He and Susan and the boys had moved back into the twice-burned house on Elsemere Avenue in August, and he set up an office there for his financial business. Hightower planted a satellite dish atop the roof, tuned into the computer program he purchased during his two-day training course in Chicago. The machinery would supply instant information on world markets, and he would get rich. Simple.

While Susan, now the mother of two, finished her master's degree in psychology, Christopher frequented the basement of a public library to attend weekly meetings of an investment club. The sixteen other members were mostly men and women at or near retirement age who had pooled some of their available cash for careful investments.

When Hightower first began attending the meetings, he impressed those around him with his caution and smoothness. He obviously knew the language of the financial world. Polite and ingratiating, he would listen to his elders speak and talk only sparingly. But talk he did. Hightower might have been a flop at Riker Labs, but he was successful at selling himself.

He threw around stock market and financial terms with the same ease he had inserted long Latin words into his conversations on science. Hightower talked so far above the heads of the average person that, rather than appear stupid by asking him to slow down and clarify what he said, they just assumed he knew what he was talking about. Only later would they discover that he didn't have a clue.

Like throwing bait to hungry fish, he dropped hints about his investments in commodities. The more experienced investors shied away from the speculative gamble, but Hightower pressed ahead, just telling them how he was doing. Once they considered how he was turning such huge profits—investments that soared fifty percent in a single day—they wanted to know more. Maybe there was something to this commodities business. If he can make money at it, why can't I?

He made a formal presentation. It was primarily a computer program that he had bought off the shelf and then spent hours to improve, he said. The data from the various world markets came over almost instantaneously, from a satellite to the dish on his roof, feeding his computer and allowing him to make trades through his Chicago broker before the overall market could react. It was almost like stealing, he said.

Greed knows no age limit. The serious men and women who had dabbled in the stock market with their life savings decided to take a flyer with their new buddy, Chris Hightower. By 1986 papers were drawn up to create the Investors Guild of Dayton, and the members chipped in more than $102,000 for Hightower to use as seed money in trading commodities. The minimum investment was $3000, and he was to report every month on how they were doing. They sat back and waited for the money to roll in.

For six months the carefully printed reports of inventory, value units, and club worth contained good news. Everything seemed to be working out just as Chris had promised. He stayed busy in his little home office, churning out charts and graphs, reading books and magazines, steeping himself in the commodities and futures game. With his telephone calls, thousands of dollars purchased and sold items in a crisp, efficient manner. There were the occasional dips, but that was to be expected in such a chance-riddled investment business.

But there came a day when one of the Investment Guild members wanted more than Blue Sky paperwork. He wanted some of his money, right now, thank you very much. So sorry, said Chris. Can't do it. All liquid funds are invested. Maybe later.

The Guild decided to have a picnic on July 7. There was sunshine and lemonade and good cheer, but Christopher Hightower, their investment wizard, did not show up. Sitting around the picnic tables, the members talked themselves into rebellion. A telephone call was made to Hightower, who broke the dreaded news they all half expected—most of the money had disappeared.

People who had up to $24,000 in the scheme were furious. Not only had they lost their money, but they had been sheared like a bunch of sheep, led on by lying reports. A group of them hurried over to confront Hightower, who welcomed them to his modest home with the satellite antenna on the roof, then sat calmly behind his desk, hands folded, and politely listened to his former friends and clients scream and threaten. He didn't even get mad. You all knew that options and futures were risky, he reminded them, but still you volunteered your cash.

"I didn't steal it. You lost it. You've got nothing on me," he said rather calmly. After all, they had been aware that he didn't even have a license to trade commodities.

When all was said and done, nine months after the Guild was created the club's original investment of $102,600 had a net worth of only $231.36. Hightower had skimmed much of it for living expenses and lost the rest.

In reviewing their documents, Guild members found that Hightower, their mentor, never invested a cent of his own money, although he listed himself as being in for

$12,000. The money that was in his name had come from his mother's retirement fund, and when the other members paid in their shares, Hightower withdrew the $12,000 and sent it back to Titusville, leaving his own investment at zero. He played the chancy market entirely with other people's money.

The irate investors could recoup precious little. The only thing of value he had was his house, so, in settlement, they accepted a $22,000 second mortgage.

No big deal, Hightower thought. Susan had finished her degree requirements and it was time to pack up the kids and leave Ohio anyway. Time to go home, back to Barrington, Rhode Island. Before leaving Ohio, he filled out the necessary forms and received a license to be a broker from the National Futures Association and the Commodity Futures Trading Commission.

Book Two

8

The Brendels

At first glance the wedding of Ernest Brendel and Alice Bobb would have seemed to be a marriage of a couple of New York go-go professionals. Both had Ivy League and advanced degrees. He was a Wall Street lawyer and she was a rising star in the New York City library system.

They were about the same height, Alice only an inch shorter than Ernie's five-foot-six, but there was a marked difference in their width. Alice was slender, almost willowy, while Ernie weighed about 160 pounds and was built low to the ground, like a football linebacker. Ernie had curly chestnut hair, and Alice wore her lighter brown hair cut to her shoulders.

Indeed, the two people standing at the altar of the Memorial Church of the Holy Cross in the center of Reading, Pennsylvania, would have seemed destined to carve a future together in New York City. They could have had a fashionable East Side apartment with a uniformed doorman, and own a splendid car hidden away in a private garage. They could dine at elegant restaurants, be denizens of the Broadway theater, and shop on Fifth Avenue.

The 100 people in the church that day knew better. Their friends knew that for Ernie and Alice, New York was just a way station. The marriage and their subsequent life together would be marked by prudence, caution, and a stubborn adherence to basic values. They would live for the future, not for the day.

That did not mean Alice and Ernie couldn't play the Manhattan game with the best of them, and indeed they had met during a social function at the city's posh Brown University Club. Both were graduates of Brown, Ernie in 1959 and Alice in 1967. He had gone on to obtain a law degree from the University of Virginia and passed the New York bar in 1964, while Alice moved to New York after her Brown years and took her master's degree in library science from Columbia University.

They were witty, ambitious, and in love. Conversations were spirited, and their choice of music was classical. Alice thrived in the museums and theater life of the big city. Ernie played softball in Central Park and was part owner of an uptown bar, Rigby. Both enjoyed the adventure of finding a new restaurant, and anything was open to their inquisitive palates.

However, Ernie's tiny apartment at 178 East Ninety-third was like a lesson in urban survival, and not their idea of how to live. They rented a slightly larger apartment on Broadway, but that too began to pale as the couple examined their future. They wanted a home, not an apartment, and eventually wanted children, but feared raising them in New York. So a few years after their marriage, they moved out of the Big Apple, settling into a house at 175 Kelburne in North Tarrytown, only a short walk from the train station where they could commute to New York. Alice still worked at the library, while Ernie tried private law practice in partnership with another attorney.

Ernie Brendel was born on March 22, 1938, in Jersey City, New Jersey, to Jacob Brendel and Jolene Breit, and his German ancestry was burrowed into his core. The United States was on the brink of World War II, and, while Jacob and Jolene had been in the country since 1929, they did not decide to become American citizens until 1936, and the necessary paperwork extended into the war years. As such, the family was classified as "enemy aliens" and forced to leave their apartment overlooking the shipping in New York's busy harbor, a natural target for German spies. When Ernie began school, he was small for his age and an easy mark for classmates who called him a Nazi. He learned to be stubborn and fight back, traits he would carry throughout his life.

He sought refuge in sports, another lifelong passion, and as a boy set his heart on becoming a pitcher for the Boston Red Sox. For practice he would haul his younger sister, Christine, out to be his catcher, while baby sister Susanne was the audience. Eventually, the war years over, the family settled in an upper-class section of Convent Station, New Jersey, in a two-story colonial house. His father, an import-export entrepreneur, was away from home half of each year, leaving the task of raising the three kids to Jolene, who was of the authoritarian European school of child-rearing.

In high school Ernie became popular with the guys, showed a creative side by writing for the school newspaper, and excelled on the baseball diamond and basketball court. But his small size prevented any hope of playing ball beyond that, and sports faded while he buckled down to his studies. He dabbled in premedicine courses, got bored with science, settled into prelaw at Brown, and later got his law degree from the University of Virginia.

His age and education removed him from the Vietnam draft, and although he served in the National Guard, he never went to war. Instead he began a career as a lawyer and as the husband of Joanne Rogers, a Kentucky girl, whom he married in 1962. They divorced seven years later, with no children.

Ernie was not charming, but a friendly "man's man" sort of character, who liked to drink beer in working-class saloons, narrate the football films shown at the Brown Club, and play squash and poker. He was stubborn in arguments, sometimes refusing to change his position despite logic and facts, and difficult to get to know, but he prized friends. Meanwhile, he worked at the law firm of White and Case, specializing in trademarks and patents. Shortly before meeting Alice, Ernie joined the giant liquor firm Joseph E. Seagram's, where he would rise to assistant general counsel before taking a lucrative "Golden Parachute" buyout in 1979.

Alice Bobb was the youngest of the three children of Arthur A. and Arlene Klinger Bobb, when she was born in Reading on July 9, 1945. The family was intellectually curious, and the desire to learn left an indelible imprint on the young girl.

Her father was a respected eye surgeon, a profession that also drew her oldest brother, Arthur. Her other brother, Donald, became an attorney. Surrounded by books and ideas from a young age in her upper-middle-class home, Alice too gave serious thought to becoming a doctor, as she graduated with honors from Reading High School.

The top grades did not slow the social life of the quick-witted teenager, who could play practical jokes as well as the piano. She dated often, her outward shyness falling away among close friends. Her laugh was her trademark.

The high school grades, however, won her acceptance at three colleges—the Connecticut College for Women, Wellesley, and Pembroke College, which was the women's division of Brown University, in Providence, Rhode Island. Although clearly sexist in its structure at the time, Brown was a coed school, and Alice chose not to surround herself only with other women.

She had a sense of adventure, and her foot would begin to tap at the sound of a jet plane going somewhere. With her brother Arthur working with Aramco in Saudi Arabia, Alice took advantage of opportunities to travel abroad. Her passport collected stamps from all over Europe, Russia, the Near East, and nations around the Arabian peninsula.

Alice loved to read, and after college her bachelorette apartment in New York was stuffed with books and periodicals. Frequently, a savory aroma wafted from the stove, as Alice became a gourmet cook. After Columbia she joined New York's sprawling public library system, working in mid-Manhattan and at a smaller branch facility, as she punched her ticket for advancement. She continued her active social life, her mother constantly commenting on the number of Alice's young men friends.

One of her beaux was the smitten Ernie Brendel, who used a considerable amount of his stubborn determination to court and win the pretty librarian from the Pennsylvania Dutch country.

New York eventually lost most of its glitter for them, and in 1980 the couple left Tarrytown, drawn back to Providence. In Rhode Island they could afford to buy, not rent. Ernie was more than ready to make the leap and open his own business. But Alice was a bit fearful of leaving her library chums and comfortable lifestyle. But they agreed that to raise a family, a move to quiet New England would be best. For $84,750 they bought a small place at 7 Thayer Street, a stone's throw from the academic whirl of their beloved Brown University. Ernie worked out of the house and Alice landed a job, first in Boston and later at Brown, only a short distance from their new home, the historic William Church house, built in 1840. Alice attended the Central Congregational Church on Angell Street, but Ernie, a lapsed Catholic, chose to stay home on Sundays. Both maintained their love of travel, and visited Spain, Israel, Egypt, and Jordan for special holidays. Ernie, remembering his German heritage and his own awkward school days when he was chided for being a six-year-old "Nazi," eagerly looked forward to touring the beaches of Normandy where the Allied forces landed in World War II, then cruising the wine country of France.

The lives of Alice and Ernie Brendel changed on June 27, 1983, with the arrival of a baby daughter they named Emily Anne. When she was born, her mother was thirty-seven years old and her father was forty-five, and the child was "the best thing that ever happened to them," a close friend recalled. Having carefully planned the birth, both parents doted on their only child. Naturally, they decided, she would go to Brown.

Actually, she went to Brown early, as Ernie and Alice would plop Emily in the stroller and walk around the hilly campus. But as good as life was at the edge of their favorite university, Brown happened to be in an urban area, and Providence, the parents felt, was not much better than New York when it came to being child-friendly. Ernie, who thoroughly investigated everything before making a decision, searched for a new place, somewhere close by, somewhere just right. He found it just a few exits down the interstate. Barrington.

9

Black Wampum

The town, which sits on a peninsula that juts into Narragansett Bay, was incorporated in 1717 and named after an English champion of religious tolerance. "A Group of Gentlemen" paid thirty-five pounds sterling to a tribal leader and his son in 1653 for title to the land, and all modern Barrington real estate transactions can be traced to that centuries-old document. Originally part of Massachusetts, the town became attached to Rhode Island in 1746.

A marvelous place of rugged wilderness and seaside glory, it is one of those little New England towns that transcends the passing years. Natural beauty abounds in mysterious bogs, swamps, and coves, and a meandering tidal line stretches for twelve miles. The Warren and Palmer rivers form the eastern boundary, and the western flank abuts the city of East Providence. The Massachusetts towns of Seekonk and Swansea lie along the northern edge, and the water owns the south.

Barrington is a place of quiet elegance, where money made elsewhere buys peace, quiet, and security. It is the kind of place where a Mercedes-Benz pulls up to a pet store, and a woman wearing a full-length mink coat buys dog biscuits for her poodle with a hundred-dollar bill, and the storekeeper won't think anything is unusual. Most homes are of substantial size and sit on spacious lots. There is no drinking allowed in public places.

The landmark of the town is the gleaming white steeple of the Barrington Congregational Church, a classic New England place of worship that has occupied that corner since 1717. The White Church would play a staggeringly important part in the looming bloody crime that would shake the village to its core.

Fresh from fleecing his investors in Dayton, Christopher Hightower returned to Barrington in 1986 a happy man, driving a U-Haul, with his young wife and his two little boys at his side. Of course, he did not have a job, but that was of little importance. They would live with Susan's parents and sister for a while in the cozy home at 10 Chantilly Lane, and he planned to set up his business as soon as possible.

Not for a moment had he considered the Dayton debacle to be anything more than the sort of lumps any financial rookie might encounter in the commodities game. Instead of learning in a classroom, he had taken on the College of Real Life. The Investors Guild of Dayton was far behind him, and he had no intention of checking the rearview mirror to see if it was catching up.

By returning to Rhode Island, Hightower had chosen a state that for centuries had been on the cutting edge of financial skulduggery. Los Angeles may have three thousand more traffic lights than all of Rhode Island, but when it comes to the fast buck, the nation's tiniest state was a major player.

The trail goes all the way back to the earliest days of the American colonies. The helpful Narragansett Indians pulled off a real estate swindle by selling white settlers land they didn't own. And when the white man decided to set a European price on the carved shells that the Indians used as currency, the Native Americans were again quick to help. A single carved seashell, known as "white wampum," was worth three English pennies. Darker shells, "black wampum," were equal to one penny. The Indians began substituting thin chips of ebony rock for the black wampum, since it was easier to chip rocks than carve seashells.

Four centuries later the Native Americans seemed like pikers compared to the grand schemes that slapped Rhode Island in the final decades of the twentieth century. The Rhode Island Share and Deposit Indemnity Corporation, a private insurance fund that protected the deposits of state-chartered banks and credit unions, crumbled after bailing out the failed Heritage Loan and Investment Company. Joseph Mollicone, the high-living president of Heritage, vanished, along with $13 million of the bank's money. Ironically, he would later ride to his own trial handcuffed to Christopher Hightower.

Hours after Bruce G. Sundlun became governor on the first day of 1991, he closed the forty-five banks and credit unions whose depositers had been ill-protected by RISDIC, which had already voted itself out of business. Some $1.7 billion worth of assets belonging to about 200,000 depositors were frozen until the mess could be straightened out.

The mayor of Pawtucket, Brian J. Sarault, was given five and a half years in prison on a federal racketeering charge in connection with a City Hall extortion ring. Movers and shakers, bank presidents and elected officials carried on the state's fine old tradition of black wampum, as if trying to live up to the state's ancient nickname of "Rogue's Island."

In 1986, when Hightower came back to Barrington, junk bonds were ploughing corporations into astronomical financial trouble, America had become the world's greatest debtor nation, and the recession was about to hit with unimagined force. But there was still money to be made on the dark side, and Chris Hightower was about to step up to the trough.

The Hightower family moved into the home of Mary Lou and Clyde Slicker at 10 Chantilly Lane in October 1986. His in-laws welcomed them with open arms, determined to help. They would not let the two boys, their only grandchildren, suffer because of a temporary financial setback. Clyde remained supportive of Chris and even helped him learn more about the stock market. Mary Lou was particularly delighted to have the little boys around.

Susan was happy to be home again, out of that dreadful existence in Ohio. The fires and living on a skimpy income were behind her. She felt much safer in her parents' house than living alone with her increasingly mercurial husband. One moment he might scathingly criticize her, and the very next he might charmingly turn up the car radio and coax her to dance with him beside a public road. The trouble was, she never knew which Chris was going to show up.

Before the year was out, Chris created Hightower Investments and rented an office on Route 2 in nearby Warwick. True, there were no clients yet, but until there were, Clyde Slicker helped pay the bills.

When 1987 rolled by without Chris being able to earn enough money to support himself and his family, Susan decided to call a family meeting. Everyone agreed. The time for a steady job and paycheck was overdue. It didn't work out the way Susan originally thought. Chris went back to his nebulous investment work, claiming it would be the height of folly to bail out now, when he was so close to bringing in the big bucks. Everyone agreed, and Clyde said he would continue to supply the couple with a thousand dollars a month for their expenses.

It was Susan who had to go out and find work. Owning a master's degree in psychology, she took over her mother's old position as secretary at the Barrington Congregational Church.

Chris Hightower retreated to his office, read the *Wall Street Journal*, toyed with his computers, printed reams of numbers, stayed up-to-date on how hog bellies were selling and, once in a while, wondered just where the hell he could scare up a client or two.

In May of 1988 Ernie and Alice Brendel settled on a big white house at 51 Middle Highway, a place with a history. Originally built as a caretaker's home on a vast estate, the house most recently was the home of one of the most flamboyant members of the Rhode Island Legislature. Leo Patrick McGowan, who was fond of loud plaid sport coats, died in 1984, and four years later his widow Doris put the house on the market. Ernie and Alice bought it for $225,000, needing only a $100,000 mortgage.

Alice continued to work at the Brown library, taking the bus into Providence. Ernie, who liked to get away for Brown football games and Red Sox baseball, set up his office in a tiny hallway on the second floor of his house. And Emily soon found herself enrolled in the ALP program of the Primrose Hill School a block from her front door.

Her parents were a bit shy and standoffish with their neighbors, but Emily fit right in. She made friends easily as she grew from a toddler to a little girl with a rosy future, and her life took on a sense of swirling excitement. She twice went to Disney World, and her mother proudly took her to lunch at an expensive restaurant in New York, where Emily was thrilled by the trays of frothy desserts. Her parents were loving but strict with their only child, and Emily grew up polite and well-behaved. Frugal, they did not spoil or indulge her, for life was a serious matter. Early in her life Ernie had obtained Social Security number 039–52–7886, for his daughter.

Like her parents, she was somewhat shy, but developed a group of pals at Primrose Hill School, and others at the various day care programs she attended after classes. In the evenings, she would return home with her father, meet her mom at the bus stop without fail, enjoy a tasty dinner, and then fall asleep surrounded by a herd of stuffed animals and wrapped in her babyhood quilt which she called "Blankie." On a shelf lay her favorite book, Chris van Allsburg's *Just a Dream*, and her pet turtle paddled about in its bowl.

There seemed to always be something exciting in her life, always something to which she could look forward.

In 1988, wearing a long white gown, gold-glitter wings and halo, she portrayed an angel in a church Christmas play. In 1989 she was the wife of the innkeeper, and in 1990 played Mary in the holiday pageant. In July, when she turned eight years old, her father took her and a dozen of her friends over to the Caratunk Wildlife Preserve, where they had an indoor birthday party on the hottest day of summer. Her parents promised that next summer she could accompany them to England and France.

Emily was a source of constant wonder and delight to her parents, but, to their dismay, she was growing up fast.

Ernie set about doing business from his home, using his skills as a patent and trademark lawyer to assist a number of companies. Word circulated that the lawyer could be a hard man with whom to work, but he paid the bills on time and accomplished his goals. As the years progressed, he obtained a stable of companies whose products ranged from pinball machines to cosmetics, and he used much of his free time to study his own investments. Brendel dodged a bullet by yanking money away from a Texas scheme before the oil market crashed, and fell short on several other occasions with his own investments. He was always eager to check out something new, whether it be wine coolers or a newsletter for nurses. The bank accounts remained healthy, but he began to have second thoughts about working alone, and sent out résumés to law firms around New England.

Shortly after starting his business in Barrington, he ran into another entrepreneur. Brendel's friend Paul Ryan, also an attorney, introduced Ernie to Christopher Hightower. The two men found they had a lot in common, and since Ernie cultivated few friends, they began to socialize. They both loved athletics, ran their own businesses, doted on their families, and liked to talk about money. Ernie, who could not nail two boards together, welcomed the handyman help that Chris would offer around the big house on Middle Highway. When Chris moved into his new office on Maple Avenue, Ernie helped lug things upstairs. The friendship increased over time, and in the summer of 1990 they took their families on a joint vacation to a home that Hightower's in-laws owned on a lake in New Hampshire.

But from the first day, Ernie was more than a potential friend to Christopher Hightower. He was also a potential customer. After many long talks, Ernie was eventually convinced to set aside his caution and make a small investment with Chris, even advancing a few thousand dollars in May 1989 for Hightower to buy equipment. The investment was a bust, but Ernie thought little of it. When the persistent Hightower approached Brendel again for an investment, Ernie demanded to see the trading results before putting up another dime. The printouts blew his mind. Hightower had turned a profit of more than 80 percent in only a few months of trading commodities.

Ernie invested more than $11,000 of his own money in May 1991, and brought some friends along with him, for a total investment of $40,000. This time when the money began to dwindle, Brendel checked with the people whose accounts Hightower had cited to lure Ernie back into the fold. The former clients said the figures lied. Hightower had lost much of their money.

Ernie exploded in rage. He had not only been swindled of his hard-earned dollars, but had been betrayed by a friend and had caused other friends to suffer unneeded financial loss. He demanded that Chris return all of the money, peppered him with threats, slammed him with lawyer talk, and took his complaints to the federal agency overseeing commodity traders. Ernie got enough from Hightower to pay back his fellow investors, but ex-friend or not, he was determined to put a halt to Hightower's scams. He was out $11,861, and while he might never get a cent of that back, Ernie Brendel was determined that Chris Hightower would never play anyone else for a sucker.

10

September 17, 1991

Christopher Hightower leaned back in his beige chair, his shoeless feet on the edge of the desk, and stared at the hole in the ceiling of his office. A cup of black Maxwell House coffee was near at hand and the soothing classical music of Solid Gold Baroque came from the tape deck. A slight breeze swept through from the open door. The three computer screens were blank, the new Epson QX-10 printer sat silent behind him, and failure was once again clinging to him like a damp cloak.

Since returning to Rhode Island five years ago this month, Hightower had changed. From a loner, a person with few friends and a lack of direction, he had found himself in Barrington. The job that Sue had taken at the White Church had a lot to do with it. No longer an outcast, Hightower began attending services with the Slicker family, then became increasingly active in church functions. The same thing happened with outside activities as his two sons grew. On this Tuesday morning, he sat in the bright light coming through the broad, curtained windows to his left, a man active in his community.

He was chairman of the Board of Christian Education at the church, taught third and sixth grade Sunday school classes, was a youth group leader, and headed the Junior Pilgrim Fellowship. He had also been one of the church members who searched for and found Rose

Amadeo, the new associate pastor, the previous year. Hightower coached the soccer team on which one of his boys played, led a Cub Scout pack, and bought the kids baseball cards.

He, Susan, and the boys now lived with the Slickers in a new house at 1 Jones Circle, a spacious place the color of sand, with green shutters, set back on a manicured lawn and bordered by a wood rail fence. And his business office was no longer a little cubicle, but a two-room suite on the second floor of a converted house at 580 Maple Street in the heart of Barrington. The Jeep Cherokee that he normally used from the family stable of vehicles was parked behind the office.

Hightower looked at the hole in the ceiling carefully and thought of the forecast of rain. The mere whisper of moisture was enough to spin the thoughts of Rhode Islanders back a month, to when Hurricane Bob slammed through, crushing seafront homes and scattering debris that still lay in thick piles around Barrington. More rain, that's all he needed. Looking outside, all he saw was the sunshine of another ninety-degree day. The classical music was too dour. He rolled the swivel chair back and went over to change the tape. *The Best of Mozart*? No.

He needed something upbeat, to fight the frustration gnawing at his stomach, so he popped in a Linda Ronstadt tape. He refilled his cup from the Mr. Coffee, resumed his chair and examined the bulletin board, where pictures of his boys were pinned, side by side. Rows of neatly printed papers were stuck to the corkboard, but they meant little, no more than the mounds of papers stuffed in boxes and drawers throughout his office. As much as he wanted to present a picture of success to the world, Christopher Hightower was still a loser, facing disaster.

First, there was the pending divorce. That morning, during a rambling conversation over breakfast, Chris had asked Sue to reconsider, think about the situation. He turned on the charm, had been contrite and remorseful. One more chance, that was all he was asking. He confessed that he had been moody and hard to live

with because of the stress caused by the continual set-
backs in his business. It could be . . . it *would* be better,
he promised. He requested that Sue make out a list of
things that were wrong so he would know exactly what
he needed to correct. Was she buying it? He honestly
didn't know. She had said only that she would think
about it.

Losing Sue would mean more than just a parting of
the ways with his beautiful wife of nine years. It would
mean he'd have to leave his children and the big house
on the circular driveway at 1 Jones Circle. It would mean
a loss of wheels too, since the Slickers owned all of the
cars. No family, no mobility, no roof. The gossip that was
certain to follow would be hard to bear. Bad stuff indeed,
but not insurmountable. He reached for a pen and made
a detailed list. Buy a rose and a card and go over to the
church to encourage her with a dose of sweetness. He
jotted a series of talking points to discuss in their next
conversation, his left hand scribbling as his mind
whirled.

Now, that done, he turned to another problem. Those
guys downstairs, Dennis Murphy and Ray DeWall, his
landlords, were getting restless because he was months
behind in his rent. As property managers, they had their
own problems trying to run a real estate business in a
depressed economy and were out of patience with their
delinquent tenant. The tension of thinking about them
made him clack his jaws together in nervousness. It was
impossible to dodge them, because the only entrance to
his office was by the stairs at the side of the building,
and they saw him every time he came or left. God, the
scene when Murphy came storming up the stairs, the big
Irishman demanding payment.

Chris had tried to play the pity card. Sue was thinking
about divorce, he cajoled, and things were tough at
home and on the business front. Confidingly he added,
"I'm thinking about terminating my lease here in a couple of months."

Murphy wasn't interested. Hightower was already late

and maneuvering to get more time on the cuff. "A couple of months, hell," Murphy yelled. "We want that back rent. Now!" Chris wasn't afraid of DeWall and Murphy and had not backed down when he and Dennis accidentally bumped shoulders during the office argument. Why should he be afraid? In the briefcase at his feet rested a 9mm Glock semiautomatic pistol. As Murphy demanded the back payment, Chris thought, Mess with me and you lose.

When the latest rent check bounced, the landlords had gone to the Barrington police. Hightower had a telephone call the previous day from Sergeant John Lazzaro, who said the check had to be made good within seven days—by next Monday—or else.

Hightower leaned over and picked up a yellow legal pad that listed a series of names. Murphy and DeWall weren't his only creditors. Banks, credit card companies, and collection agencies also were demanding money that he didn't have. His talent at kiting checks, making threatening telephone calls, and generally muddying the financial waters had bought some breathing room, but they all still wanted their money. He smiled. As a money man himself, he knew his creditors would grant almost any extension if a promise of full payment was at the end of the trail.

There was a partially completed poem on the pad, and he worked on it a few minutes before laying it back on the clutter of papers across the desk and returning his gaze to the hole in the ceiling. Now that hole—that was truly serious.

The guy from Financial Securities Information Systems down in Florida had come up to the office and repossessed the leased computer equipment that linked him with the outside financial world. The ragged hole was left when they pulled out the cable that went through the ceiling and connected with a small satellite dish on the roof. Hightower had been cordial to the technician, even helping carry the stuff downstairs. It wasn't the guy's fault. Financial Securities just rented out the equipment, not the highly specialized service that came over it.

But the loss of the machinery was a serious blow, for with the data that marched across those colorful computer screens, he could keep abreast, minute by minute, of the wide world of commodities and futures trading. A bumper crop forecast in Colombian coffee? A storm on a Kansas wheat field? A strike by the black miners working South Africa's thick reefs of gold? Chris Hightower had the word as fast as anyone on earth. Such knowledge was critical in providing his clients a clear trading advantage.

Without the machinery, Hightower could be relegated to a technological backwater. The data bouncing off the satellites in geosynchronous orbit high above would belong to his competitors, not to him. The hours he spent combing through those voluminous electronic reports were the happiest moments of his workdays. The office, shorn of that magic technology, looked naked.

The loss of the satellite feed would directly hinder his ability to go service his clients. Clients! That was a joke, he thought bitterly. He didn't have any.

But there was an even bigger problem.

He hissed a deep breath of exasperation as he picked up the thick complaint from the U.S. Commodities and Futures Trading Commission. Today, Tuesday, was the deadline for him to respond to the allegations made against him. He felt bile in his throat, like a bitter pill. Everything seemed to be happening at the same time.

His old pal, Ernie Brendel, had turned on him and called in the feds, claiming Chris had signed him as a client by using cooked numbers. Ernie had been hounding him for months to get his money back. Once, the two men had worked closely together, Chris in his computer-studded Maple Avenue office and Ernie at the desk in the upstairs hallway of his home. But the CFTC document had driven them into separate legal corners.

Ernie, Ernie, Ernie. Hightower was frustrated and angry.

Ernie knew that futures and commodities were risky. It was the old risk-reward ratio—the higher the amount of risk on an investment, the higher return might be expected. But flying high also meant that it was easier to crash and burn. *Ernie knew that. What's wrong with him?*

Hightower viewed the CFTC complaint as potentially the biggest nail in his professional coffin. Rent could be juggled, wives mollified, and computer gear replaced. But if federal investigators sided with Ernie, they might jerk his license as a commodities broker. That would be the end of it. He would lose his trading ticket and that would force him to the sidelines of the fast-moving business that he loved. He was haunted by the memory of being cut from the basketball squad years ago in junior college when he didn't measure up. The possibility of being kicked out of this game, too, was more than he could bear.

He tossed the CFTC paper back onto the desk, crossed his arms and leaned back in thought, the bones of his jaws grinding together with audible cracking sounds as he became lost in concentration. If Chris Hightower knew he had anything, he had brains, and he was depending on those smarts to once again get him out of a tight jam. He knew he could do this. Bend a rule here, dodge a creditor there, use money from Peter to pay Paul. Keep the hounds at bay until things shake out. Find a couple of new clients, solve some problems, settle Sue down, get Ernie to drop the legal action, and Chris Hightower would be back on his feet.

In Washington, Supreme Court nominee Clarence Thomas was ending his testimony before the Senate Judiciary Committee. The U.S. was awaiting word of a hostage release in Lebanon. A judge dropped charges against Oliver North while, in Miami, the trial of former Panamanian dictator Manuel Noriega was reaching stalemate. Chris Hightower read those headlines in the morning paper, but could not have cared less. He had enough troubles of his own.

All he needed was a plan by which to extricate him-

self. Already one was beginning to glimmer in the back
of his mind. But right now it was time to go find a suit-
ably soapy card and a flower and talk to Sue at the
church.

Susan Slicker Hightower paid little attention to the
small gifts and quickly put them aside after her husband
left the office. Too much had happened between them.
Too much to make up for with a card and a flower and
more empty promises. She was no longer the teenage
girl who idolized a mature, older man, but an educated
woman with two children. The man who just left her office, she felt, was really a stranger.

Instead of paying attention to her, he preferred to
hide out in that office over on Maple. Instead of being a
part of her life, he preferred slouching on the sofa and
watching *Goodfellas* or *The Godfather* and other such mov-
ies that fed his morbid fascination with organized crime.
Instead of paying bills, he constantly carped and criti-
cized, not only her, but her parents too. He was never
overtly violent, but there was a scariness just below the
surface that frightened her. Like when he threatened to
hit one of the boys with a plastic bat. He would whirl on
her during an argument, eyes big and blazing in anger,
and call her vile names. Nine months of marriage counseling had not helped. The relationship that had started
so sweetly had turned sour.

Chris made big plans, big promises, and always came
up short. Instead of making big money, he hardly made
any at all. The only bills he paid around the house were
business-related telephone calls. No taxes. No car payments. Sue paid rent to her mother and the monthly
bills. When Mary Lou Slicker told Chris to quit fooling
around and go get a job, he visibly blanched at the idea.

The only plus, it seemed to Sue, was that he did spend
time with their sons. He was a good father, but not a
good husband. To the rest of Barrington he might be a
good guy, but the rest of Barrington didn't have to live
with him. She had thought it over carefully. The mar-

riage was dissolving before her eyes. She had taken it as far as she could, and felt that Chris was becoming increasingly distraught and unstable. Another chance? No. For her own peace of mind and the future of her boys and parents, she was going to see a lawyer. With quick determination, she took off her wedding ring.

When she arrived home at 1 Jones Circle after work, Sue found Chris eating dinner with Bobby. "I don't want to get into an argument," he said, glancing toward the boy. "But I have one question. Did you think about what I said?"

"Yes," she replied. "I thought about it. And I don't think it can work."

She once again saw the frightening change in his face, which signaled the turmoil he was feeling. His eyes bugged out and his forehead reddened. Neither spoke as Chris took the boy in hand and headed out the door for an afternoon soccer practice. She sat very still until she heard the engine of the Jeep Cherokee come to life and the car drive away.

11

Tuesday Night

The big house on Jones Circle was tense when the Jeep Cherokee rolled back into the driveway a little before seven o'clock. Mary Lou Slicker was away in Ohio, visiting a terminally ill sister, while Clyde Slicker was still out, playing tennis. The courage Sue had felt earlier, when she told Chris their marriage was at an end, had fled, and she was now acutely aware that once the boys were put to bed, she would be alone with her husband. The idea filled her with dread.

Finally, the kids were asleep and the house was quiet, except for the sound from the television set that she and Chris watched in discomfort from the couch in the family room. The silence between them was almost a physical thing. Chris, as usual, had taken off his shoes. Even with the hearing problem in her right ear, Sue could hear him grind his jaws together. He said not a word, moved not an inch, and his dead calm terrified her.

As the program changed at nine o'clock, he abruptly went to the liquor cabinet. He threw ice cubes into a big glass, poured a deep draught of scotch whiskey, and drank it in a gulp. He refilled the glass and came back to the TV, moving to a nearby easy chair, suddenly seeming nervous. Hightower knocked back the second drink and got a third, then returned to his seat, still silent. He was almost through with the third whiskey before he spoke. Sue, who had rarely seen him drink anything stronger than a glass of wine on a weekend, was intimidated.

Commercials came on at nine-thirty. Chris stared at her, his face a mask of contempt. "What do you know about guns?"

"Not much," she replied. "I don't know the difference between them or what different kinds the policemen carry or anything. I just know the difference between a small one and a big one." She didn't press the matter, because she knew Chris had several weapons stashed around the house.

He asked if she had a will. No, she said, neither do you.

"Do you know how much a human life is worth?"

He had never harmed her, not once in their nine years of marriage, but she was suddenly gripped by fear. "No. I don't know how much it's worth."

"Let me tell you. A human life is worth five thousand dollars, and that's what I've paid someone to kill you if you try to take my children away from me during a divorce. I paid another thousand to make it look like an accident."

Sue sat rock still, afraid to even move. The situation had dissolved in an instant from a marital conflict into a threat of execution. He was going to have her murdered!

There was more. Chris said his ex-wife and daughters also would be on the assassination list. Clyde and Mary Lou and Sue's sister Kathy would also be turned over to the paid killer if they tried to take possession of the boys. Chris rambled back and forth across his bizarre threats, repeating that he would have her and others killed if they fought him in the courts and accusing her of being unfaithful. "You fucking whore!" he hissed. "You bitch!"

In earlier arguments, Sue had held her own, once even shaking him by the shoulders to keep him from walking from the room until he heard her out. He had threatened to slap her then, but she had not backed down. But this was different. She would rather that he yell, show some kind of emotion. It was the icy tone that was frightening. Susan Hightower was afraid for her life and the lives of those two little boys asleep upstairs.

After the barrage of threats, name-calling, and accusations, the most welcome sound she had ever heard was the noise of her father's car coming into the driveway.

Chris heard it too. He stood up, wobbly, and took the last sip of whiskey from his glass. Then with a great swing, he hurled it against the fireplace. Glass exploded in a flare of shards, needling into the carpet and bouncing off the bricks. Hightower picked up his shoes and lurched toward the stairway. Without turning he said, "I don't know about you, but I'm gonna sleep very well tonight. You don't ever have to worry about me coming after you. I won't. But I'm gonna sleep well tonight."

He spat another warning over his shoulder before climbing the stairs. "You can tell anybody you want about this. You can never prove it. There's no tape recording. It's just my word against yours." Then he went upstairs and vomited in the bathtub before going to bed in Bobby's old room, where he had been sleeping alone for two weeks while the kids bunked together.

Sue was still sitting in the family room, frightened and angry at the same time, when her father walked in. A glance at her face and the debris of broken glass on the hearth told him the tenuous marriage had come to a dangerous crossroad. He was not surprised, since Chris and Sue hardly spoke anymore.

Their battles hurt him, for Clyde Slicker was from the old school. Marriages were sacred and were supposed to last forever.

He immediately moved to comfort Sue. Naturally, if he had to make the hard choice between them, he would side with his daughter.

With a growing sense of shock, Clyde listened as Sue told him about how Chris had gotten drunk and threatened to have them all killed by some hired gun. Together, as if it were some solemn ritual, father and daughter picked up the broken glass, almost as if gathering pieces of the shattered marriage. They decided that the first thing Wednesday morning, Sue should go see her attorney.

As Sue pulled out the vacuum cleaner to gather the smaller pieces, a numb and worried Clyde Slicker went to his own bedroom. As he was putting away his tennis gear, there was a knock on the door.

Chris stood there, looking disheveled and out of sorts. When he spoke, the words were slurred. "I think I've had too much to drink. Would you wake me up in time to pick Bobby up from kindergarten?" Clyde, aware that his son-in-law moments before had told his daughter that the family might be as good as dead, only replied that he would do so.

In a less civilized environment switchblade knives may have flashed in anger long ago in a similar marital dispute. But this was Barrington, a place of genteel civility, where people could always solve their problems simply by talking them out. Or so it was thought.

When Chris told Sue that he was going to sleep well Tuesday night, he wasn't just talking about the three shots of whiskey that he drank during their argument. He was physically exhausted.

Unknown to anyone in the family, he awoke in the wee hours Tuesday and went for a long walk, hoping to quiet the demons playing in his mind. Hightower had slipped into his flannel shirt, jeans, and sneakers and walked out shortly after midnight. He had heavy thinking to do, and something he had to find.

Barrington police had reports of break-ins around Brickyard Pond, and Patrolman William Dorney, riding the midnight shift, was watching for suspicious activity. As he drove along the lonely bicycle path that meanders through the neighborhood, he spotted someone in the darkness. At 1:11 A.M. Dorney cautiously pulled to a stop and asked the man for some identification. Christopher Hightower politely obliged, showing a valid Rhode Island driver's license. Dorney called it in to headquarters for a check with the computer, but there were no outstanding warrants, nor a question of any sort. So he handed the permit back and said Hightower could go.

Still, Dorney was suspicious of why the guy would be in such an overgrown area at that time of night. It was unusual behavior for any Barrington resident. He drove a quarter mile to Middle Highway, parked and waited. When Hightower did not emerge within a few minutes, the policeman drove back down and saw the man still walking, slowly, toward the highway. Dorney passed without stopping, drove down to the YMCA, turned in the spacious parking lot and retraced his route. Hightower was still walking. The cop, puzzled, decided the guy was preoccupied with something, but since he was white, obviously middle class, and polite, Dorney decided to let it go and returned to normal patrol duties.

Hightower was happy to finally be free of the cop. He persisted with his nocturnal stroll, easily finding his way by the bright half-moon that was waxing toward full. Finally coming out on Middle Highway, he turned north, heading toward the Brendel home, and cut to the right when he came across a path used by the cross-country runners at the St. Andrew's School. It led at an angle to a huge, rolling field that sprawled like a meadow behind the exclusive private prep school. About a hundred yards in from the highway, it joined a rude road used by service vehicles.

He poked around the thick brush. The place was convenient and hidden from passersby. You could not see past the outer tangle of bushes. Just right, he thought. He might have to come back here soon.

Scuffling around, he found a pair of steel stakes like the ones road departments use for mileage markers. He dropped one at the intersection of the trail and the service road, then tossed the other casually near the small opening he had made in the thick briers, weeds, and bushes. If he had to find the place again, he could.

He was home in bed before dawn broke shortly after

6:30 A.M. Before Tuesday was over, enough bad things would happen to set him off on a deadly rampage.

Jittery, almost as if dreaming up goblins, he noticed another uniformed policeman working on a road detail near 1 Jones Circle that morning. Before leaving for work, Hightower went over to the cop and asked what he was doing. Routine assignment, the policeman said. Three hours later, with the policeman still hanging around, Hightower again asked what was going on. He got the same answer. Like I told you before, the officer said, just routine road duty.

Hightower was beginning to feel very uncomfortable. In reality, the encounters with the two patrolmen were nothing more than chance. But he felt the hounds were at his heels, and he had done nothing worse than argue with his wife. It was obvious the cops were in on the conspiracy against him.

Just be cool, Chris Hightower told himself. Stay calm and work through this thing. You can still do this. You're smarter than they are.

12

Wednesday

The Brendel house at 51 Middle Highway and the Hightower home at 1 Jones Circle were more than separate structures on the morning of Wednesday, September 18, 1991—they were separate worlds. One Jones Circle was shrouded in dark clouds of doubt and worry, while 51 Middle Highway was a place of happy bedlam. The two would soon be linked by murder.

Alice Brendel was up first that day, rising from her single bed in the upstairs bedroom and lacing on running shoes for her morning jog just before the sun came up. It was another pleasant day, the big trees around Barrington donning their fall finery of bright leaves, and she padded easily around the neighborhood, unafraid. One of the beautiful things about living in such a peaceful suburb was the sense of total safety she felt. When she finished her run, she stood on the wide front porch a few minutes to cool down and scan the headlines of the *Providence Journal-Bulletin* that had been delivered at 4:00 A.M. Her fastidious Ernie insisted the paper be tossed directly onto the porch each day, not left in the driveway.

Her morning jog, the newspaper delivery, the fact that she would now go back inside, shower, and dress before awakening Ernie and Emily, were hallmarks of a family oriented toward a set routine. It was the same every weekday morning. Routine was good and comfortable and eliminated awkward surprises.

Later, as she drank black coffee and Ernie settled in over a cup thinned with milk, they discussed the day's schedule. Great. Nothing important. She would be at work, he would work out of the house, and Emily would go to school and then over to the YMCA. The usual. She rinsed the cups in the kitchen sink and put them in the rack of the rickety Kitchenmaid dishwasher, a rattling relic of the 1950s that had come with the house.

Alice and Ernie had carefully examined the options of her getting to work. Since she could not drive a stick-shift car, they leased a 1988 Toyota Camry Deluxe for $286.24 a month. But driving into Providence during the morning rush hour was a zoo, and parking was expensive, so the Toyota sat in the garage beside the sporty black Audi that Ernie preferred but had not repaired. It was better, they agreed, if Alice just took the number 100 RIPTA express bus downtown.

She tied her comfortable sneakers and stuffed work shoes, umbrella, and book into a straw Kenya tote bag. Then she picked up her purse, kissed Ernie on the cheek, and set off down County Road for the little sheltered bus stop. At 7:56 A.M. the big blue and white bus stopped before the wooden structure, and Alice dropped eighty-five cents into the box and settled into a seat, nodding to a few other frequent bus passengers whom she recognized. She pulled out her book as the bus headed down the Wampanoag Trail for the quick drive into Providence. Getting off at the Kennedy Plaza terminal at 8:13, she walked the few blocks uphill to the modern Brown University library.

Emily Brendel had turned eight years old on June 27 and considered herself a young lady now, almost too old for the Alternate Learning Program in which she participated at the Primrose Hill School. She had been in the program since kindergarten, among sixty kids spread among three teachers who taught the mixed class based upon interest, not automatic lesson plans. She still loved going to the red brick school, and rarely missed a day. So on this morning Emily almost pushed her father out of the front door. Parents were so infuriating sometimes. Didn't he know that she had to get there early so she could chat with her friends in the cafeteria before beginning the day?

The conversation would focus upon the class trip planned for Friday, when everyone would go down to Newport to see the Viking ships, or she would chatter about her pet turtle. But with her closest friends, Emily could share scary dreams she had been having and the stories that she had written about them.

She called one "The Dream That Would Never Go Away," and although she knew it was just a stupid dream, it still disturbed her. "One night as I was going to bed, I had this strange feeling something awful was going to happen," she wrote. "When finally I got to sleep, I drempt an awful thing. This viking was chasing me and I couldn't get away."

Stupid dream. Almost as stupid as the one she wrote about in "The Land of the Gnomes," when two best friends show up for school and find all of their classmates are standing around and talking about something they cannot understand. Emily knew they were only dreams, and dreams cannot hurt you. Both her father and mother said so.

When Ernie left her at the door of the school that morning, he knew his little girl was growing up fast. It would not be long before she would be in Barrington High, then in Brown. Of course, she would go to Brown, just like her parents did. Brown blood ran in the Brendel family. Already he was squirreling away money for her college education. Her Rhode Island Hospital Trust Bank savings stood at $3,627.59, and the 701.853 shares in the Washington Mutual Fund Investors were currently worth $11,019.09. By the time Emily was ready for Brown, Ernie would be ready for the hefty Ivy League tuition. There were many years before he had to pay that, however, and right now the little girl running into the school was only eight years old and just beginning to really enjoy life.

Ernie Brendel walked back to the big white house, grabbed another cup of coffee in the colonial-style brick and beam kitchen, climbed the thirteen steps to the second floor and settled into his chair, checking the big calendar that lay upon the desk. Today was the Jewish holiday of Yom Kippur, it informed him. An appointment scheduled for just after noon had been canceled, but he glanced at the 7 scribbled into the Thursday box. The Dean Witter financial seminar up in Dedham. And on Saturday he would drive to New Haven and meet Jim Page for the Brown-Yale football game. Jim would spend Saturday night with them, then go on over to Nantucket for a few days.

Brendel swung around to examine the papers showing his financial status. Since taking a "golden parachute" payment when he left Seagram's in New York, he had carefully invested his money and watched it daily. He knew he had a reputation of being tight with a dollar, but so what? Contracting to repaint the big house one side at a time was practical. Turning to the financial pages of the newspaper, he checked his mutual funds. He had four of them with the Tucker Anthony brokerage, the largest, with he and Alice as co-owners, today standing at $100,248. The other three, with a total of $44,379, were also doing well, and the Hospital Trust savings accounts stood at $89,832.

Alice's own mutual funds, according to the quotes, were worth an additional $41,000, and her pair of retirement funds bubbled along nicely near $71,000. With his conservative money management, all of the money should grow nicely over the next decade, before he had to seriously consider shifting it into rock stable retirement funds. With Alice's weekly income of $523, her insurance coverage, a low amount of debt, and the money he pulled in free-lancing as a patent and trademark attorney, they lived well within their means. Even with substantial life insurance policies—$250,000 for him and

$200,000 for Alice—by Barrington standards, they weren't in the upper financial league. No yacht, no waterfront property, no Ferrari, but the Brendels didn't care for that sort of thing. They were financially comfortable and would stay that way, as long as Ernie paid close attention to the money. No matter what his friends said, painting the house one side at a time made economic sense.

He took a short break to finish hooking up the new combination fax and telephone answering machine. It had cost him more than $500, money he hated to spend, but would be worth the investment in the future. When he was away from his little hallway office now, he wouldn't miss any calls and also could enter the wonderful world of faxes. As a bonus, he could screen incoming calls after his self-imposed deadline for business conversations at seven in the evening, when MacNeil/Lehrer came on television.

He thumbed through file folders of his current business accounts—Del's Lemonade, Traner International, Distlefink Designs, Waco Industries, Blatzwax, World Peace 2000, Change Your Attitude, LoCal Industries, his partnership in the Newport Trading Company. He had to decide what to do about a load of toy slot machines in the garage, but nothing was pressing.

Ernie spent a moment going over a letter from Page Taft Real Estate down in Guilford, Connecticut, firming up the listing agreement to sell the condominium in West River Village. This was a difficult one, for he and his sisters were moving their mother, Jolene, into a nursing home, and had to arrange the disposition of her goods and the sale of her town house. The place was actually owned by Ernie and his sister Christine Scriabine, who lived nearby in Guilford, and they had decided to market the cedar-sided condo with a rock garden, near the swimming pool, for $119,900.

The entire family had been down there only last weekend, clearing out Jolene's closets and dressers, cleaning the place, helping her move forward with life. Ernie had not wanted to put his aging mother into a nursing facility, but there was no choice. He had failed in an attempt to get Barrington officials to grant a zoning variance to convert the outbuilding at the rear of his property into an apartment, and his house was simply too small for another adult, particularly one who could not handle stairs. So instead he examined almost every nursing home in a three-state area, until he finally found a suitable one in Hudson, New York.

Last Saturday, as they had packed boxes for Goodwill Industries, each kept some personal mementos. In a plastic shopping bag bearing the Lord & Taylor logo, Ernie carried a set of steak knives and the odd item that had been the subject of so many family jokes—an old police nightstick of thick wood that his mother had come up with somewhere. He tossed the bag into the back of the Toyota Camry and drove back to Barrington with Emily and Alice, after telling Christine that he and Jim Page would come see her in Guilford after the football game next Saturday.

Signing off on the nine-month listing agreement, Ernie pushed back and stretched. His business duties were already done for the day, and it wasn't even noon. He didn't have anything pending until he picked up Emily at five o'clock. Ah, the glory of working for yourself. This is why he left New York!

Ernie allowed his mind to wander, hoping for one specific telephone call. He was expecting Joe Mazza of the National Futures Association to give him an update on whether that skunk Chris Hightower had met the NFA deadline on his complaints.

Chris had not needed a wake-up call from his father-in-law. The throbbing in his whiskey-fuzzed brain was an early alarm. He awoke naked and lay in the narrow bed for a while, listening to the emptiness of the house, a place that suddenly seemed alien and hostile. The rancid taste of yesterday's whiskey lay in his mouth like sour cotton, and in his hangover he thought it was Thursday, not Wednesday. The argument with Sue slowly came back to him, and he did not regret a word of it. Nobody would push him around anymore! He had not scratched his way up from poverty just to be jettisoned at the convenience of other people. There was work to be done today. He got up, showered, and dressed in jeans, a polo shirt, and Top-Siders. Putting a blue Chicago Cubs baseball cap on his head and grabbing his worn green Army fatigue jacket, he walked the few blocks to his Maple Avenue office, hurrying up the stairs so he did not have to confront Murphy and DeWall.

The door closed, he clicked on some music and began to make his daily list of things he needed to get done. Before he could really get started, as the coffee was still brewing, the telephone rang and Joe Mazza from the NFA quizzed him about missing the deadline. Chris ground his teeth in frustration. Damn these people! He said that personal problems had come up unexpectedly, mainly some trouble with his wife, and that he had forgotten about the NFA time limit. I'll get right to it, he promised Mazza.

Hightower had no wheels that morning. Sue had the Jeep over at the White Church, Mary Lou had one car in Ohio, and Clyde drove the third car to school that morning. Earlier he had loaded his heavy Sears Craftsman toolbox into the Jeep and arranged for Sue to deliver it that morning to 580 Maple so he could help dismantle the rooftop satellite dish. Despite the threats, she kept her promise, and he met her downstairs. They hardly exchanged a word as he picked the heavy box out of the vehicle and she drove away. Upstairs, he removed the snub wire cutters and the black steel pry bar, transferring them to his briefcase.

He slid back into his chair, picked up the yellow legal pad and, since he had no customers and no computer data that might allow him to at least *pretend* he was working, began doodling with his latest poem, letting his pent-up emotion flow into the rhythm of the phrases, writing about a trip "down the path of life." Hightower wrote that life was "like a circus" where one could lose a bag of popcorn "when the dive bomber came crashing down."

He said that the "bumper cars" of life might result in "knocks and bruises," but he expressed real worry about the Ferris wheel stopping "on top of the world."

One by one the things and people he depended on for support were falling away. He was broke, Sue was talking about divorce again, the NFA was hounding him, Ellen was pestering him about overdue child support payments, the landlords were demanding rent, Ernie was showing no signs of letting up on that all-important complaint, and now even his mother had enough of his empty words. After almost losing her $12,000 in retirement savings in the Ohio scam, Chris had recently turned to her when he ran into business trouble in Rhode Island. When he sent a packet of documents to Titusville, promising huge returns if she would just let him have some money again, Margaret Hightower took the material to a lawyer. Not that she didn't trust her first-born child, but she had learned the hard way to be careful when dealing with him. The lawyer examined the papers and warned that if she signed them, she would be putting her Florida home on the line for any of his business losses in Rhode Island. Margaret Hightower did not sign. Chris was enraged that he couldn't even depend on his own mother anymore, for God's sake.

He took up the legal pad again and very carefully started adding up the due bills. One Optima card, a Discover, two from MasterCard, two American Express, five Visas, a savings and loan payment, back rent, telephone, the data connection to get back his repossessed satellite dish, and a few others. The total was $3,766 due this month, just to get even on his current bills. Hightower didn't want to think about the money he had pirated in the commodities business from his few clients and the approximately $50,000-plus that he had borrowed over the years from his in-laws.

He had to come up with some cash, quickly. Luckily, his fertile imagination provided several ideas. Ernie, of course, would have a stash of money somewhere around that flaky house of his, and maybe he could con Ernie into still another loan. He was going to have to go over there soon anyway to convince Ernie, one way or the other, to drop that complaint. No use trying to talk to the NFA guy until Ernie was in line. One way or the other.

Then Hightower had another bright idea. He picked up his pen and pad and began to scribble a note to pass to a bank clerk. He warned that "a very large explosive device" was in the building, and that, unless his instructions were followed, "a lot of people will die." He wanted only "all the 10's and 20's from the front register" and said that all police calls were being monitored. "If our scanners pick up a police dispatch, we will immediately blow up the building."

He looked at it with pride of authorship. *Who am I kidding? I'm a commodities broker, not a bank robber. Anyway, how can I rob a bank today? I don't even have a car!*

At five o'clock Ernie Brendel backed the Toyota out of the garage, down the long drive and onto Middle Highway. Hitting the electronic button on the visor, he closed the rolling door as he drove away.

Exactly ten minutes later he was at the YMCA to collect Emily, signing the pickup sheet.

Alice Brendel had covered her computer terminal at the library, swapped her work shoes for her tennis shoes again, and reversed her morning route. She got on the Hampden Trail RIPTA bus across the street from the courthouse, exactly at the same time Ernie was picking up Emily. When the bus pulled to the side of the road twenty minutes later, Alice stepped off alone, ready for one of the favorite parts of the day, a little ritual that marked the start of the Brendels' family evening.

Ernie had parked the Toyota nearby in the East Bay Mental Health Center parking lot, chatting with his daughter as they waited for the bus to arrive. When it did, the passenger side door of the car flew open and Emily bounced out, running to give her mother a hug.

Being as polite as possible about the uncomfortable situation, the Hightowers gathered for dinner that night. It was a mark of how things were expected to be done that Sue, who had sworn out an affidavit for divorce, and Chris, who was writing crazy poems and bank robbery notes and threatening to kill her, could dine together without incident.

During the meal, he reminded her that someone would have to be home Thursday night to watch the kids. He had to attend to some private business and might not return until Friday morning.

It was the last time they would ever be together as a family.

13

Thursday

Storm clouds formed over the Atlantic coast, heavy and gray with the promise of rain. Storm clouds of a different sort hung over Chris and Sue Hightower as they arose Thursday, September 19, in separate bedrooms and faced the ordeal of breakfast, getting the boys off to school and readying themselves for the day. Their conversation was clipped and chilly, but not openly adversarial. Neither wanted to tip their hand on what was going to happen in the critical hours to come.

Sue left at 8:30 A.M., wheeling the Jeep Cherokee out of Jones Circle onto Nyatt Road, turning left on Rumstick Road, just as if she were heading for work at the White Church. Instead she drove right by the big church, its steeple pointing sharply at the gray clouds above, and headed for Providence and her 9:00 A.M. appointment with her lawyer.

Chris left the house a short time later, driving the Chevrolet Caprice station wagon, following much the same route as he headed to nearby Swansea, just across the Massachusetts state line. As he passed the church he noticed that the Cherokee was not there. He would check later. He drove to the Sears store in the Swansea Mall and, using one of his debt-riddled credit cards, bought a new pair of black, high-top Reebok sneakers.

Wearing his new shoes, he drove the Caprice down busy Route 6, cruising past the strip malls, gas stations, and drowsy little stores until he reached Thompson's Sport Shop, a dark red brick building crowned with a cupola and weathervane. Eight big front windows were jammed with sporting gear and advertisements. Inside the double front door Hightower saw a jumble of water skis, St. Croix fishing rods, Eureka tents with Gore-Tex fabric, racks of rifles, canoes, and a cornucopia of outdoor clothing. He walked past a spotted dog sleeping beneath a rack of winter parkas and headed for the left rear of the store. He had been there before, lingering amid modern bows and arrows that hung from overhead pegs like nightmarish stalactites.

"Hi, Chris. How are you? You in for the sale?"

Bill McGovern, a tall and slender man with a slight beard, had sold Hightower a small, pistol-like crossbow two months ago. Now, Hightower said he liked the little crossbow, but it didn't have enough power to bring down the pesky crows and one particular raccoon that were giving him trouble. He was interested in something bigger.

McGovern had just the thing, last one left in stock. He handed Hightower a fully assembled Bear Devastator crossbow, a huge, yard-long weapon in a camouflage pattern. The salesman demonstrated its power by showing Hightower how hard it was just to cock it. He put a foot into the steel stirrup and pulled back the drawstring, his shoulder muscles shaking as the tension in the crossbow increased to 150 pounds of pressure. The twenty-six-strand steel string finally clicked into place, and McGovern flipped the safety away from the red firing position and handed the empty weapon to Hightower. If Hightower's little crossbow wasn't much more than a slingshot, this thing was a cannon.

He grasped the pistol grip with his left hand and brought the square cheek rest to his face, peering through the folding rear sight. The Devastator, made of magnesium alloy and extruded aluminum, felt cold to his touch, but coiled with unimaginable power, like a giant fist ready to lash out.

After examining the weapon for a few more minutes, Hightower handed it back to McGovern and said he wasn't ready to buy at the moment, but he might be back later. He thanked the salesman and left.

Sue's attorney, Mary June Ciresi, was ready for some quick legal moves by the time her client showed up at the Family Court building in downtown Providence. Much of the detail work had been done weeks earlier, so she was able to expedite the normally cumbersome process.

Even couched in lawyer language, the affidavit filed that morning spelled out a menace that, months later, would jump off the page.

> The Defendant informed me that he would be taking my minor children and that he has paid the sum of Five Thousand ($5,000.00) Dollars to make sure that it looks like an accident and that he would be sure to have an alibi.
>
> Defendant further advised me that if my parents attempt to take my minor children, he would have them killed also as he has a sufficient amount of money hidden away to accomplish this act.
>
> I am in fear for my life and the safety of myself, my children and my family.

Filing for a divorce can sometimes be as difficult as swimming in mud, but the threat of violence from Chris greased the legal skids. Sue Hightower was in and out of court in an hour and a half.

By the time she returned to her car, the judge had allowed the filing of a complaint for divorce, ordered a constable to serve a domestic abuse complaint against the husband, approved a motion for temporary allowances that gave Sue exclusive custody of the children, and okayed a restraining order to throw Chris Hightower out of the house.

Today was her thirtieth birthday, and the judge gave her freedom as a present.

Chris Hightower left Thompson's and returned to the White Church. The Cherokee still wasn't there! *Where is she?* He drove through the heart of Barrington's small shopping district, looking in restaurant windows. No Susan. *Just where in the hell is she?*

Passing the church again shortly before noon, he saw the Cherokee pull into the parking lot and immediately drove in next to her.

"Where have you been?" Hightower shouted, still behind the steering wheel of the Caprice. His face was red and his eyes huge, enraged.

"I've been out," she called back, still in the big Jeep. "What do you want?"

"Nothing!" he yelled back.

He was hounding her but had nothing to say? What was this? "Are you leaving?" she asked.

"Yes." Then the words began to tumble out of him. "I've been following you. I knew you didn't go to work. I knew you went somewhere else. I've been following you." He threw the car into gear and hurried out of the parking lot.

No, you haven't been following me, she thought, gripping the wheel with relief. You have no idea where I've been or any clue about what I've done today. She was nervous and more than a little frightened as she got out of the car and went into her office, locking the door behind her. Sue picked up the telephone and called home, telling her father that she had filed for the divorce, and the restraining order would be served the following day, on Friday.

As they spoke she saw the Caprice pull into the lot again and Chris, obviously angry, approach. By the time she hung up the telephone, he was pounding on the locked office door, demanding entry.

"Tell me what you want," she called from the far side

of the glass, determined not to be caught alone with him in the small room.

"Let me in!"

"No. You tell me from that side of the door."

"Either you let me in or I'm going to break it down!"

Sue realized that could lead to disaster. She saw her keys were still out on the desk. Picking them up, she went to the door, unlocked it, and walked right past Chris, leading him outside to the driveway between the church and the adjacent office building. Cars were passing by on County Road, giving Sue an element of comfort, knowing that other people could see them.

"Where have you been?"

"None of your business." She was terrified, but felt stronger out in the open air with potential witnesses driving by. The argument continued and she withstood his barrage of questions, refusing to tell him about the court visit and the pending restraining order. Soon, she knew, it would all be over. The legal train was finally moving and would soon carry him out of her life.

Chris was implacable, yelling that they were still married and that he had a right to know the movements of his wife. He had a right to know everything that she did, everyone she saw, everything she said! Just outside the church where he was considered a leader and example to young people, Christopher Hightower blew his top, on one hand warning that he had been following her all morning, and on the other demanding that she confess all to him, right there, right now.

Just as he seemed at a breaking point, another car pulled into the parking lot. Kathy Slicker, bringing Sue three birthday roses—one for each decade—drove directly past them, parking beside the river behind the church. Knowing of her sister's actions that day, Kathy was worried. Chris was standing with his hands on his hips, glaring at Sue, who had her arms crossed and folded, defiant and protective. Trouble was in the air, but Chris said that Kathy could come over. When she approached, Sue put an arm around her sister's waist and received Kathy's arm around her own. Never had Sue been so delighted to see Kathy, never in her entire life. The sisters now presented a united front.

Hightower was furious. He had failed to bend Sue to his will, and now Kathy was there. Kathy, who had lent her brother-in-law $8,500 that she was certain she would never see again, was no friend of Chris Hightower, and would not stand by and watch him bully her big sister.

Chris glared at the two of them, spun away, and in moments the Caprice station wagon shot out of the parking lot.

Right on schedule, Ernie Brendel came into the YMCA Thursday afternoon to coax Emily away from her afternoon of play. She had been with the Y for more than a year, ever since her father had taken her out of the after-school program of the House of Little People over on Maple Avenue. And in all that time, Emily's mother had only picked her up about a half-dozen times. The Y staff could almost set their watches by the brusque Ernie Brendel collecting his daughter precisely at 5:10 P.M.

Usually he had little to say, other than a brief hello. All business, he wanted to get the little girl and go. But on Thursday afternoon he lingered a moment to tell Pam Poirier, the program director, that Emily would be a little late on Friday because the Primrose Hill ALP class was going to Newport. He would pick her up at the regular time. Poirier said that would be fine. A late bus was arranged for the ALP kids.

Ernie and Emily walked into the parking lot, hand in hand, and left to pick up Alice at the bus stop. They wanted to be on time, since it had begun to rain and a light fog was drifting in from the coast.

That was too bad, Ernie thought. After an early supper he had to drive up I-95 to the Dedham Hilton for the Dean Witter investment seminar tonight. Martin Parquette, a broker, had contacted him months before with a tantalizing investment idea. Always ready to check out a financial opportunity, Ernie agreed to attend the seminar, but made no promises to buy. Now, looking up at the drizzling dark clouds, he considered canceling. But an appointment was an appointment, and Ernie was always on schedule. It started at seven o'clock and he wanted to be a few minutes early.

Dinner was not pleasant at 1 Jones Circle that night, although Chris wasn't there. He had spent the day at home with the kids, but as the clock approached Sue's arrival time, he went to his office. If he had hoped to escape from the tension in his life, he was badly mistaken.

The telephone rang at five-twenty and a less-than-cordial Joe Mazza of the National Futures Association told Hightower that he wanted to come up to Barrington tomorrow, Friday, along with his supervisor, Timothy Wigand, and audit the books at Hightower Investments. The allegations brought by Mr. Brendel were serious, Mazza said, and you missed the deadline for either paying back the money or answering the complaint. We have to talk about this immediately.

Hightower told Mazza it would not be convenient to see them tomorrow. He would be busy all night tonight and just would not be up to such an important meeting. If you can call back later, we'll set something up. It was a puzzled Mazza who hung up his telephone in New York. This guy Hightower was a case, all right. His license was in jeopardy and he was stalling a meeting that might settle the problem.

About six o'clock, as darkness gathered, Hightower left 580 Maple and, turning up his collar against the rain, went to the Caprice parked in the rear. He drove home, dashed through the open garage door, into the house, and saw his family already at dinner. Mumbling, "I gotta go get something," he picked up the checkbook and went back out into the rain.

* * *

Bill McGovern was still working when Chris Hightower came back into Thompson's, shaking rain from his jacket. He wanted to buy the Devastator.

Fine, said McGovern. What about bolts—as crossbow arrows are called. Hightower added two sets of camouflaged Jennings bolts, three in each set. Points? McGovern asked what kind of arrowheads Hightower wanted. Displayed on a rack were a wide array of razor-sharp arrowheads powerful enough to bring down a bear, but Hightower made a strange choice. Instead of the exotic, multipointed arrowheads, he chose the almost-blunt bullet points. When McGovern rang it up, the total came to $314.99, and he was glad to close the day with such a nice sale.

Hightower carried the assembled weaponry outside, while McGovern shoved the crossbow's large box into the rear of the station wagon. Across the top of the white box was stenciled the word DEVASTATOR.

It was dark and raining hard when he turned off Route 6 and went through the triangular intersection that put him on County Road leading to Barrington. He made two stops, carefully hiding the crossbow and picking up a shovel and pitchfork, then drove back to Jones Circle as the windshield wipers beat a loud tattoo that matched the drumming in his brain. Everything was falling apart! Susan nagging at him all the time, Mazza and the NFA demanding an audit, overdue rent, repossessed computers, pending lawsuits, and that cocky Ernie Brendel would not drop the complaint. Chris had telephoned Ernie only last week to ask him once again not to press the charges, and Ernie, brusque as always, refused. Chris had not really wanted to carry out his emergency plan, but they had forced his hand. The responsibility was on their heads.

His mind churning, he ran back into the house, past an astonished Clyde Slicker and straight up the stairs to his room, where he changed into a long-sleeve plaid shirt and jeans, and grabbed a heavy coat. Carrying his old olive-drab Army fatigue jacket, he trotted back down the stairs.

Hightower had not seen Sue, but on the way out he told Clyde he would not be home until very late, if at all. The heavy downpour had stopped during the half hour he was upstairs, but it was still raining. He walked into the steady drizzle without hesitation, vanishing into the darkness on foot. How odd, thought Clyde Slicker.

Down Rumstick Road he walked, finding the Bike Path and following it to Middle Highway. Hightower was headed toward Ernie Brendel's home to settle things.

First there was a dirty job to do. He ducked behind St. Andrew's School, and, guided by the two steel posts he had laid down as markers on Tuesday night, was quickly swallowed from view. The shovel and pitchfork were laying just where he had left them. He could not take the chance of being recognized, so from his jacket pocket, he pulled a large square of blue cloth that he had found among Mary Lou's sewing material. Putting it over his head, he adjusted the eye openings and secured it like a hood.

Then he began to dig.

At the Brendel home a disagreement was in progress when the telephone rang at one minute before eight o'clock. Emily wanted to have her ears pierced and her mother was refusing. The gentle argument actually had been going on for a few months, but with Ernie out of the house tonight, there was some time for girl talk, and Emily was pressing her case.

The little girl answered the telephone. It was her aunt Christine, and Emily launched a plea for her to help convince Mom that plenty of girls her age had pierced ears and that there was nothing wrong with it. Christine, always ready to stir things up, was considered somewhat of a bad influence on Emily by Ernie and Alice. She had a relentless sense of humor, like when she would tell Emily they were going to run away and join a band of Gypsies. But Emily could not draw Christine in as an ally tonight, and soon their conversation became silly. Emily, frustrated, simply hung up.

Christine redialed. This time Alice picked it up and said she would call back after doing the dishes and getting Emily into bed. A half hour later she did return the call, and spoke to Christine for eighteen minutes. Christine wanted to tell Ernie she had been feeling guilty about putting their mother into the nursing home and would visit her this weekend. She would not be home if Ernie and Jim Page wanted to drop by after the football game. Alice said she would give him the message.

After she hung up, Alice heard the Toyota in the driveway and Ernie rush onto the porch. She was happy he had stopped beside the stairs rather than taking the car all the way into the garage and getting soaked running to the back door.

The two of them had a laugh about the bad weather, he told her the seminar was no big deal, then they shut off the lights and went upstairs to bed as thunder rumbled and lightning cracked.

For Chris Hightower the heavy weather was both good and bad news. It was hell to be getting drenched, but he couldn't have asked for better conditions for the task at hand. He looked at the windows all around the Brendel house. They were dark. The big crossbow lay at his feet.

From a pocket he removed the short steel pry bar that had been in his toolbox and felt for the back door, his fingers running over the little metal sign that read, PEACE BE UNTO ALL WHO ENTER HERE. He wiped the water from his glasses, placed the sharp toe of the pry bar beneath the wooden doorjamb and gave a sharp push. Nothing. He moved the pry bar down a few inches and pushed again, harder.

The door sprang inward and was yanked to a sudden stop by a little chain that locked it to the wall. Before he could reach inside, Hightower heard the *peep-peep-peep-*

peep of an alarm system. He was startled, because he knew Brendel had terminated the alarm service, considering it a waste of money. Who needed an alarm in a place like Barrington? Hightower grabbed the crossbow and retreated across the backyard, to hide in the trees as the rain beat down on him.

Ernie was also surprised at the chirping sound. He found the noise was coming from the little speaker upstairs, but he had to go all the way down to the main box by the front door to shut off the alarm. He quieted the thing, then discovered that it probably had been set off when the wind blew open the back door. He flipped on the outside light for a moment, saw nothing but sheets of rain, and turned it off. Closing the door, Ernie Brendel went back upstairs to bed.

Hidden in the woods, Hightower was soaked. The first part of the plan had gone well, the secret hole was dug. But the alarm threw off his timing. Now he had to improvise, since he could not get into the house tonight. He needed to find shelter and rest until tomorrow morning, when Ernie would be alone.

The garage! Hightower spotted a narrow window in the big building, pried loose the heavy screen and broke the glass. Pushing the crossbow ahead of him, he slithered up and into the building, stepping on the shards that littered the floor.

He knew this place. It was here that he and Ernie had stored a shipment of wine they had bought from a defunct Boston restaurant, a purchase that would later have major importance. The cars would be parked on the right, so he felt around the corner of an interior wall until he found the opening to the three horse stalls that had been empty for God knows how many years. He had to go slowly, so as not to bump the bicycles or any of those idiotic slot machines Ernie had stacked all over the place. It was musty and dank but would afford him a dry place to sleep.

He burrowed into a stall, and, as the rain slammed

against the roof, the Devastator crossbow at his side, he began a fitful doze. At the rear of the garage rested a large cardboard rainbow, below which children had written, *Mr. McGowan's Garage Is A Fun Place To Be.*

14

Friday

Alice was embarrassed. As matriarch of a household that always ran on schedule, she had somehow failed to check her purse Friday morning. Only when she arrived at the bus stop did she realize she did not have the eighty-five-cent fare. Chagrined, she walked back home, shielded from the heavy rain by a little umbrella. Ernie had taken Emily to school and was back at the house, in a good mood because he was twenty-four hours away from going to watch the Browns and Yales play football. No problem, he said, I'll drive you in today. They walked to the red Toyota still parked in the driveway and joined the morning rush hour to deliver her to the front door of Brown's Rockefeller Library. By 8:30 A.M. she was at her desk, and for the rest of the day Alice would tell people how nice it was that Ernie interrupted his own work to drive into Providence. The enjoyable morning interlude, a break from the schedule, would be the last time they would see each other alive.

Christopher Hightower heard the Toyota leave. That wasn't part of his plan. Ernie was supposed to stay home. Alone. The alarm last night had already put a dent in his scheme, now Ernie was driving away!

Hightower felt absolutely rank and dirty. A man who prided himself on cleanliness and appearance, he had gotten soaked by the rain last night and was unable to dry out. The dampness and continuing rain left him shivering during the night, and being inside the garage had added a layer of dirt to his already befouled appearance. Hunger gnawed at his stomach, since he had not eaten since a quick bite during his afternoon errands the day before. There was nothing he could do but get on with the plan first and bathe later.

He wandered through the garage, which was illuminated by the dim light coming through the row of small, square windows across the top of the rolling front door, two big windows on the north wall and the two narrow windows through which he had gained entrance at the south, rear. Chances were good no one could see in from outside. The shiny black Audi was parked on the far side, the slot normally occupied by the Toyota empty. He took the electronic door opener from inside the Audi.

As the rain slapped the steep roof he picked up the big Devastator crossbow, put his foot into the cocking stirrup, and pulled the string back until it locked. He wanted a practice shot before Ernie returned.

Carefully, he loaded an arrow as long as his forearm into the slot and searched for a target. There was a bag of peat moss along the north wall, sitting in front of some junk. Hightower took aim and squeezed the trigger. With a hard *chunk* sound the arrow flashed from the crossbow and needled all the way through the obstructions and into the garage wall itself. What a powerful weapon! Silent and deadly, the perfect assassination tool. Hightower loaded another arrow and lay the crossbow aside. He reflected again on his plan to force Ernie to drop that complaint to the CFTC and get the NFA off his back. There were no further flaws in it. Faced with such a weapon, Ernie would surely be as meek as a lamb. Hightower settled back to wait, listening to the rain slapping at the barn.

By the time Ernie drove back into the driveway and tapped the garage door opener above his visor, Christopher Hightower had slunk back into the far southwest corner, hidden from view. The rolling wooden door rose like a dirty curtain in a theater of death, and the Toyota coasted inside, braking to a stop behind the Audi's left rear fender.

Ernie Brendel's first clue that something was amiss was when the door started to roll down behind him. He had not touched the switch. The door clattered slowly toward the floor, cutting visibility as if a dark cloud were settling inside the garage. He got out of the car.

"Ernie!"

Brendel saw a shadowy figure come around the corner of the stalls, a man, carrying something strange in his hands. "Chris?"

Christopher Hightower stepped out of the shadows and stopped. He was filthy, as if he had taken a mud bath, but Ernie Brendel hardly noticed the appearance of his former friend, for his eyes were focused on the huge crossbow Hightower held at waist level, pointed at him. Brendel's surprise quickly gave way to a surge of anger. "What in the hell are you doing here?"

Hightower ignored the question. He would do the talking this time and he got right to the point. No use trying to reason with Brendel. "You're ruining me, Ernie. This is all your fault. We're going inside the house and you're going to call the NFA and tell them you're dropping the complaint."

"You're crazy, Chris. Put that thing down. Let's talk."

Hightower bristled at the insult. "No. I'm not crazy. But you leave me no choice. Now put your hands up and move away from the car." The thin arrow stayed on Brendel.

"You cheated me, you son of a bitch. I'm not calling anybody. You're not going to get away with that kind of crap anymore, not if I can help it." Brendel kept his hand on the door, hoping to dive into the car and lock it. "Put that thing down and maybe we can make a deal."

"I'm through talking. Don't be stupid, Ernie. Don't make me shoot. Make the call."

Ernie Brendel was furious, worried not only about his own safety, but what this maniac might do to Emily and Alice. A strong and active man, his thoughts turned briefly to disarming Hightower. He always thought he could take Hightower in a fight, but now, gauging the distance between them, he doubted that he could get close enough. His choice was to get back into the car, and he jerked the door handle.

Hightower squeezed the trigger as Brendel turned. *Chunk!* The arrow hurtled from the crossbow, and its sharp point sliced into Ernie's left side, just above his buttocks, penetrating almost parallel to the floor all the way across the fleshy part of his lower back. Ernie screamed in agony and fell to his knees, his powerful hands trying to rip the metal bolt from his side. Chris watched him fall, heard him scream. Savoring his victory, he began the cumbersome process of reloading the Devastator. Finally, he was in control!

Ernie staggered backward toward the door, away from Chris, who was struggling to cock the crossbow again. His hand found the edge of the Toyota's trunk and he dropped to his knees behind the car just as Hightower slid another arrow into firing position and raised the weapon, this time circling closer to the Toyota and carefully aiming at Ernie's bobbing head. *Chunk!*

The arrow slashed across the open space, nicked the edge of Ernie's left ear and burrowed into the lower panel of the garage door, trailing blood.

Ernie Brendel knew he was badly wounded, but he refused to surrender to the madman stalking him. He had survived two arrows, but the pain in his hip was excruciating. In his rage he managed to snap the metal shaft of the arrow in his side, leaving a sharp and ragged edge protruding from his body. He had to reach shelter if he was to survive. Chris had stopped near the Toyota to once again cock the crossbow, and Ernie used the time to crabwalk between the car and the garage wall in an effort to reach the Audi. If he could get in there before Hightower fired again, he could lock the door and perhaps even drive it away, smashing through the garage wall if necessary.

Hightower looked up from cocking the crossbow and

saw Brendel reaching for the Audi door. His quarry was getting away. Chris shoved another arrow into place and moved to the open area of the garage, toward Ernie. Hightower forced himself to slow down, brought the crossbow to his cheek, sighted carefully on Ernie's broad chest and squeezed the trigger. *Chunk!*

Ernie was slammed backward by the force of the sharp arrow. It punched into his right chest and dug into his lungs. He was spun around by the impact, the broken arrow at his hip gouging deep scratches in the blemish-free dark finish of the Audi. Blood gushed from the deep chest wound and Ernie tried to remain conscious. The wounds were too much. He could fight no longer. With his last bit of strength, he opened the passenger door of the Toyota and he lurched inside, knowing his life was about to end, but still trying to escape, to survive. He would never give in to Chris Hightower.

Things were not going according to plan for Hightower. Once again he had been thwarted. Ernie should have died instantly. Chris, when playing the scene in his mind, had envisioned a nice, clean one-shot attack with a minimum of blood and only a few seconds between pulling the trigger and the death of his enemy. Clean. Neat. Instead, Ernie refused to roll over and die like he was supposed to. The man was stuck full of arrows, bleeding profusely, and still challenged the authority of Chris Hightower, mocking him! He would not tolerate that! Not today, not ever again. Ernie was supposed to die, and die he would! *To hell with this crossbow.*

Hightower dropped the Devastator and reached into his pocket, his fingers closing around the cold steel of the claw-tipped pry bar. He pulled it free and stepped between the two cars. Ernie had managed to wrest open the door of the Toyota and was half inside when Hightower overtook him with a combination bear hug and football tackle. Ernie tried to struggle but was too weak from the loss of blood, which was spraying around the car like a crimson fountain as his heart pumped madly. Chris raised the pry bar and struck heavily on Ernie's head as he crawled on top of him. The arm went up and he delivered a second blow, and a third, a fourth.

He was wild, berserk with anger, slashing away at Ernie, reducing the man's head to a pulp. His frenzy carried the one-sided battle into the backseat as he hammered the steel bar down and crushed the head and face of Ernie Brendel. Blood was everywhere. Hightower did not notice that none was coming from the massive head wounds he had inflicted. The heart had stopped pumping blood when Ernie died, just as he reached the sanctuary of the car. Christopher Hightower was beating a corpse.

Reveling in his blood lust, he hauled Ernie's body from the driver's side of the car and laid him, faceup, on the concrete. Panting with exhaustion, Hightower summoned a final bit of energy and reloaded the Devastator one final time, locking it into place and inserting an arrow. Standing above his fallen prey, exulting at his victory in a life and death struggle, he put the point of the arrow a few inches from Ernie's stilled heart. *Chunk!* The force of the penetrating shaft made the body jump in one final convulsion. It was done. Hightower staggered away, sat on the concrete floor, leaned against the wall and surveyed the carnage. Ernie's blood dripped from his left sleeve and puddled onto the floor.

Let this be a lesson to them all. I did what I had to do. Ernie would not cooperate, so he had to die. It was not my fault. He made me do it.

Hightower's breathing slowed. He was tired beyond belief, but flush with his deadly victory. Unfortunately, he could not rest. There was no room in the plan for rest.

A little while later, Christopher Hightower arrived back at 1 Jones Circle, riding Ernie Brendel's bike and looking as if he had been in a train wreck. Although it had long since stopped raining and the sun was out, he was drenched, his hair stuck to his balding head, with great streaks of dirt clinging to him, and his glasses bent at a

cockeyed angle. He parked the bicycle in a thicket behind 1 Jones Circle and went in through the back way,
happy to see the Chevy station wagon was still in the
drive. He planned to clean up, then drive the station
wagon back to Middle Highway and haul Ernie's body
away, either to the little grave he had dug or far into the
New England woods.

Clyde Slicker, with no classes that Friday at Rhode Island College, was home alone, puttering in the basement workshop. He was shocked by the filthy state of his
normally well-groomed son-in-law, who muttered something about needing a shower and proceeded upstairs.
Clyde thought the boy looked hungry too, so he went to
the kitchen and poured a glass of orange juice and laid
out a couple of granola bars for Chris.

Chris did not notice that his father-in-law seemed nervous, but Clyde was quite concerned that Chris would
find that his guns were missing. On the advice of her
lawyer, Sue had decided to get rid of several weapons in
the house. She and Clyde had gathered a rifle from a ce-
dar closet in the basement, along with a gun bag containing parts of another weapon. From upstairs, they
took a .22 caliber rifle Chris had secretly bought as a
Christmas gift for their older son. A family friend took
the guns to the police station for safekeeping, but Clyde
worried that Christopher was going to be quite annoyed
to find the weapons missing. The police were already annoyed, for when they looked into the gun bag, they de-
duced that Hightower had sawed off a shotgun, making
it a particularly lethal weapon, and it was missing.

While Chris was upstairs taking a shower, Clyde stepped
into the garage with a portable telephone and made a
nine-second call to Sue at the Barrington Congregational Church, telling her that her husband was back.
Sue called a constable. That dive bomber that Chris envisioned in his bizarre poem was just about to attack.

Then Clyde observed a truly unusual sight. Chris
Hightower stuffed his stained and muddy clothes into

the washing machine. It was the first time that Clyde
had ever seen Chris, who considered washing clothes to
be women's work, use the appliance. Hightower, wearing
a white T-shirt, jockey shorts, and dark socks, ate the
food and set to work, with Clyde's advice, to straighten
his glasses.

Oh, yes, Clyde said, someone from the National Futures Association telephoned this morning and wants
you to call them. Chris acknowledged the message and
went upstairs again. Clyde called Sue at the church for
a whispered conversation that lasted fifty-three seconds.
Chris was still at the house, he said.

Six minutes after he hung up, Hightower dialed a
number in New York and, seemingly upbeat, advised
Timothy Wigand of the NFA that all was well—Ernie
Brendel had decided to drop the complaint. Mazza and
Wigand did not need to come up for the audit after all.
Wrong, Wigand replied. We need that information in
writing, from Mr. Brendel. Until then the complaint
would remain in force. Hightower did not change his
tone of voice, but when the call was over, he cursed beneath his breath, nervously chomping his jaw. *That's not
part of the plan! Ernie can't write a letter now.* Chris would
have to make another adjustment.

What happened next was totally unexpected. His
worst nightmare came knocking at the front door in the
form of Constable Vincent DeFalco, Jr., and three
Barrington policemen. Clyde opened the door and took
DeFalco and Sergeant Rick McInnis into the den as
Chris ambled in from the kitchen. Two patrolmen had
fanned out around the yard, concerned about the missing sawed-off shotgun. When Hightower saw the badges,
his heart skipped and his knees went weak. Had they
found Ernie already? He was hardly able to absorb what
DeFalco was saying. Nearby, a dog barked. No, they said
nothing about Ernie at all. Something about a restraining order, court papers, a judge's decision. When he finally took a breath, he realized he was just being
divorced, not arrested for murder.

"Let's go upstairs," McInnis told the numb Hightower, guiding him through the process of gathering a few clothes. Although he told the officers he had thrown away the sawed-off shotgun, they were not about to leave him alone in the house until they knew the fate of the weapon for certain. DeFalco and McInnis had seen other husbands go into shock like this. They never believed the little wife would get a court order to make them go away and not come back. Violence was a clear possibility.

Before they ushered him out the front door, Hightower threw a stare of cold hatred at his father-in-law. Moments before they had been washing clothes and fixing eyeglasses together, and Hightower now realized he had been deliberately set up by Clyde Slicker, the last person he thought would ever betray him. The con man had been conned, big-time. Clyde Slicker had become an enemy too.

The stunned Hightower handed over his keys to the house and cars before walking out, carrying only a briefcase and a brown paper grocery bag stuffed with clothes. The police did not know a murderer was strolling away from them with a large pistol in his briefcase.

Clyde Slicker had noticed a large cardboard box in the silver-gray station wagon, and summoned the police to take a look. An empty white cardboard box, partially draped in a dark trash bag, had the word "Devastator" stamped across the top.

Meanwhile, Hightower was on the verge of screaming, numbering his limited alternatives as the house at 1 Jones Circle grew smaller behind him. Clearly, he would never live there again. Even Clyde had turned against him! His inner rage against Sue knew no bounds. He hated her with all of his soul, but the hatred would have to wait, for he had more pressing problems at the moment. He had no money and was suddenly among the homeless. He could not use the station wagon to get rid of the body. He could not get the bicycle he had stashed in the trees behind the house, or the cops would become curious. And in the garage back at 51 Middle Highway, Ernie's battered body waited with the infinite patience of the dead, seeming still to mock him.

It wasn't supposed to happen like this! This was not part of the plan!

15

Friday Night

Time was another enemy. If there were any chance at all that Christopher Hightower could carry out his already damaged plot, he had to make some quick moves. He had originally thought that if he could get back to Jones Circle and retrieve the station wagon, he could put Ernie's body in it and drive it far away to a secure hiding place where it could never be found. And no one would ever know he was involved. He also suspected that Ernie kept a cache of money around the house, money that Hightower desperately needed and intended to find. Once Ernie was gone for good, Chris could persuade the CFTC to drop its investigation. Then he could resume business as usual, mend his marriage, and everything would work out all right.

But now that plan lay utterly in ruin. The police had just thrown him out of his own home, and he could not use the station wagon to transport the body. Still, he was confident that he could handle things. Just like on the basketball court, one had to maneuver around obstacles in order to score. As he walked on, the restraining order burning a hole in his pocket, his mind almost exploded with things that had to be done. He looked at his wristwatch. It was almost one o'clock. Little Emily Brendel suddenly became his number-one priority.

She was to get out of school at 2:00 P.M. sharp, which gave him only an hour to present himself and collect the child. It would not do for her to be stranded at school, because people would start to wonder about the absence of the predictable Ernie. Someone might come over to 51 Middle Highway and snoop in the bloody garage. No, that would not do at all.

Chris, at the wrong end of Middle Highway and with the clock ticking, decided to play a White Church card. Susanne Henderson, who had served on church committees with him, was surprised when she opened the front door of her neat home at 275 Middle Highway and found Chris, sweating, standing there wearing a winter coat and a meek smile. He wanted a favor. He was late for an appointment just down the road, and could she give him a lift? Henderson, about to head out on errands anyway, readily agreed. Five minutes later, after a pleasant chat, she stopped at the Lutheran Church next door to the Brendel home and Hightower politely thanked her for the lift. That he was disturbed about something was written all over him, and Henderson asked if he was all right. I'm fine, he said. Thanks for bringing me. Henderson drove away, concerned about her out-of-sorts friend.

Using Ernie's keys, Hightower let himself into the house, went straight to the telephone and dialed the Primrose Hill School. When secretary Gwen Groves answered, she heard a gruff male voice. "This is Mr. Brendel," it said. "I would like for Emily to walk home today."

Groves said no crossing guard would be on duty. Why not? Well, Emily and her class were on that trip down to Newport and would not arrive back until three o'clock. The man on the telephone paused, then said Emily was "a big girl now" and would be able to safely walk the one block to her house. Groves said she would leave the message with Principal Elizabeth Durfee. The man, seemingly flustered, hung up. Three o'clock! An hour later than Hightower expected. It was as if the conspiracy was still working against him, and he fought to steady himself, to maintain control of the deteriorating situation.

To make use of the extra time, Hightower rifled Ernie's upstairs desk. He found no cash, but did come up
with two checkbooks. Hightower called the Rhode Island
Hospital Trust Bank to determine the precise accounts
balances, citing checkbook account numbers for verifica-
tion, then set about cleaning them out. He learned that
one account contained $3,028 and a second one currently
had $1,737. Hightower wrote out two checks—one for
$2,700, the other for $1,500—and slipped them into his
wallet after twice forging the name of Ernest Brendel.

When the school bus pulled back into the parking lot
at 2:45 P.M., Durfee took Emily into the office to telephone her father and settle the nagging question about
going home alone. After getting no answer, Emily
boarded the YMCA bus as planned to join the after-
school program.

Moments later Christopher Hightower walked across
that same parking lot and introduced himself to Jane
Pezzulo, one of the teachers who had been on the trip.
"Can I help you?" she asked.

"I'm looking for Emily Brendel. Has the ALP field trip
bus returned yet?"

Pezzulo's guard went up. A man she did not know was
asking about one of her kids. She directed him to see
Durfee. Calm and courteous, the man said there must
be some miscommunication, and Pezzulo saw him walk
away, heading back toward the Brendel home.

Hightower may have appeared calm, but a caldron
was bubbling in his stomach. *Emily had escaped!* Now he
had to take even bigger risks and kidnap her from the
YMCA.

He cleaned the bloodstained Toyota's windows with
Windex and sprinkled baking soda on the backseat,
backed the car from the garage and drove to the Y. Once
there, his efforts again turned to ashes when Pam
Poirier refused to recognize his authority to take Emily
home. This meant going back to the house, getting Ernie's wallet from his pants, taking out the license, calling the YMCA to again imitate Ernie giving permission,

returning to the Y, and finally, at four o'clock, convincing the staff he had the proper credentials to take her away.

By the time the Toyota drove away with the elusive Emily inside, Christopher Hightower was running on adrenaline alone. His store of energy had long been used up in this hellish day. He chatted with Emily, and once at the house, sent her upstairs to play, telling her that Ernie was off at an appointment and her mother would be home soon. The little girl had no reason to doubt Mr. Hightower, the family friend.

He checked the time. Alice, about to get off work in Providence, would be the next obstacle, and he would keep the kid quiet and in the house until her mother showed up. At last he had a little time to himself, time to put his plan back on track.

Wrong again. An unexpected knock on the door sounded like thunder to a man whose nerves were stretched like piano wire. *Now what?* Hightower took a deep breath and opened the front door. A muscular young man stood there, effortlessly holding a large, wrapped item.

Bill Shorten of T & B movers saw a bespectacled man open the front door, but not the screen. The house was silent behind him. "Delivery man. I've got a box springs from Apex."

Hightower's mind was spinning, but he maintained his calm facade, telling Shorten something unexpected had come up and the people who ordered the bed weren't home. They would reschedule the delivery. Hightower had to get rid of this guy before Alice showed up. It would ruin everything if Alice saw them on the porch and started asking questions about Ernie before she entered the house. Hightower sweated it out, peering through the front window as Shorten, seeming to move in slow motion, loaded the box springs back into the truck, handed the paperwork to someone in the cab, cranked up and drove away.

Alice's bus arrived at the East Bay Medical Center shortly before six, and she was astonished to find no welcoming committee. No Ernie. No Emily. Other people on the bus also noticed the bouncy child was not there to rush up and hug her mother. Alice walked up the street, past the Primrose school and then one block farther to her home at 51 Middle Highway.

She let herself in the front door and called out to Ernie and Emily. There was no answer. The car was in the driveway, but no one was home. Puzzling. Moving to her left, she took off her tennis shoes and neatly laid her raincoat across the back of a chair in the dining room. When she turned, Christopher Hightower was standing in the doorway—a black pistol in one hand and Emily in the other.

Time. Time. Time. Precious minutes ticking away.

An angry Hightower rushed a bewildered Alice and a suddenly frightened Emily through the kitchen and down the stairs to the basement. With a thick rope, he tied them to a vertical beam in the middle of the room. The dank cellar was walled with heavy stones and dirt, with only a single small window high on one wall. The washing machine and dryer stood to one side on a raised wooden platform. Otherwise, almost all of the floor was dirt. Screams would not be heard, but he gagged them anyway, hurrying, hurrying. The banks would be closing soon. He left.

Alice, frantic with fright but trying to keep Emily calm, heard the telephone ring upstairs. It rang and rang, unanswered, each ring meaning someone was trying to reach them. The recording machine clicked on and Jim Page left a message that Ernie should meet him the next day at the train station in New Haven. Alice heard the machine do its work and felt totally helpless, locked in terror. Her little girl was here, sobbing quietly, and they were in mortal danger. Where was Ernie? She had a dreaded fear that he was already dead, for nothing short of that would stop him from rescuing them. Had Chris gone mad?

Hightower dashed over to the Rhode Island Hospital Trust bank branch in Barrington, where he cashed the

$2700 check at 6:13 P.M. Eleven minutes later he was at the Citizens Bank, where he deposited $800 to his personal account, bought an $1,800 treasurer's check in the name of Dennis Murphy to cover the back rent, and kept a hundred dollars for spending cash.

Things were finally going his way! Cash jingled in his pocket. It had been a harrowing, terrible day in which little had gone right, but he had overcome all obstacles, and finally Christopher Hightower felt his confidence oozing back.

To celebrate, he went to Sears and bought some new clothes, using one of Ernie's credit cards.

Back at the house on Middle Highway, Hightower descended into the basement, where the sense of terror was almost tangible. He no longer thought of Alice and Emily as anything more than a couple of things with which he had to deal in order to punish his enemies. In fact, as he checked the knots binding the females he had captured, he felt a dark thrill in their fear of him.

Infused with a feeling of power, he went back upstairs to be alone and map his moves for the next day. He telephoned his treacherous father-in-law, fighting to keep his emotions under control, to ask for the keys to the Maple Avenue office and also for Clyde to look up the address of his ex-wife, Ellen.

"How are you planning on getting them, Chris?" asked Clyde.

"I'll pick them up at the soccer game tomorrow morning."

"You're not supposed to be there."

"I don't think it will be a problem," said Chris, adding that the court directive primarily banned him from the house on Jones Circle.

"Well," said Clyde, "I think you better read that restraining order again."

After that inconclusive call, Hightower played back the tape that had recorded a day's worth of calls to Ernie Brendel. There were many, but one burned him and another disturbed him. There was the voice of an obviously happy Dennis Murphy, his landlord, crowing to Ernie that the police had been by that morning, looking to serve divorce papers on their mutual pal, Hightower. Then there was a call from Jim Page, obviously referring to a Saturday morning meeting with Ernie. Chris would have to do something about that.

No problem. He had plenty of time to think about what came next. He was back in control. He had money. He had the rent check. His nemesis, Ernie, was dead in the garage, and the woman and girl were tied downstairs.

At 10:00 P.M., exhausted, Chris Hightower lay down on the couch and slept well.

16

Saturday

He killed them both the next morning, after a muffin, a shower, and a few chores.

Chris was baffled by the computer on Ernie's desk. His own stuff was top of the line IBM and he had no idea how to run that boxy Apple Macintosh, which used a completely different system. To make the CFTC-NFA letter seem legitimate, it needed to be written on Ernie's printer. So he hauled the despondent, desperate Alice up from the cellar and forced her to type while he dictated. Alice must cooperate or he would hurt Emily, he threatened.

Then Hightower made Alice telephone Jim Page in New York. In a voice that betrayed nothing, knowing Emily's life was at stake, Alice told Page that Ernie's mother had taken a sudden turn for the worse and he had left to see her. Ernie would not be at the football game. Page said that was fine, and for her to tell Ernie he hoped Jolene was okay. It was 7:07 Saturday morning when they hung up.

That done, Christopher Hightower simply had no more use for Emily and Alice Brendel. Every second they breathed represented another opportunity for something to go wrong, and his plan had been derailed too many times already to take any further chances.

In the kitchen he whipped up a strange cocktail, fruit juice laced with twenty crushed sleeping pills that he had bought from a drugstore. Downstairs in the cellar of horror, holding his pistol to their heads, Hightower forced them to drink the syrupy dosage. Within moments they slouched almost unconscious at his feet, one on each side of the basement pillar, Alice reaching out to cradle Emily in her arms.

Alice was first. He tied a long white scarf around her neck and pushed hard against the slipknot. It bit into the soft flesh, gagging her. Mesmerized by the drug, she could not resist, but was aware that he was killing her. Alice Brendel went to her death knowing she was leaving her beloved child, Emily, at the mercy of a killer.

The eight-year-old girl was barely conscious, aware something was hurting her mother and that her father was not around. Emily's eyes were open when Christopher Hightower came to her, but she saw only hazy colors, her brain aswim with the sleeping potion. Hightower had now killed twice. The ability to wield the ultimate power over someone touched him almost like an aphrodisiac. He had used a crossbow and a steel bar to kill Ernie, and had slowly strangled Alice with a scarf. For little Emily he simply used his hands.

He wrapped his strong fingers around her thin neck and squeezed. The eyes opened wide, staring into his own, as he increased the pressure. A trickle of blood ran from the corner of her mouth. She could not struggle, could not call out, could not even cry. All she could do was die.

He was glad that it didn't take too long because he had things to do, places to go, people to see. The plan was back in motion.

With hardly a blip in his pulse rate, Christopher Hightower pedaled Ernie Brendel's bike down County Road to the Barrington police station. He had already walked away from cops after killing once, and now marched straight into their lair after having killed twice more. He was thrilled to realize how much smarter he was than all of them. *If they only knew!*

With a sense of accomplishment, he handed over the $1,800 check to Sergeant Rick McInnis, saying it was in settlement of a rent dispute. Would the sergeant please telephone Dennis Murphy and tell him it was ready? Thanks.

Out the door with a smile. Coffee time, where else but at the Newport Creamery, where he could spend time thinking about and refining his day. He still needed money, because the amount he had snatched from the Brendels' account would not last long. A measly nine hundred bucks. His scheme took a novel turn as Hightower molded a foolproof way to land some really big bucks.

He pedaled over to Maple Avenue at 9:25 A.M., but without keys he could not get into the upstairs office. One of his landlords, Ray DeWall, pulled into the rear parking lot, and Hightower walked around the building to meet him. To DeWall, Hightower seemed depressed, but calm, as he explained that the check for back rent was waiting at the police station. Opening his wallet and pulling out a twenty-dollar bill, he asked DeWall to leave a new set of keys in the mailbox, then rode away on the bike, heading for the grassy expanse of Haines Park, ready to coach his son's soccer team.

Hightower would clean up the unsightly mess back at 51 Middle Highway later. Right now he had to put his team through stretching exercises. About thirty-five parents milled about.

A fellow coach, Bob Pearson, was surprised to see the busy Hightower. Sue had telephoned Pearson to advise him that Chris would not be at the game because of the divorce action. Hightower calmly explained he had every legal right to be there because he was the coach.

That dream faded when Sue Hightower drove up. She was in no mood for nonsense. She didn't want to talk to him, to see him, or have him anywhere around her children. While she waited in the car, refusing to let the boys out, her friend Diane Hutton called for police assistance. Ten minutes later a patrol car rolled up and

Barrington Patrolman Bart Stanzione approached Hightower.

"Wonder what he's here for?" Pearson asked Hightower.

"Probably the restraining order," Chris replied. "Would
you go and talk to him?"

Pearson, not wanting to get drawn into a marital dispute, refused. Hightower ambled over to the policeman.

By now everyone in the park realized something more
interesting than a kids' soccer game was afoot. The officer asked Chris to leave, but Hightower responded he
had a right to be there because he was a coach. The policeman was unimpressed. Hightower looked over the
man's shoulder and saw Sue and the boys, still sitting in
the car. His gaze was one of pure hatred, and Stanzione
saw the look, thinking the man might resist him. The
policeman shifted to a position that would allow him to
move instantly, and warned Hightower that he risked arrest if he stayed any longer.

Hightower felt humiliated. These people with their
kids were his friends, they respected his abilities and
had known him for years. They knew he was a good person! The kids depended on him as their coach! He made
a brief tour of the clusters of parents, shaking hands and
telling them how much he had enjoyed being a coach,
but that he probably would not be able to continue.

Looking like a man who had been dreadfully wronged,
he climbed onto the bike and pedaled away, disgraced in
public by Sue, the awful embarrassment of the moment
burning in his bones, his thoughts in havoc. He had been
kicked off the soccer field, but he was still getting away
with murder.

He returned to 51 Middle Highway. Enough of the bike.
Using the Toyota, as matted as it was with Ernie's blood,
he set out to cruise the Barrington area, attend to little
errands and await darkness.

Back at Sears, he used Brendel's credit card to buy
two red plastic gasoline cans, remembering how helpful

those Dayton fires had been. Each could hold five and one-quarter gallons of fuel.

Hungry, he went by McDonald's drive-in window and picked up two quarter-pounders, a large fries, and a vanilla shake, then drove down Route 6 to Somerville Lumber in Seekonk, where he bought four one-gallon containers of muriatic acid.

Susan Hightower had another shock in store. As she went to the police station to complain about her husband breaking the restraining order, she saw a happy Dennis Murphy coming down the steps. Murphy showed her the $1,800 check and said Chris had paid off the overdue rent. Sue exploded in anger. Her deadbeat husband had left her with a mountain of unpaid bills and no money to support his children, but was able to write a $1,800 check for his landlord? As Murphy left, she was using some most unusual language.

Darkness found Hightower hard at work in the garage, using the acid and a scrub broom to clean up blood. Then he drove the Toyota inside and closed the door.

He loaded Ernie's stiff body into the trunk, some final drops of blood oozing from the deep lung wound, and slammed the lid closed. He punched the button, and the garage door wound noisily up, opening onto the night.

Hightower backed out, not using the lights, for he had ugly work to do and wanted no attention. As a result, the left rear fender crunched into the porch steps with a loud, grinding noise. He pulled forward, then back up again to park on the grass, with the car's trunk facing the back door. From the basement, he brought up the body of Alice Brendel and wrestled it into the backseat. Then he made the trip again for the tiny body of Emily, which he dumped atop her mother. Checking to make certain they could not be seen over the edge of the windows, he closed the house and drove away, turning on the lights as he hit Middle Highway.

Circling the St. Andrew's School field, he made certain the area was empty, then steered down the track until he reached his secret place. Moonlight filtered eerily through the overhanging branches, but there were no sounds.

Hightower found the hole he had dug earlier. Picking up his tools, he dug another one three feet away, at an angle to the first. With plenty of time, he had made the first hole rather spacious—five feet, seven inches in length and five feet wide, two feet deep. Now he was working faster. The new hole had to be deeper, so he went down three feet. But it was only four and a half feet long, two and a half feet wide.

Sweating and nervous, he popped the trunk, pulled Ernie to the bigger grave and dumped him in. Emily was next, and he lay her body on the floor of the second, deeper grave. Her mouth was open, almost as if she was just asleep. Alice's body was placed atop her daughter. The dead adults would not fit into the short graves, so Hightower bent them at the knees.

Then, by the light of a harvest moon, Christopher Hightower shoveled dirt onto the bodies until the ground was level. Before leaving, he found two short branches and, on the grave containing the bodies of Alice and Emily, arranged them in the form of a Christian cross.

17

Sunday

Christopher Hightower steered the red Toyota off the Connecticut Turnpike at exit 58 and promptly got lost. His destination was 435 Colonial Road, the home of Ernie Brendel's sister, Christine Scriabine, and her husband Alex. But it is virtually impossible for an outsider to find any address in the town of Guilford, Connecticut, without stopping a few times to ask directions.

Established in 1639 along a section of the Long Island Sound, Guilford is a maze of twisting, turning streets that meander through alleys of thick trees, beside marshy fields of cattails that grow ten feet high and along sloping grades that wind around hillocks and gullies. When the trees are thick, as they were late on the evening of September 22, many Guilford homes cannot be seen from the road.

It had been a gloomy ride down Interstate 95 from Rhode Island in the desecrated car that wore the marks of the ferocious battle in which Ernie Brendel had died. That was fine with Chris, because he counted on the shock value to accomplish the job at hand. He had wanted to avoid using the vehicle entirely, but the damned Audi wouldn't start, leaving him no choice. By the time he reached Connecticut, he had figured how to turn the messy car to his advantage.

With directions from a fireman at the station on Whitfield Street, just off the rectangular village green,

Hightower finally located Colonial Road, a dipping and winding two-lane route that led toward Sachem Head harbor. He drove past homes that bore names like the White House and Breezy Knoll, past a sign that advertised rabbit hutches for sale. At a battered black mailbox perched on a square pillar beside a plastic sleeve for the *Register-Courier*, he turned right and accelerated up a sharply inclined asphalt driveway that curved around a few tall trees.

Money. As he had motored down I-95 he thought of the big cash payoff he anticipated within hours. His plan depended only upon his nerve and brains, and he felt confident that he would soon take the Scribianes for a bundle. Violence would not be needed this time, just some good old-fashioned extortion. With the cash, he could settle a few final scores with people who had done him wrong, then disappear.

As usual, Chris Hightower had overestimated his ability. He had thought Ernie Brendel was about as stubborn as a person could be, but Hightower had not yet met Ernie's sister, Christine.

Before leaving Barrington Sunday afternoon, Hightower had returned to Somerville Lumber in Seekonk Square and paid $11.94 in cash for a fifty-pound bag of garden lime, a fifty-foot garden hose, and a wire brush. He used his purchases to scrub down the garage. Afterward he went inside the house, but could get no rest. There was a knock at the back door and two little girls wanted to know if Emily could come out and play. Christopher Hightower said Emily was not at home.

Later he went to church, not to attend services, but to use the photocopying machine in his wife's office when he thought everyone was gone. Associate Pastor Rose Amadeo came in while he was running papers through the machine, chatted briefly with him about the pending divorce, gave him a reassuring hug and left. Hightower, his mysterious mission complete, departed a few minutes later. On the way back to 51 Middle Highway, detouring near his former home at 1 Jones Circle, he spotted a woman he knew walking along Rumstick Road, and offered her a ride in the bloody Toyota. She declined.

So at four o'clock, after making sure everything he needed was in the car, he left Rhode Island and headed for Guilford.

Christine Scriabine had returned from the weekend visit with her ailing eighty-two-year-old mother in New York, feeling somewhat relieved of her pangs of guilt. Dinner Friday night was at a Japanese restaurant, where Jolene had enjoyed shrimp tempura before spending the night in Tarrytown at the home of Susanne Pandich, Christine and Ernie's sister. Saturday was spent at a craft fair, followed by lunch and some more shopping before Christine headed back to Guilford. Four guests were coming for dinner, bringing lobsters, and Christine had to prepare the salad.

When the four women arrived, Alex Scriabine had not yet started to pour the wine and the front door was not even closed when someone else showed up. The guests went into the kitchen to toss the lobsters into boiling water, while the Scriabines met the latecomer on the front stoop, a balding man neatly attired in a short-sleeve blue shirt with button-down collar, blue jeans secured by a blue-and-white-striped belt, and large black high-top sneakers.

"I'm Christopher Hightower," he said. "I'm a friend of Ernie's and I have to talk to you." In his hand was a little address card taken from Ernie's Rolodex.

The Scriabines explained that dinner guests had just arrived but that they could give him ten minutes if it was important. Hightower said he needed more than ten minutes, and that he would come back later. "It's a very important matter. How long will they be here?"

The Scribianes dodged the question with one of their own, already alert to the strangeness of the situation. Alex had never heard of Christopher Hightower, but Christine recalled Ernie mentioning the name a couple of years earlier. "Is it an emergency?" Alex asked in his distinctive Latvian-Russian accent.

"No," Hightower replied.

"Is it a matter of life and death?"

"No." Hightower politely retreated from the house, allowing the Scribianes to get on with their dinner after scaring the hell out of them. Christine telephoned Ernie's house, but there was no answer other than the machine. She felt it was unusual for nobody to be home on a Saturday night, and began to feel uneasy about the stranger who had come calling.

Hightower had some time to waste. While the lobsters were being devoured in the big house on Colonial Avenue, he downed some hot dogs at Chuckie's, drank a soda at McDonald's, gassed up the car, drove around and got lost again. He finally showed up just as the guests were leaving to catch a train back to New York. Alex asked the peculiar stranger to wait in the library while they made their good-byes.

When the front door closed and the three of them were alone, Hightower walked from the library back into the hallway, followed the Scriabines into the kitchen and launched into one of the most bizarre crime stories ever concocted.

His story, as told to the Scriabines, had a little bit of everything—organized crime figures, mass kidnapping, severe beatings, ransom demands, armored cars, walkie-talkies, Mafia thugs watching their every move, and long explanations of his own genius in running investments up to huge profits for his financial clients. It was like some kind of loony, macabre Hollywood script. The Scriabines could barely keep track of where the conversation was going as the time rolled by and they tried to piece together what this guy who was drinking black coffee at their kitchen table was really saying.

Christine, an historical consultant with the Museum of American Political Life at the University of Hartford, and Alex, a physician, had spent their lifetimes dealing with facts. Tonight, facts were hard to come by.

But the evidence that Hightower did present was horrifying enough to lend credence to other parts of his wild tale. He first produced Ernie's wallet, a fanfold of her brother's credit cards and receipts, his driver's license, and Alice's wedding rings.

He said that Ernie, Alice, and Emily had been snatched by the Mafia, along with his own wife and two little boys, and that he was acting on precise instructions given to him over the telephone by the kidnappers that afternoon. Hightower had been allowed to speak on the phone with the kids, Alice, and even Ernie, who had trouble talking because he had been badly beaten. Alice said everyone was all right, except that Ernie suffered a broken jaw when he resisted the kidnappers. Hightower's wife and children were okay too, Alice said. Nobody else would be hurt if Chris followed the instructions.

Hightower said the kidnappers told him to come up with a ransom of $300,000. Evidence of their actions could be found in the Brendel garage, and that he should always remember they would be watching his every move. He went over to 51 Middle Highway, and in the garage found the blood-spattered Toyota and a number of other items, proving something evil had happened. Ernie told Hightower on the telephone that he could only raise $50,000 and that Chris should go into the house and find Christine and Alex's address on the Rolodex. They will know what to do, Ernie had said. They can get the money.

The Scriabines were aghast at the information spilling from their visitor. There was no way they could come up with such a huge amount of money on a weekend. Who keeps that kind of cash lying around?

Not to worry, said Hightower, revising his figures on the spot. I can raise $175,000 by putting up my business as collateral, but the kidnappers want $75,000 in cash by Tuesday morning. I'm to rent an armored car from the First Federal National Bank in Boston, and when we deliver the first payment, they will turn loose some of the hostages. Simple addition would show those two sums came to only $250,000, a great deal short of the kidnappers' demands, but the Scriabines did not catch the numerical shift immediately.

They wanted two things. Let's call the police, they said. No, Hightower replied. The kidnappers said they would kill everyone if the authorities are notified. Well, why are they doing this horrible thing? Hightower explained that he had invested substantial funds and made great profits for some men with connections to organized crime. When Ernie advised him to drop them as clients, they became very upset and kidnapped both families in retribution because the moral Hightower refused to continue trading their accounts with his secret computer program.

Organized crime, right? asked Christine. Yes, he said. Organized crime. Mafia. Worst kind of people. Dangerous. Christine explained that she had a friend who was a criminal lawyer who dealt with such people on a regular basis. He had contacts. We'll call him to set up a dialogue. It was her understanding that the Mafia did not kidnap children, and these people had taken three kids.

Hightower blanched, the color draining from his face. *No!* he almost shouted. The kidnappers were very insistent that they call nobody. He had another shock coming when Christine excused herself, went upstairs and changed into black jeans and a black sweatshirt. She planned to sneak out of the house, evade the watchers and reach another home, from where she could call the FBI. *No!* Hightower quickly talked her out of that one too. Much too dangerous, he said, thinking that this stocky woman was more stubborn than her brother. *Why don't these people just do as they're told?*

Hightower decided the time had come to back up his story with hard proof, and escorted Alex and Christine out to the Toyota in the driveway. It was too dark, so Alex had Hightower drive it into their garage, where he turned on the light.

It was a horrible sight. Hightower gave the middle-aged couple a ghoulish tour that would haunt them with nightmares. He pointed out stained sections of the seats where blood had caked, a backseat covered with a white powdery substance that Hightower said was baking soda to hold down the smell. There was blood on the windows, blood in the door gutters, blood on the visors and on the seats. He opened the trunk and a block of foul odor rose, causing Christine to twist away from the rising smell of old blood. The doctor part of Alex's brain began to work on its own. Hightower said the only injury was that Ernie's jaw had been broken. No jaw in history had ever been broken in a way to set loose so much blood! Something was dreadfully wrong, he felt, but said nothing at the moment.

But Christine also was fed up with Hightower's rambling story. Too many things didn't fit. The Scriabines knew that something terrible had happened, feared for the worst, and began to take control away from a surprised Hightower. She went upstairs, moistened some cotton swabs, tapped them into the bloodstains and put the soiled swabs into a plastic kitchen bag.

Christine began turning the screws. Hightower's story was just too nutty to be believed. She wanted more proof. It was suggested that Hightower change cars and leave the Toyota behind. He could take Jolene's car, which was just sitting in the garage, unused for the past six weeks. Hightower reluctantly agreed, but that car would not start and they called a Texaco gas station for help. The mechanic was unable to get it started, leaving Hightower still behind the wheel of the blood-drenched Toyota.

While Hightower sat in the living room, Christine popped through the doorway and snapped a photo of the startled man, whose mouth hung open and eyes bugged out. He had the look of a trapped guppy. She demanded more evidence, and Hightower gave her his own overdrawn American Express Gold Card.

Now she wanted a statement, and brought out a little

tape recorder, which failed to operate. So about 11:00
P.M. she took him upstairs to her office and turned on the
goose-neck lamp on the captain's table. Christine adjusted the pillow on her chair, sat down before the IBM-
clone computer, and told Hightower to start talking. As
he dictated, she typed the extraordinary yarn: everything, all about the kidnappers and ransom and the Mafia, even wandering off track to the fact that his wife,
Sue, was missing part of a toe on her right foot and that
he pulled down 150 percent profits for one of his old clients who turned out to be part of the mob.

When her Panasonic KX-P1090 printer produced two
copies, she put one into an envelope addressed to her
husband's office in Branford, Connecticut, and told
Hightower to drop it in the mail. She eventually gave
him something else—the words he had been waiting to
hear all night. Christine, wanting to get this guy out of
the house as soon as possible, told him they would raise
the necessary money as soon as the banks opened Monday morning and would put off contacting the police.

A little after one o'clock on Sunday morning, after
spending about five hours with the Scriabines, Hightower piled back into the driver's seat of the Toyota and
headed out of Guilford, glad to be rid of the troublesome
and snoopy couple. He headed back to Barrington, quite
satisfied. The Scribianes were about to cough up
seventy-five big ones for him.

Before he could rest, he had one last job to do. Back
at the garage, he reloaded the big bag of Lee Lime into
the Toyota and drove to the fresh graves, finding his way
in the silvery moonlight. He ripped a corner from the
bag, scraped back about two inches of dirt, and poured
the white substance into the holes. The lime would help
decompose the bodies. In his haste he forgot something.
The torn edge of the lime bag fluttered into one of the
holes and was covered up, unnoticed, as he pushed the
dirt back into place. That missing corner would later
point like an arrow straight out of the grave at the man
who had purchased the lime.

He was a bit nervous when he finally lay down to sleep on the couch at 51 Middle Highway. He had the creepy feeling that he could not trust Alex and Christine. He was right.

She had already called the FBI.

Book Three

18

Arrest

Am.RIPOLBCST.TXT
BARRINGTON POLICE DEPT.
RI0010100
PICK UP AND HOLD FOR INVESTIGATION FOR THIS DEPART-
MENT. USE CAUTION.
CHRISTOPHER J. HIGHTOWER—WHITE MALE DOB 08/20/49.
DIRTY BLOND HAIR-BALD ON TOP. 5 FT 11 INCHES 190 LBS.
BLUE EYES—SOC SEC #263868171, RI LIC 38980712. SUB-
JECT WEARS SILVER WIRE-RIMMED GLASSES. SUBJECT MAY BE
OPERATING RI REG AB-343 A 1988 RED TOYOTA VIN
3JT25V21E3J3289142, REGISTERED TO ITAL AUTO LEASING
INC. GENERAL ELECTRIC CORP., PO BOX 310, BARRINGTON, ILL.
60011. IT IS POSSIBLE THAT THIS SUBJECT MAY BE IN POSSES-
SION OF A 12 GAUGE SAWED OFF SHOTGUN. ANY INFORMATION
PLEASE CALL BARRINGTON POLICE DEPT. 401-247-1910 DET.
SGT LAZZARO.
    AUTH SGT LAZZARO   SENDER PETERS

Christine Scriabine's telephone call to the FBI at 1:20 A.M. on the morning of Monday, September 23, set a manhunt in motion.

The duty officer rolled Special Agent Ralph DiFonzo out of bed at 2:30 A.M. to make the initial contact. Since a kidnapping was suspected and state lines had been crossed, federal laws came into play. DiFonzo thought he had heard just about everything in his twenty-two years with the FBI, but the story relayed by the duty officer proved he had not. The Mafia has snatched two respectable families in Rhode Island and wanted a Connecticut relative to pay a $300,000 ransom, to be delivered by a rented armored truck in Boston. He ran a hand through his thinning hair, knowing it would be a long day.

DiFonzo stopped by the Guilford Police Department, then went to the Scriabine residence, where he spent two hours. In the normal course of events he might expect a witness to give a partial account of their experiences. To his surprise, the Scriabines gave him not only the full story, but also cotton swabs they said contained blood samples, film containing photos of Christopher Hightower, a neatly typed copy of a statement he allegedly dictated, diagrams of stains and items in a red Toyota, and a couple of telephone numbers the suspect jotted down. By the time DiFonzo left, he had a detailed report that was hard to believe. Before dawn he returned to New Haven and began making telephone calls.

In Barrington things were also stirring. Patrolman John Alfred, a clean-shaven young cop, was handling the midnight-to-eight shift. A car wreck that sent one person to the hospital had been the only action until 2:45 A.M., when he got a call from the police in Guilford, notifying him of the possible disappearance of a Barrington family. Alfred sorted through the records for the previous two days and found nothing on file, so he climbed into his patrol car.

Driving past the house at 51 Middle Highway once, he saw nothing unusual. Quietly, he coasted into the long driveway at 3:05 A.M., turned off his lights and motor and sat for a moment. The blackness was complete and silence smothered the place like a blanket. He stepped onto the driveway. The stairs leading to the porch of the big house that loomed above him seemed askew, as if they had been rammed. Little alarm bells of his training sounded in his head, and Alfred decided not to walk around the property or shake doorknobs or shine his flashlight into windows. The Gulf War veteran wasn't afraid, but if he stumbled around the house, he might ruin important evidence, such as a footprint. Instead he got back into his cruiser and left.

The early actions of the veteran FBI agent in Connecticut and the young cop in Barrington were to set an unusual pattern. As the case unfolded, law enforcement officers would be extraordinarily careful to preserve evidence and to conduct exhaustive, detailed interviews with people involved in the crime. In a case that would be solely constructed on circumstantial evidence, they had to build a mountain, pebble by pebble. Dirty Harry would have hated it.

By early morning the game was afoot. The parking lot of the blocky police headquarters beside the Barrington River filled rapidly, as cops of many stripes descended upon it. As one law enforcement officer trotted up the steps, he could not help but notice that a jurisdictional mess might be in the making. *Oh boy. We're going to have problems here.*

The crime was at risk of being overwhelmed by the administrative problem of who was in control. Would it be the FBI, with their huge array of trained agents and federal resources? Would it be the Rhode Island State Police, backed by the attorney general, whose people would handle the prosecution? Or would it be the Barrington Police Department, men and women who had served their community for decades? Egos, turf battles, one agency "big-footing" another, or someone squirreling away a private bit of evidence could wreck the case. It was imperative they work together, but everyone involved questioned whether they could. As much as hunting for kidnapped families and a man riding around in a bloodstained car, the cops were treading on eggshells just dealing with each other.

Barrington Police Chief Charles Brule juggled a ticking time bomb. Telephones were ringing off the hook. Every chair had someone in it, cops roamed the halls, the stairwells, hunted for fresh coffee and tablets for notes. The headquarters simply was not designed to accommodate such a deluge.

The tiny size of Rhode Island began to play a part in solving the dilemma. Most of the cops in the decision-making loop had been working at their jobs for decades and had crossed paths somewhere with most everyone else. There was an undercurrent of mutual respect, which eventually translated into cooperation. There were enough elements of this crime to satisfy everyone. Instead of animosity, teamwork emerged. The case would eventually be noted for the courtesy and coordination extended between the various departments. It wasn't planned that way. It just happened. Screw the flow chart, they said, let's go get the Bad Guy.

Even while the shuffling of the law enforcement deck was under way, warrants were being pecked out on a typewriter by Jim Lynch, a state police corporal who resembles a tanned lifeguard. Lynch had been summoned because, after working in narcotics for years, he could sail through paperwork, particularly search warrants. He knew, for instance, that a cop can't just bust in the door of a rented office, because a suspect may be living there and have certain rights of tenancy. Without a court's permission, everything found in such a search could be blocked from coming into evidence in an eventual trial. While the chiefs palavered about who would drive this train, Lynch and the rest of the tribe were already busy stoking the boiler. He wrote the warrants, a judge signed them, and the search began.

The big problem, at the moment, was that nobody yet knew what, if anything, had happened. The only firm cards were an almost unbelievable tale from Christine Scriabine and the report of the policeman on the overnight shift that all was quiet at 51 Middle Highway. That changed in a hurry.

As the morning wore on, teams of patrolmen, detectives, and FBI agents fanned out to look around the White Church, Hightower's office on Maple Avenue, with one team dispatched to the house at 1 Jones Circle to check on the Hightower family. They quickly learned that there had been no kidnapping involving the family, as Hightower had told Christine Scriabine. One of the boys was in school as usual on Monday morning, one was home sick, watched over by a family friend, and Mrs. Hightower—Susan—was at work at the White Church. They were told police would be posted nearby in case Hightower turned up, because he was wanted for questioning on some rather peculiar matters. At that point the family had no idea of the magnitude of the storm that was about to break around them. Sue only knew that police were looking for Chris, and it had nothing to do with the divorce and restraining order. The news, or lack of it, frightened her.

A cluster of police cars also swept up to the white colonial house at 51 Middle Highway at 10:15 A.M. "Never seen so many Fords in my life," commented one neighbor as a fleet of police vehicles rolled over lawns and flower beds. FBI agents and uniformed Barrington officers prowled the exterior of the house, garage, and outbuilding, finding them all locked.

John Medici, a burly patrolman with thirty years on the Barrington force, went across the street to the fire station and borrowed some bolt cutters to snap the padlock from the garage door, and a long steel crowbar. As they entered the musty building, they found a dark Audi sedan parked near the rear wall. Medici easily popped the trunk open with the crowbar. Nothing unusual was found.

A ladder was brought in to examine a loft. They looked around the horse stalls. A broken window was noted at the left rear of the garage, and between the Audi and the door the searchers discovered a large damp area.

Next they went to the smaller outbuilding, broke the lock and pushed back the old door on its overhead rollers. A cloud of dust blew out. The police quickly determined the place was devoid of interest.

They decided to go through the back door of the house. Instead of using the crowbar, Medici gave the wooden door a vicious kick just below the knob. It crashed back against the wall, snapping off the little chain.

Medici, the first one through, felt a strange chill, as if something awful was watching him. He never wore a bullet-proof vest, but with the hairs prickling the back of his neck, he wished he had one on this morning. He rested his palm atop his pistol.

The team went from room to room, careful not to disturb anything more than absolutely necessary. All of the telephone cords were disconnected or missing, some wrapped around the receivers. There was an unearthly quiet about the place, as the police and FBI agents saw all of the belongings of a family, but not a soul in sight.

In the cellar they found a wooden beam in the middle of the room, dirty on the top and clean on the bottom half. The whole building had an eerie and frightening quality, as if the house was holding its breath.

Medici edged up the narrow staircase to the second floor and peered into what was obviously the bedroom of a child. A little girl's clothes were scattered about, stuffed animals stared blankly at him, books lay open and a blue kazoo was on the dresser. It was much like the rooms of his own children, but silence sat in it like a heavy rock. Medici, whose own father had been the Barrington police chief for decades, did not spook easily, but this time he felt a stab of bitter premonition, thinking, *This room will never get any older.*

He plugged in a telephone and called Brule. "We have some problems," he said, reporting that the house was empty and suspicious stains were found in the garage. There were no bodies, no obvious signs of violence. But there was no mistaking that something evil had been in the old house.

The officers withdrew until forensic experts could arrive, and carefully searched the grounds. Twenty feet from the back door a sliver of white caught their attention. It was a simple business card, standing on its side, wedged upright between blades of grass. They read the name of Martin Parquette, a stockbroker. It could be nothing, it could be something, but they logged it as a piece of evidence. It would turn out to be very large.

Two old war hawks sat across a cluttered desk from each other in a tiny office of the Barrington police station. As supervisors, they had done everything necessary and were now just throwing ideas at each other. The hunt was on, and Barrington Detective Sergeant John Lazzaro and FBI Special Agent Jack McGraw were confident that sooner or later the red Toyota bearing Rhode Island tag AB-343 would turn up and the mysterious Christopher Hightower would be arrested.

They had no idea where the man might be. The alleged crime had taken place in Rhode Island, he had made the alleged extortion attempt in Connecticut, where he had mentioned going to Massachusetts, and early interviews turned up the fact that he was familiar with property in New Hampshire. This character could be anywhere in New England, and if he thought police were on his trail, he might have headed west, down the Connecticut Turnpike, toward anywhere in the United States. They didn't even want to consider that possibility. Knowing a couple of generations of crooks, they guessed he was probably pretty close to home, near places and things familiar to him.

They were equally as confident he would be taken into custody. But for what? All they had was the strange report from Christine Scriabine and the early results of officers who had gone through the Brendel home and Hightower's office. Getting divorced wasn't a crime, and Hightower on Saturday had paid the bounced rent check. Something was cooking, but they only knew whatever it was had a most peculiar smell.

McGraw, out of the Providence office of the FBI,

headed the teams of special agents being brought in to
work on the case, which would be the final major one of
his long career. He was nearing the FBI's mandatory retirement age and wanted to close things out with a solid
performance. Sitting across from him was Lazzaro, the
senior police detective in Barrington, who would be his
department's pivot man on the investigation. The two of
them had spent lifetimes in law enforcement and knew
a crime developed its own tempo. As supervisors, there
were times, like this, when it was best to stay out of the
way and let the field crews do their jobs. But as time
passed, the lure became too strong. Even the most professional cop did not like to sit still when a mystery was
at hand. Both hated being stuck with the paperwork end
of things.

They decided to take a ride. Never without a police radio except when his wife Kathy forced him to go on a vacation cruise each year, Lazzaro plucked a walkie-talkie
off the recharging rack, stuffed it into a coat pocket and,
with McGraw at his side, went outside. Bored with sitting around, they declared it was time that the supervisors, meaning themselves, took a look at 51 Middle
Highway.

In an unmarked car, Lazzaro and McGraw came out of
the parking lot, turned right and joined the stream of
midday traffic heading north on County Road. In seconds they were in the heart of the tiny business district,
approaching the Barrington Plaza shopping center, heading north.

It was 1:38 P.M., and Patrolman Joe Pine was also coming up on Barrington Plaza, heading south, and braked
to a stop. Less than a mile from the police station, he
had caught the red light where County Road intersected
with the shopping center parking lot on his right and the
red brick St. John's Episcopal Church parking lot on his
left. Pine did a double take when he scanned the oncom-
ing traffic. Facing him, only a few feet away and on the
other side of the road, was a red Toyota bearing Rhode
Island plates AB-343. He quickly scanned the bulletin

about the car that police were hunting throughout New England. A 1988 red Toyota, AB-343. A balding man with wire-rimmed glasses was driving. *It was him!*

The bulletin warned that the suspect might have a sawed-off shotgun, so Pine grabbed his microphone and reported his sighting. Four hundred feet away Lazzaro and McGraw almost jumped as Pine's words came over their radio. The patrolman was right ahead of them, so they must be closing in behind the Toyota, which was obediently waiting for the red light to change. Lazzaro swept up beside the car and tapped his siren.

Christopher Hightower had seen Pine's patrol car across the intersection and was staying cool, ready to drive away, observing the speed limit. After walking away free so many times, he felt he was invisible. He was also feeling good because he had just cashed the forged $1,500 check and was flush with money. But then he heard the brief wail of a siren, so close that it seemed to be inside his ear, looked to his left and saw two stern-faced men staring back at him. The driver pointed, and yelled for him to pull to the side of the road. Hightower steered into the large parking lot of the Red Church.

Lazzaro stopped directly behind the Toyota, Pine pulled his patrol car into line, and a fleet of other cars soon flooded into the lot. After Hightower had eluded the law for so long, police seemed to be raining from the skies.

Lazzaro, a bear of a man with a surprisingly gentle demeanor, and McGraw, the serious FBI agent, did not even pull their pistols. They read this guy as a wimp. Lazzaro had told Hightower a week ago that he might be arresting him today. At that time a bounced check was the question. Now, as Hightower felt steel handcuffs bite into his wrists, he faced some of the most serious crimes on the books.

19

Questions

The detective's room at the Barrington police station was an eighteen by twenty-two box containing four desks, eight chairs, two telephones, Christopher Hightower, and a bunch of cops. The two-minute ride to the station had been made in total silence, after the arresting officers had looked inside the stained Toyota, where they found the grisly material described by Christine Scriabine, and more. A huge crossbow lay in the trunk and three human teeth were in the backseat.

Hightower surrendered without a fuss, saying he wanted to help authorities, and spread the contents of his pockets on the trunk. He was carrying $1,500 in cash, some of his own credit cards, and American Express, Sears, and Discover cards bearing the name of Ernest Brendel.

From the outset, in the church parking lot, Lazzaro gave Hightower the required Miranda rights—saying he did not have to talk to them and that he was entitled to a lawyer. Hightower replied that he only wanted to help. He did not mention that three people had been kidnapped, much less say they had been murdered and buried in the dark of night.

For Lazzaro and McGraw, the Miranda rights was paramount. They wanted it on the record that the suspect now sitting before them to be interviewed had been properly advised of his constitutional guarantees. As they went through the five-point process again, Christopher Hightower's name was typed on a printed form containing the information and he initialed each part. Hightower said he didn't want a lawyer, didn't want to make any telephone calls, but did want to help police with their inquiries. Fine, they said. Sign this paper, here and here and here. Hightower signed.

No tape recorder or videotape machine documented the agreement, one of the few missteps police would make in the case. Hightower knew that whatever he signed, it would be his word against theirs.

Lazzaro paused before starting the questions. Now that the prisoner was in custody, the detective sergeant really didn't know what to ask. Early reports were sketchy, no bodies had been found, nor any real proof of foul play. But he knew the blank spaces had a way of filling themselves in, given enough time.

The detective recalled one murder case that was solved when he ordered a pizza. A woman had been shot to death, and another woman who knew the victim's husband had been brought in for routine questioning. Police did not even suspect her, but when they were kind enough to send out for food, the woman confessed on the spot. Anything can happen, Lazzaro thought, deciding to let the interview go where it would.

He rolled a five-carbon sheet into a typewriter and, at 2:30 P.M., began to type as he asked questions.

"Q. Would you like to speak with us in reference to the disappearance of the Brendel family, and why you were in possession of his car?"

"A. Yes."

Off they went. At the end of each page, Hightower, Lazzaro, and FBI Agent Kevin Ray Eaton signed. The tale was similar to the one that Hightower gave the Scriabines, but diverted wildly on some important points.

When questioned about the demands made by the kidnappers, Hightower told police, "They were holding the Brendels and wanted $200,000"—$100,000 less than he had demanded of Christine and Alex. He added that

he knew his family was safe, although he had told the
Scriabines "that my wife and children had been taken
hostage. I did not want her to think they were in this
alone." The interview had hardly begun, and the suspect
already admitted telling lies.

According to Hightower, he had known Ernie Brendel
for three years, but they were having difficulty because
Brendel suspected "discrepancies" in a $15,000 financial
account Hightower managed for Brendel. Hightower
claimed he last saw the Brendel family late Friday, when
he spent the night on the couch at 51 Middle Highway.
The family was still asleep when he left the next morning.

Saturday night he slept in his Maple Avenue office
and received a frightening telephone call about 6:00 P.M.
Minutes later he changed that, saying he made a mistake, the call came in at noon on Sunday. "The male
caller stated that they had the Brendels as a hostage and
wanted money for them."

The caller said Hightower would find personal items
belonging to the Brendels in the red Toyota. When he
went to the Brendel garage, he not only found what he
was told, but discovered acid on the floor and blood spat-
tered all over the car. "A real bad smell [was] in the car.
I went into the house and got some baking soda and
Windex. I put the baking soda on the stain in the rear
seat and washed the windows of the blood."

Then he took the Rolodex card bearing the Scriabine
address from inside the house and relayed the ransom
demand, he told the typing Lazzaro.

For McGraw this was too much. He had better things
to do than sit around and listen to Hightower weave an
obvious pack of lies. The FBI agent got up and went to
the door, but before he left, he turned to Hightower.
"Chris, you know what happened to the Brendels. Tell
these guys."

Hightower suddenly understood the police weren't
buying his yarn, no matter how friendly Detective

Lazzaro seemed. But it made no difference. He had his story and was sticking to it.

Lazzaro and Eaton asked him why he purchased such a big crossbow.

"I just wanted it. To have it."

Why do you have a sawed-off shotgun?

"I was having problems with maybe the mob and I wanted protection." He added that he carried a Glock pistol in his briefcase.

Why go to Ernie's sister?

"Ernie had told me that they were well off." That also changed as Hightower added that the person he thought was Ernie specified that he should go see his sister in Connecticut for money.

"Did you kill or injure any member of the Brendel family?"

"No."

"Do you know if anything happened to them?"

"No. I do not."

Hightower read the nine-page statement, made and initialed eight changes, then signed each page.

The world had not stopped turning while Hightower made his statement. Right outside the police station a tanker truck filled with heating oil skidded and flipped onto its side, blocking the street. Voice traffic on the open police scanner channels, cryptic most of the day, burst into life as rescue personnel hurried to the scene. A photographer from the *Barrington Times*, only a block away, came over. While the dazed driver was pulled from the wreckage, a policeman drifted near the busy cameraman and whispered, "This isn't even your biggest story of the day."

Teams of law enforcement personnel, including an FBI agent with a pistol tucked into the waistband of her miniskirt, closed in to search 51 Middle Highway and 580 Maple Avenue. Others went to the White Church, to 1 Jones Circle, and around Barrington to question people who knew Hightower. That part of the case was coming together well.

Indeed, information came in from Connecticut that Hightower had called Christine Scriabine at 7:00 A.M. Monday morning with new information. He said he had spoken with all of the kidnapped adults and everyone were fine. Further good news, he said, was that his business clients had come up with $45,000 in cash, and he could get the rest of the needed money himself. The Scriabines did not have to put up any money at all. The ransom would be paid on Thursday afternoon, not Tuesday. The hostages would be driven in a van in downtown Providence, where men with walkie-talkies would decide the final location of the money delivery. And, he said, since the Scriabines were no longer required to pay anything, they should not have to notify the police.

Then he called Alex Scriabine at his medical office at 8:55 A.M. with a similar story, adding that Ernie's face had been lacerated in the fight, that was where all the blood had come from. Hightower said he had arranged with the Federal Reserve Bank in Boston to get the needed cash. He repeated there was now no reason for the Scriabines to call the police.

By the time the interrogations were under way, officers were aware of the huge discrepancies in Hightower's improbable story and waited to hear what he had to say about them.

In police work, if an arrest is not made within the first forty-eight hours following a crime, statistics point toward a harder road for authorities. In this instance, they had grabbed a culprit almost immediately. Little did they know that the statistics were wrong on this one—the tough police work would stretch on for agonizing months.

Something important was still missing. There was absolutely no indication of the whereabouts of Ernest, Alice, and Emily Brendel. It was as if the family had vanished into thin air.

A formal family photograph of Emily, Alice and Ernie Brendel. (Courtesy of Barrington Police Department)

Above: A candid photo of Emily, Alice and Ernie Brendel, taken in 1987. (Courtesy of Fred Bobb, Palm City, Florida)

Left: The Brendel home at 51 Middle Highway, with floral tributes in the driveway while the family was missing. *(Providence Journal-Bulletin* photo)

Left: Emily Brendel's last school photo, 1990, age 7. (Courtesy of Fred Bobb, Palm City, Florida)

Below: Emily mugs for the camera on the front porch. (Courtesy of Fred Bobb, Palm City, Florida)

Above: Christopher Hightower at his arraignment. *(Providence Journal-Bulletin* photo)

Left: Emily Brendel on a field trip, September 20, 1991, a few hours before her death. (Courtesy of Rhode Island State Police)

Christine Scriabine identifies Hightower in court.
(Providence Journal-Bulletin photo)

Susan Hightower testifies against her husband.
(Providence Journal-Bulletin photo)

Above: Defense Attorney Bob George shares a laugh with Christopher Hightower in court. *(Providence Journal-Bulletin* photo)

Above: Assistant District Attorney Mike Stone. *(Providence Journal-Bulletin* photo)
Left: Assistant District Attorney Pat Youngs. (Ken Franckling photo)

Christopher Hightower, against the advice of his attorney, testifies. *(Providence Journal-Bulletin photo)*

Above: State Police Sergeant Mike Quinn displays Devastator crossbow to jury. *(Providence Journal-Bulletin* photo)

Right: The Barrington Congregational Church. (Photo by Robin Murphy)

All of the activity erupting around Barrington blew away the veil of secrecy. Neighbors, friends, and residents started to piece together that something terrible had happened in their quaint little town. They did not know exactly what, but would find out soon enough.

There was no doubt, however, for Susan Hightower. Authorities had contacted her shortly after she arrived at work, and stayed in touch throughout the morning. They tried to keep their interest in her husband low-key, but when they asked for a photograph of Chris, she realized something serious must have happened, and she had no idea where Chris might be. Since her mother was in Ohio visiting a sick relative, and her father and sister were also at work, she arranged for friends to stay with the boys at Jones Circle. Shortly after Hightower was arrested, FBI agents showed up at her desk at the White Church and asked her to come to the police station with them. Horrible scenarios raced through her mind, but she was told that her family was in no danger, everyone was fine.

Once at the station, she was questioned for a while in a different room from Chris, and never saw him while they were in the same building talking to police. Officers did not know what to expect of her, since most wives, when they learn that their spouse is in trouble, will automatically become protective of him. That was not the case with Sue Hightower. She had already pulled the plug on their marriage by filing for the divorce, and she was openly fearful of Chris.

It did not take long for her to realize that he was involved in something truly awful. The Brendels had disappeared, and police believed Chris was deeply involved with it. From the first moment, she believed the accusations, and sought to put distance between her husband and her family. Chris had already shown, by coming to the soccer field, that a court's restraining order would not keep him away. But the police—*the FBI!*—had him in custody, and she made up her mind in the little police station that she would do everything in her power to help them put Christopher Hightower behind bars, put him somewhere that he could not bring harm to the family. Officers found that Mrs. Hightower and her family would be among their most cooperative witnesses in the months to come.

It was 8:00 P.M. before local police and the FBI were through with their questions. As a final gesture, Lazzaro ordered an Italian grinder and a Coke for Hightower, thinking that if a pizza worked once, there was no telling what a monster sandwich might do. It did nothing. After Hightower ate, he was turned over to Rhode Island State Police investigators for another round of questions, and again waived his right to a lawyer, saying he only wanted to be helpful.

This time he confirmed that he believed the mob was after him, and told Lieutenant Richard Hurst that he was about $60,000 in debt. Hightower also said that after he bought the crossbow, he took it over to the Brendel house, where he and Ernie fired a practice shot.

Hightower also claimed he helped Ernie clean up an oil spill in the garage Thursday night by spreading acid on it, and that later Ernie counseled him privately about both the money that Chris owed him and about the pending divorce. Because of his marriage problems, Hightower said he had been spending a lot of time at the Brendel house.

Alice was already up, making coffee, he said, when he awoke Friday morning, and he left about the same time she departed for the bus. Later that morning, he was given the divorce papers and ordered out of 1 Jones Circle, so he returned to 51 Middle Highway.

Hightower freely answered the questions, confident that he was in control of the situation. He knew he was smarter than these guys, smarter than all of them. All he had to do was stick to the story and they would have to let him go. After all, he knew they had no bodies, no evidence that he had been anything other than a reluctant messenger trying to carry out the demands of mobsters.

Hightower had already babbled too much, but it seemed as if he could not stop himself, for he could not resist being the center of so much attention. He enjoyed mind games, talking just to hear himself talk. The police were treating him as someone special, and a sense of importance swelled within him.

But at 1:30 A.M. the euphoria fled as police made him strip and seized his clothes for evidence. They asked about the abrasions on his legs, and one queried, "What did you do with the Brendels?"

Hightower fought to keep his temper, but it was difficult. Sitting there naked, he no longer felt in control. Suddenly, he was being treated as a common prisoner.

He told the state patrolmen that Ernie and he spent time Friday afternoon cleaning up some oil that had spilled in the garage, and later went inside to again talk about Chris's deteriorating marriage situation. To take some of the pressure off of his friend, Ernie said forget the $2,000 you owe me, Hightower said. The helpful Ernie also wrote checks for Hightower in the amounts of $1,500 and $2,700, then asked him to pick Emily up at the YMCA. When Alice came home, she made them a nice dinner of steak and vegetables.

Saturday morning, Hightower said, he left early, while the Brendels were still asleep. He had breakfast at the Newport Creamery and made good on the bounced rent check before going over to the soccer field, where he was forced to leave because of the restraining order. He spent the rest of the day and that night in his office, sleeping on a blanket on the floor and mulling his personal and financial problems.

Then, at noon on Sunday, came the fateful telephone call from the kidnappers, which launched his odyssey to Guilford.

Hurst, whose sleepy-eyed look belied his determination, was astonished at the frivolous detail Hightower was throwing into the story. The state policeman had walked into the interrogation room trying to keep his mind open. But over the next six hours, he became convinced the man before him was simply trying to pull off a scam.

"You're lying," Hurst said in a soft voice.

Hightower's jaws began to click like castanets. He was tired, his skin was flushed, and he broke into a sweat.

"In the name of God," Hurst pressed, "if you know where the Brendels are, tell us."

The man began to shake and broke into tears, putting his head into his hands, playing his role to the fullest. "I wish I could, but I can't," Hightower mumbled. "I don't know where they are."

The tears were not for his victims, but for his own failure. Hightower realized he had failed to persuade any of the policemen. So he decided to get a lawyer.

At 3:00 A.M. an agitated Christopher Hightower was taken to a jail cell, and John Lazzaro pulled up a chair nearby to be sure the prisoner did not harm himself. An hour later Lazzaro received a call and stood up to leave his post.

A curious Hightower asked Lazzaro where he was going, and the detective replied that suspicious tire tracks had been found at Boxwood Court. He was going over to take a look at them.

The prisoner, who had just spent thirteen hours insisting he knew nothing about the disappearance of the Brendels, nodded, then spoke. "Sarge," said Hightower. "You're wasting your time. They're not buried there."

20

Search

The arrest of Christopher Hightower left law enforcement officials in a quandary. It was plain from the grisly discoveries made in the Toyota and from Hightower's kidnapping fantasy that something awful had befallen the Brendel family. But Hightower had fallen silent while still maintaining his innocence, and there was not a shred of direct evidence to prove murder. The cops had a suspect, but no victims.

The Brendels had vanished, so police were forced to conduct an exhaustive search for the family while simultaneously launching a meticulous investigation for circumstantial evidence.

Until Monday, September 23, Barrington was sleepily unaware of the painful event that lay on its doorstep. The Barrington High School Eagles soccer team had just captured first place in their division, but the football team had been beaten 26–6 on Friday by Tolman High, over in Pawtucket. Village schools were opening the academic year, hopefully on a cheerful note. The previous year had been strife-ridden when taxpayers tore $400,000 from the school budget when teachers refused to take a cut in promised pay raises. Stores were holding sales and the Barrington Police Athletic League was raising money for its annual White Christmas fund.

Over the weekend, a rumor began that someone had

been murdered in Barrington, as unbelievable as that seemed. The truth seeped out when police sealed off 51 Middle Highway with strips of yellow tape, making it a crime scene.

The initial search found the house still hauntingly empty, with the personal possessions of the Brendels lying about undisturbed, as if the family had stepped out for a few minutes. Two things were obvious departures from the ordinary—the wide staircase leading from the lawn to the front porch had somehow torn from its foundation, and three empty chairs were lined up in a row at one side of the kitchen table. But there was no evidence of violent struggle.

A detailed search, during which every piece of paper would be examined, every pocket in every piece of clothing emptied, every cupboard and drawer opened, and every book thumbed through, was just beginning.

A tow truck backed up to the garage and hauled away the Audi, with its telltale bloodstains and scratches. Dark areas that appeared to be blood on the floor of the garage were sampled, and damage similar to what might result from an arrow's impact was discovered in a wall. A window, with its covering screen torn away from the sill and curled outward, drew their attention. The work continued long after nightfall, with emergency lights illuminating the scene bright as day.

Over at Maple Avenue police found a number of things in Hightower's cluttered office, including two new, empty red gasoline cans, a stash of documents, and the missing sawed-off, pump-action shotgun.

But the investigation uncovered not a clue to the whereabouts of the Brendels. There had been no word from them since Alice's telephone call to Jim Page on Saturday morning. "We had us a mystery," a police officer recalled.

By Tuesday everyone in Barrington knew that the family was missing, and the rumors began to swirl, some of them wild imagination and all untrue. The Brendels had been seen dining in New York City. Chris Hightower had spirited the family away to save them from a mobster's threat. Alice had a spat with Ernie and had taken Emily back to Pennsylvania. Body parts had been found on a bicycle path. The family was hiding in Florida, in the care of the FBI's witness protection program.

The only person who knew the truth was Christopher Hightower. "He's done a lot of talking, but told us little," Chief Brule said. "He has justified some of the happenings or places he was, but he did not give us anything on the location of the family."

One item that came from the early interviews was that Hightower had almost completed a doctoral degree in science, convincing police that they were dealing with "a brilliant guy."

After a conference it was agreed that stronger protection would be needed for Hightower than could be provided locally. He was loaded into a squad car and taken to the Adult Correctional Institutes, Rhode Island's state prison, in Cranston, where he was locked in a cell by himself. To keep him there, Hightower was slapped with seven assorted federal and state charges, ranging from possession of the sawed-off shotgun and a stolen car, to the attempted extortion of the Scriabines.

After a few hours of sleep, he was taken to an interview room of the ACI to meet John Hardiman, who had been dispatched from the Public Defender's Office to represent the destitute prisoner. Without realizing it, Hightower had drawn an ace. The dapper, bearded Hardiman was not some kid working his way up through the ranks, but a skilled attorney who would have at his fingertips all of the state resources he would need to mount a competent defense. After a brief talk with Lazzaro, who brought him up to date on the case, Hardiman had two pieces of advice for his new client. He told Hightower to shut his mouth and keep it shut.

Hardiman quickly added the services of Michael DiLauro, another veteran public defender, so that instead of being just another oddball loser without a prayer, Christopher Hightower suddenly became someone with expert legal representation.

On the other side of the ball, the case exploded Monday morning at 72 Pine Street in Providence, where Attorney General James E. O'Neil's offices were located. The lanky O'Neil, tall and with salt and pepper hair worn long and swept back over his ears, knew a hot case when he saw one. He was serving his third term as A.G., and was responsible for the prosecution of all felony crimes in Rhode Island. This Hightower thing had all the earmarks of being trouble, particularly with Hardiman and DiLauro handling the defense.

It became apparent the case would not be routine when O'Neil's chief prosecutor, James Ryan, head of the attorney general's criminal division, had to withdraw. Ryan lived in Barrington. His son played soccer at Haines Park. Ryan knew Hightower. Ryan was out.

In Rhode Island, again because of its size, the representative of the Office of the Attorney General is the top law enforcement officer at a crime scene. The job fell to a most unlikely looking lawyer, the bagel-munching, tall, quiet Pat Youngs. His scholarly demeanor was misleading, for Assistant Attorney General Youngs enjoyed putting away bad guys.

The house on Middle Highway and the office had been secured by police overnight on Monday and the serious searching began Tuesday morning. Teams gathered at the Brendel home about 8:30 A.M. and started a meticulous room-by-room search, filming and making note of the little things they saw, as well as the big ones. The cords of all telephones were unplugged. Emily's double bed was unmade and fluffy stuffed animals stared vacantly across her upstairs bedroom. A blue plastic musical toy lay atop her messy dresser. Ernie's hallway office was little more than a small, cluttered desk.

Investigators felt the same icy foreboding that had

made Patrolman Medici jittery. Then one of them saw Emily's neatly printed documents, "The Dream That Would Never Go Away," about the "awful" bad dream in which she could not escape the "viking" chasing her. Such things threatened their cold and impartial police outlook.

On a white refrigerator covered by colorful magnets holding pieces of paper in place was another of the child's poems, which began, "I am Lady Emily, builder of castles, tamer of dragons and conquerer of the black knight." The cops went through drawers of socks and underwear, examined Ernie's John D. MacDonald detective novels, stacked side by side on a shelf, and found a TV program guide still open to last Wednesday's programs. Such things tore down the protective curtain of the investigators and made them start to care about the victims.

"We got to know them, going through every scrap of paper in the desk, every piece of clothing in the closet. They became real to us," said one policeman. "It got personal."

While the cops made their rounds in the house, they could hear the shrill whine of a chain saw. In the garage, investigators carved out a wall section containing the broken window and torn screen. U-Haul trucks were backed onto the property and loaded with scraps of paper, clods of dirt, pieces of wood, and bags of other material. Eventually, hundreds of pieces of potential evidence would be stored in empty cells at the State Police headquarters or sent south to be examined by the scientists in the FBI's crime laboratory.

With the investigators busy inside, grid patterns were laid out to govern a massive outdoor search. It would be an extraordinary task in any locale, but was even more difficult around the craggy landscape of Barrington, where at least one lake was said to be bottomless, coastal tides sucked things out to sea twice a day, and falling leaves covered vast wooded acres.

Police fanned out in the woods, crawled through thickets of briers, poked sticks into piles of leaves, and hunted alongside trails. They found absolutely nothing on Tuesday. Nothing on Wednesday. Nothing on many other days yet to come.

On Thursday afternoon, September 26, the bleak sum of their work was revealed during Hightower's arraignment in District Court in Providence. Patrick Youngs could not charge Hightower with murder. After two days of searching, he said there was "evidence of weapons being discharged and blood on the property." But it wasn't enough.

Nevertheless, Youngs asked Judge Stephen Erickson to set a substantial bail. Hardiman argued for a reasonable bail, claiming his client had no previous criminal record and was not some common criminal, but a man known and highly regarded within his community.

Erickson was unmoved and set bail at $100,000. It made little difference. Hightower was penniless and had bilked too many people in the past for anyone to lend him anything.

As the search intensified, the prosecution coalesced into a team that would see the case all the way through. Since Hightower had Hardiman and DiLauro—"two tough guys," in the opinion of the prosecutors—O'Neil added Assistant Attorney General Mike Stone to the State's team. The choice was crucial, because Stone's strengths exactly complemented those of Youngs'.

Youngs has infinite patience, teaching deaf students for a year at Gallaudet College, where his father was a dean. A graduate of Catholic University in Washington in 1978, Youngs spent four years working as a public defender in the nation's capital before applying to the Rhode Island Attorney General's Office for a job while on a visit home to Maine. At six feet two inches, he has the look of someone raised by a family of friendly giraffes.

In contrast, Stone is a restless, wannabe cop. Youngs

ate bagels, Stone ate doughnuts. Youngs, a walking file cabinet of legal knowledge, preferred working in the courtroom, while Stone liked to prowl crime scenes and get his shoes muddy.

The son of a former mayor of Warwick, Mike Stone wanted to follow the footsteps of his uncle Walter, who spent years as superintendent of the Rhode Island State Police. But bored with Boston College, he joined the Army during his first semester in 1966 and quickly found himself graduating from Officer's Candidate School during the early Vietnam buildup. The same day that Bobby Kennedy was assassinated in Los Angeles, Mike Stone caught a Viet Cong bullet in his right knee as his platoon suffered thirty-three casualties. For his leadership in Dragon Valley that day, Stone was awarded the Bronze Star, though he never received the medal. His dream of being a cop was shattered that day, but a few years later Stone came out of the New England School of Law—working during the day to support a family and taking classes at night—and joined the A.G.'s Office. At five-foot-nine, he has, when angry, all the friendliness of a hungry piranha.

Over the coming months, changes in law enforcement ranks put the final members of the prosecution team in place. In Barrington, John Lazzaro was promoted, and while he would continue to play an important role, he was replaced on the street by Detective Kenny Schauble, a serious officer who had come into the Barrington force two decades before as Lazzaro's clerk. Schauble was paired with broad-shouldered Detective Sergeant Gary Palumbo, who stoically endured thousands of bad puns because his name and job remind people of television cop Columbo.

From the Rhode Island State Police came Jimmy Lynch, newly appointed to the rank of sergeant; Sergeant Mike Quinn, a forensic wizard who constantly chewed a toothpick while thinking; and Sergeant Doug Badger, an affable ex-Marine with a talent for solving problems.

Before the case was done, Christopher Hightower would

get to know the names of Youngs, Stone, Schauble, Palumbo, Badger, Quinn, and Lynch very well. At least Lazzaro had been civil to him. These guys gave him no slack at all. When someone would refer to the prisoner as "Mister Hightower," Badger would snap, "He's not a mister, he's a monster!"

Each member of the prosecution team became obsessed with the case. The Brendels, whom they had never met, became their friends. Emily became their child.

Palumbo kept one of Emily's toys, a little comic button that flashed pictures of Bugs Bunny. Over the months, he would carry it in his pocket, rubbing it like a rosary bead as he thought of the little girl. His thumb eventually wore away the rubberized backing, but Palumbo would not part with the button until the case was settled.

Search groups of more than fifty people lined up at arm's length to sweep densely forested areas, at times getting down on their hands and knees to push through the brambles and thick underbrush. They worked the area behind St. Andrew's School, along the bike path, behind 580 Maple, Haines Park, compost piles, a baseball field, a bird sanctuary, stables, farmland, and other places where Hightower could have secreted bodies. They found nothing.

Kenny Schauble, who grew up in Barrington and thought he knew every path and pond, stalked the fields on his own between search sweeps. Each time he looked into the eyes of his own eight-year-old daughter, he also saw Emily, and that would send him back out the door to search places the organized groups might never reach. Working sometimes twenty hours a day, he prowled shadowy parts of his hometown, but each night came home empty-handed.

Where are they? he would ask himself on his lonely walks. Where in the hell did he put them?

21

October

October came in with a rush. On the international scene, the fighting in Croatia continued unabated and a military coup ousted Haitian President Jean-Bertrand Aristide. On the domestic front, hearings began on President Bush's appointment of Judge Clarence Thomas to the U.S. Supreme Court. The Atlanta Braves and Los Angeles Dodgers were in virtual deadlock for the National League West pennant with only four games left in the season.

Interesting stuff, but in Barrington there was only one story, and it was going nowhere fast. A week had passed since Christopher Hightower had been arrested, and nothing had been heard from the missing family of Ernest, Alice, and Emily Brendel.

Daytime temperatures were comfortable, in the low seventies, and a hint of rain was in the air as a cold front swept in from the west. The weather made little difference to the search parties fanning out each day to examine piles of leaves, stacks of debris left over from Hurricane Bob, and the immediate waters that hug Barrington. They were bleary-eyed and exhausted, tired to the bone.

After seven days of fruitless work, the ground search was temporarily suspended on the first day of October, while the police and FBI took stock of the situation. They had turned up nothing that might help them, but relied on gut feelings that *something* must turn up, sooner or later.

The Federal Bureau of Investigation is a monster when it comes to gathering data. Material from across the nation pours into FBI offices, where experts grind it through computers. The result is an extraordinary amount of information. FBI charts, based on thousands of situations, can suggest a pattern when a crime seems to be a unique act. There is no such thing as a new crime. Everything has been done before, by someone, somewhere, and the FBI has it all recorded. Want to know how a serial killer operates? The Behavioral Science Unit can make an almost perfect forecast. The same is true of car thieves, burglars, and a murderer who has to dispose of several bodies. Statistics and probabilities are powerful tools in law enforcement.

It was FBI information that confined the search in Barrington, rather than spreading all over New England. The numbers said a killer needing to hide multiple victims usually does so very close to the murder site. For instance, Jeffrey Dahmer disposed of his seventeen victims right in his own residence. John Wayne Gacy buried most of his thirty-three victims beneath his suburban Chicago home. This was the sort of pattern on which the law enforcement team was betting, hoping that Christopher Hightower would not break ranks with the many murderers who had gone before him.

"Our opinion was always that they were buried around here somewhere," Lazzaro would say later. "We weren't discouraged. That's something you learn early in police work. You check, then you recheck and you recheck again."

About one hundred officers, volunteers who had come from throughout Rhode Island, some all the way from Cape Cod and Connecticut, converged on Barrington on Wednesday, October 2, for the most intensive single search of the campaign. Fifteen trained dogs trekked along, trying to pick up a scent. Some of the animals were put into rubber rafts, to sniff the ponds and coastline. Helicopters clattered overhead, loaded with sensitive infrared gear, searching for heat patterns in disturbed soil.

The ground search was confined to areas Hightower had last been seen walking, primarily near the Glendale Acres development, close to Brickyard Pond, and later to the Lion's Head development not far from the Brendel home. The dogs would go in first, followed at twenty-minute intervals by the ground teams, who would leave yellow police ribbons on limbs and bushes to mark places that had been searched.

Such a concentration of forces roused media interest, and they, in turn, attracted crowds of sightseers. Barrington became tied in gridlock traffic as a macabre circuslike atmosphere gripped the town.

Police rolled the dice, hoping that by showering the most likely areas with maximum attention, something would be found. One by one the teams reported back to headquarters, dirty and tired, bearing the slashes of sharp branches. They had found nothing.

Barrington Police Sergeant Richard McInnis said afterward that the hunt would be the last of its size. "There will be no more searches on the scale that you saw today," he announced.

The report was a bitter pill for Barrington, where emotions were running high. The community was confused and sorrowful, and no resolution for their agony appeared in sight. A symbol of their grief could be seen every day. At the foot of the driveway at 51 Middle Highway, below the yellow police tape, a somber little garden took shape. Unbidden and without planning, the families and neighbors and friends of the Brendels built a shrine of hope.

Potted plants, formal bouquets, and loose gatherings of wildflowers were placed in a line across the driveway, in memory of the family that had lived in the big white house.

At the Barrington Congregational Church, ministers and congregation alike flung a protective cloak around the

Slicker family while being plainly bewildered why Chris Hightower, whom all of them knew to be a Christian gentleman, could be accused of such a heinous crime. "He was the best Sunday-school teacher I ever had," said one of his former pupils.

But that was merely recognition that Hightower had once been there. He had been arrested on September 23, and by Sunday, October 6, the church members knew their mission was clearly to take care of the Slickers and those two kids. The plight of former Sunday-school teacher Chris Hightower quickly became secondary to the plight of his family. The Slickers, Sue, and the kids nervously arrived a bit after 10:00 A.M. that Sunday, knowing that all eyes were upon them and feeling the strain of having been placed in a media fishbowl. But they were greeted, not with disdain, but with a warm outpouring of affection and support, hugs and promises of help. "They came to a place where they found great strength," said one parishioner. "They carried on with a great deal of courage."

The Reverend Joe Dye, who had been at the church for three years, was a close friend of the Slicker family, worked daily with Sue in the office and had provided marriage counseling for Sue and Chris, who was active in the church. Dye's involvement in the stressful situation in the coming months eventually would lead him to resign to take a job near Chicago. But in October he had a congregation in crisis, and although he encouraged them to look for "that light in the darkness," there was little question that a lot of darkness hovered around the White Church on this day. TV cameras lurked in the parking lot, for the White Church, with its splendid steeple, had become part of the gruesome story.

Clyde and Mary Lou Slicker issued a statement on that Sunday, saying their grandchildren—John and Bobby—"are innocent victims, who need our best efforts to find a stable life in the midst of tragedy over which they have no control." In unconscious proof of the incredible stress that the family was enduring, seven-year-old John had a tough time in the sanctuary, making an airplane of folded paper, sobbing, covering his ears with his hands during a hymn. When he walked out of church, he was muttering to himself and everyone who saw him felt their hearts break.

Two days later Sue Hightower met with FBI and Rhode Island State Police officers for an in-depth interview. Her manner was low-key and she was totally collected in her thoughts, telling them that the pressure she felt was more for the children than herself. She explained that the family planned to spend some time at the vacation house in New Hampshire to escape the media insanity that threatened to swallow them whole. With her attire impeccable, her makeup perfect, the police realized that she was feeling more comfortable now with the idea that Chris was never going to get out of jail, and never again be a threat to them. She was, as always, cooperative and helpful. Her worry was solely for her children and for the missing Brendels, not for the man who once was her husband.

As the weeks of October passed, thoughts turned to upcoming Halloween celebrations, a time when children put on their costumes and knock on doors, asking for candy. This year, the little witches, ghosts, Ninja Turtles, princesses, clowns, and beasties would all be escorted by their parents, for the memory of the child who would not be with them dominated the community. The children might not understand the hoopla going on around them, but knowing that Emily would miss Halloween made them mournfully aware that something was wrong in their world. Orange pumpkins carved with triangular eyes and snaggle-toothed grins joined the floral monument on Middle Highway.

Nearby, at the Primrose Hill School, students in the ALP class grew agitated by Emily's absence. Her hand-painted desk stood empty in the classroom, awaiting her return.

* * *

Chief Brule wrote a letter to the people of Barrington, telling them the lack of success did not mean the police were on the verge of surrender. "We want to reassure this community that the police department will never cease investigating and searching until all members of the Brendel family are found," he wrote. The chief also urged residents to be alert for anything unusual. A confidential post office box number was obtained for responses to police pleas for assistance. Anything would help, for at the end of the second week of searching, and then again at the end of the third week, the police still had no idea where the Brendels were.

All they did have was a smug and silent Christopher Hightower, and a growing sense of unease with a case that had a murder suspect but no bodies.

The St. Andrew's School, at 63 Federal Road, is a college preparatory school for some 127 students. Both girls and boys attend the boarding school, which offers instruction from grades five through twelve and employs thirty-two teachers. It was founded by the Reverend William Merrick Chapin as a school for homeless boys in 1893.

With an endowment of $4 million and a physical facility valued at about $9.6 million, St. Andrew's is among the upper echelon of New England's prep schools, and has the added attraction of being located in the quiet countryside of coastal Rhode Island. With an average class size of only eight students, instruction is personal and apparently successful. Every member of the Class of 1991 went on to college.

Only a mile from the center of Barrington, the campus is a collection of sturdy stone buildings and manicured grounds that slope away to playing fields, a thick stretch of woods, and a vast open meadow that creases through a valley. Most of the ninety-six-acre campus is open space, laced with trails for runners.

Classes began September 11, and the Parents' Weekend and Fall Fest were held October 25–27. Parents paying $17,900 a year to board their kid at St. Andrew's

were not thrilled about what was happening around the
school: searchers crunching through fields, helicopters
churning overhead, and headlines concerning missing
bodies. It was all quite disturbing. The kids were aware
of what was going on outside the classrooms, because
while practicing soccer or field hockey, they only had to
look around to see a police dog with its nose to the
ground passing by. They could pick up almost any newspaper and a story would be up front on the forlorn
search. The students were right in the middle of it, for
the house at 51 Middle Highway was less than a mile
from their beautiful campus.

Everyone watched television, and the cameras were always there for the searches. Tabloid, bucket-of-blood coverage is rare among New England's newspapers, deemed
to be rather inappropriate. Television, however, went by
different rules, with much of its offering unfiltered
through the layers of editors present at any newspaper.
As a rule, TV did an adequate job on the story of the
missing Brendel family, with one station being an extraordinary exception.

Viewers tuned to WPRI-TV in East Providence
watched in amazement as Logan Crawford of the Eyewitness News Team breathlessly announced "exclusive
information Channel 12 may have uncovered." Learning
that Hightower purchased cans of muriatic acid, Crawford went out and bought some too, and concocted a
story about what acid is capable of doing to flesh.

With the camera rolling, he snapped on a pair of red
rubber gloves and declared Channel 12 "may have uncovered the truth!" The acid was poured into a metal
can and Crawford then produced the centerpiece of his
scoop, a supermarket package of turkey legs. Using a
pair of steel tongs, he snared a drumstick and dumped it
into the acid.

Twenty-four hours later the camera again was on the
TV sleuth as he clamped the tongs around the turkey
leg, pulled it from the vat and proudly held up what he

termed "the stomach-turning result." Indeed, the turkey drumstick had been reduced to a mottled, destroyed piece of meat that hung from the bone in fleshy, wet strings.

Crawford's gory report clearly indicated he was of the opinion that the flesh-destroying acid was why the cops had not found any trace of the Brendels. His sensationalist fantasy, with not an ounce of evidence to back it up, horrified viewers and angered police. The Eyewitness News reporter was as wrong as wrong could be, but from then on the media would travel a hard road in talking to Barrington residents, who were understandably outraged.

By the end of October the grinding, repetitious search had flung its arms wider and wider. It looked as if Hightower had broken the FBI's statistical mold, because every square inch of Barrington had been searched, from its ponds to its darkest stretch of forest, and not a trace of the Brendels had been found.

They dug where a psychic predicted the bodies would be and came up empty. They went through the 450-acre Norman Bird Sanctuary in Middletown, took tracker dogs onto Aquidneck Island, and searched as far away as Newport, along scenic Ocean Drive and at Brenton Point State Park, where Emily only a month earlier had watched the Viking ships. They checked around the Swansea Mall and the mushy ground behind the White Church. They followed the barren land beneath the long power line beside the Gate of Heaven Cemetery.

Autumn departed and the peak of foliage season was gone, the trees discarding their coats of many colors. Temperatures began their yearly dive toward winter as calendars were flipped to November. The litany of news had a familiar ring. Jesse Jackson was trying to decide whether to run for President. Middle East peace talks were foundering. Clarence Thomas became the 106th Justice to sit on the Supreme Court. *Star Trek* creator

Gene Roddenberry died. The Braves had won the National League pennant and lost the World Series to the Minnesota Twins.

But there was still only one story of interest in Barrington. On October 20 grappling hooks were used by searchers to probe the river behind the White Church. At the end of the month, as kids got ready to trick-or-treat on Halloween, police with a backhoe dug up a brush pile at St. Andrew's. Nothing.

State Police Sergeant Doug Badger and Barrington's McInnis composed a lengthy official report that gave precise dates and places of October's searches, who was involved and what they did. After seven major efforts between September 23 and the end of October, Badger wrote: "During all these searches, no evidence was found." The mood around the police department was glum.

Unknown to all, unexpected help loomed on the stormy eastern horizon. E.T. was on the way.

22

Discovery

Hurricane Grace came late in the season, but packed enough wallop to leave Bermuda reeling under its high winds and waves before trudging north into the deeps of the Atlantic Ocean. Its track should have taken it far to the west, letting the hurricane vent its fury in open waters. Nature had other plans.

Grace wasn't the only storm of October. Another swirling dervish had stalled beneath a ridge of high pressure near the Canadian Maritimes, and it sucked energy from the remnants of the hurricane, which was moving north. The upper Atlantic was thrown into chaos, and the new storm, fighting the powerful weather ridges to the north and east, had no recourse other than to move west, straight toward the belly of New England.

Temperatures plunged as the storm headed for land. Mountainous seas forty-two feet high were reported off the Georges Bank near Cape Cod. Heavy surf pounded the beaches and a howling wind echoed along the coast from Maine to the Carolinas.

Meteorologists said it was an Extra-Tropical Depression and unofficially dubbed it "E.T." Hurricane Bob had been bad news for Rhode Island in August, but it was a pussycat compared to the new blow of October.

Huge clouds of purple and gray bouldered along the horizon as E.T. slammed ashore as if it had a score it had to settle. A Narragansett fisherman was swept to his death. Summer cottages were uprooted and went bobbing away to sink in the angry sea. A helicopter crashed trying to rescue capsized mariners off Long Island. By high tide at 2:00 A.M. on the last day of October, incredible damage had been done.

Not even the President of the United States was exempt from its fury. Walls and windows caved in at President George Bush's family mansion at Kennebunkport, Maine, when fifteen-foot waves curled over the roof.

The rowdy storm created wicked Halloween weather across the entire upper tier of the nation. But it is truly an ill wind that blows no good. In Grand Island, Nebraska, police arrested a motel robbery suspect by following footsteps in fresh snow to his front door.

A similar piece of good fortune was about to befall the exhausted law enforcement officials in Rhode Island, who were cursing the horrible nor'easter for interrupting their search. Walls of water and gale force winds pounded Barrington without mercy, pushing around everything not solidly anchored. It seeped into cracks, bubbled around doorsills, rattled storm windows, scoured the coast and drenched the fields. Where dirt was loose, the heavy rain compacted soil.

In the woods behind St. Andrew's, beside a trail used by cross-country runners, two sagging depressions appeared as the rain pounded down, hour after hour. Leaves spun in the saucer-shaped craters and settled like gentle cover when the weather finally moderated.

E.T. had done a little police work in Barrington.

Isabelle and Pedro, as usual, were taking Katherine McCloy for their morning walk. It was about seven o'clock on Thursday morning, November 7, with a nip of autumn in the air, so she put a down vest over her sweatshirt before stepping from her Cape Ann style home. The dogs sped through the open door, into a vast field that separated the houses on Winsor Drive and the St. Andrew's School.

Because much of the search for the Brendels had cov-

ered the immediate grounds, area residents had a
heightened awareness of their surroundings. The family
had been missing since September 23, forty-four days,
and for the people of Barrington there was a feeling of
something unfinished. They had been through a media
circus, and residents wanted nothing more than for their
town to return to normal, and they knew that would
never happen until the fate of the Brendels became
known. Nearly seven weeks had passed, and the mystery
lingered.

Barrington residents still could not comfortably go for
walks, play in the parks, or splash along the coast without taking notice of a new gap in the brush or broken
branches or leaves that had fallen in a strange pattern.
Homeowners knew their land and kept a macabre watch
for anything out of the ordinary.

But with the fruitless results of the police searches,
Winsor Drive homeowners and St. Andrew's students
were finally falling back into normal routines. Katherine
McCloy was mentally organizing the busy day ahead as
she followed her two mixed-breed dogs through the big
field, her breath forming little puffs of vapor in the
morning chill. Within ten minutes they reached the top
of their loop, near Middle Highway, and turned onto a
familiar wooded trail, McCloy's feet automatically following the path she had strolled almost daily for several
years. Her husband, Steve, would be getting ready for
work in Providence, the kids would be preparing for
school. A warm cup of coffee had an appealing lure.

McCloy noticed that Pedro dashed busily ahead. Normally, Isabelle would have taken the lead, but today the
fourteen-year-old dog, almost deaf, wandered about a
dozen feet into overgrown thickets near the trail and refused to come when called. McCloy raised her voice,
clapped her hands. Isabelle ignored her. The dog snuf-
fled around, sensitive nose to the ground, pawing at
leaves about fifteen feet into the thicket. The spot would
have been unreachable only a few weeks earlier, but the
recent storm and the autumn weather had thinned the

foliage. McCloy had a horrible thought. She had seen a mother skunk and its four black-and-white furry babies there earlier in the year. Isabelle might be courting disaster.

McCloy pushed aside some branches, moving closer to the dog. Wet ground in two spots had settled a few inches below the rest of the area, both places camouflaged by the damp leaves. As a gardener, she recognized the result of loose ground that had settled after a rainfall. She saw traces of a white powderlike substance, and deep in her mind the wheels began to turn. She was afraid to believe what she suspected.

With a sense of horror, she pulled the inquisitive Isabelle away, noticing as she did that two branches about four feet in length lay in a cross on the ground. Taking a deep breath to steady herself, Katherine McCloy cut short her walk and headed across the field for home, where her family was having breakfast. She quietly confided her suspicions to her husband, and they decided to get the kids off to school before doing anything. After seven weeks another half hour would make little difference. When the house emptied, she steeled herself for an ordeal, picked up the telephone and dialed the police.

McCloy was on a first-name basis with dispatcher Carol Reavey, who sat at the Barrington Police Department's exotic communications console that morning, monitoring the rows of telephones, radios, and video screens surrounding her position. Maps and memos were clustered in the office, and a rack of coffee cups was beside the door. Reavey, her silver shield pinned to a dark blue sweater, was surprised to hear the polite Katherine McCloy on the line, apologizing for disturbing her, then reporting her mysterious find.

Reavey had been poised for just such a call. She switched McCloy to John Lazzaro, who was sorting through the overnight reports. He also knew Katherine McCloy, and trusted her information. This would not be one of the hundreds of crank calls and letters that had inundated the weary investigators. He listened, and keeping his voice calm, told her to return to Middle Highway. Someone would be right there.

As Lazzaro passed the information to Detective Sergeant Gary Palumbo, who dashed for his car, Sergeant Rick McInnis commented that the area had already been thoroughly searched, but since it was so large, something may have been missed.

Palumbo, wearing a clean raincoat over his suit, found Katherine McCloy waiting as instructed when he pulled up in unmarked police car C-10. They walked down the soggy edge of the field, and McCloy led him about fifteen feet into the underbrush to the depressions. To Palumbo the area seemed to be an empty box, with walls of ivy, vines, and brambles, and overhanging tree limbs. One could not see it from a few feet away, but not so much as a skinny stick of a tree stood upright within the little open space.

The detective kicked at the leaves and saw that the dirt beneath was of different colors. Unusual. He pressed his foot against the soil and felt a springiness. He rubbed some of the white powder between his thumb and forefinger. Palumbo wanted to see more, but needed a shovel, a tool in the trunk of every police cruiser, although missing from unmarked cars like his.

When Palumbo called McInnis, who went to a fire station to request a shovel, McCloy volunteered to fetch the new long-handled Craftsman spade she had recently purchased at Sears. Fine, replied Palumbo, and off she went. Alone, he bent down and carefully brushed some leaves away from the oblong areas McCloy had discovered.

Kenny Schauble, still in uniform after an overnight shift, was driving up the Wampanoag Trail, heading out of Barrington to East Providence, when he heard Palumbo's radio call. He spun his patrol car around and reached the site within minutes. McCloy returned about the same time with her big shovel.

* * *

After dispatching Palumbo, John Lazzaro snatched a list of important telephone numbers from his bulletin board and dialed one. On any other morning, Doug Badger would have come in, grabbed a cup of coffee, and spent some time with Lazzaro before going upstairs to a room set aside for the Brendel case. It had been Badger's routine for weeks, but today, of all days, the State Police detective sergeant instead had gone to the State Police barracks, miles away in North Scituate.

Badger answered on the first ring, only to slam the phone down as soon as Lazzaro told him there was a strong possibility the search was over. Badger's red Ford peeled rubber skidding out of the headquarters lot and his speedometer pegged at 85 miles per hour, simply because it could not record the faster speed at which Badger was flying back to Barrington. Lazzaro also headed over to the site, where he would establish a command post.

Kenny Schauble paced the clearing, and like Palumbo, felt sponginess beneath his feet, surprisingly different than the surrounding hard ground.

He dug the pointed blade into the dirt, placed a foot on it and shoved. It slid in easily, meeting no resistance from a tangle of roots, as he had expected. Already there was a foul smell, possibly the result of Isabelle's digging through a vapor barrier that had contained the odor below the earth.

Schauble inserted the blade again, deeper, until it bumped against something, then came up with dirt fringed in white lime. He looked up at Palumbo, their faces mirroring the unpleasant inevitability of the discovery. "Oh, shit," whispered Schauble. The spade had hit the knee of Alice Brendel.

Schauble, Palumbo, and McCloy backed away. Strict orders had been issued that when a discovery was made, the scene must be protected at all costs. McInnis showed

up, and wearing a face mask and rubber gloves, confirmed the findings and reached for his radio.

McCloy felt as if she were watching an outdoor play, in
which she had inadvertently inherited a leading role.
She now knew for certain what her dog had found, and
had no desire to stand around to see the bodies. She
asked Palumbo if she could leave, and the detective escorted her from the site and volunteered to drive her
home. Although still shaken from the discovery, she
declined and went back to Winsor Drive.

Rick McInnis's voice crackled over the secure FM radio channel 4, one heard only by law enforcement personnel. He had a question for John Lazzaro. "Does
anyone know what time is sunrise tomorrow?"

Sunrise! The word galvanized everyone who heard it
that gloomy Thursday morning at 9:13 A.M., a day that
would be without sunshine for them all. It was the code
word to be used only when the bodies of the Brendels
were found.

In Providence, Attorney General Jim O'Neil got the report and dashed for his car, seeing Mike Stone on the
way. He shouted that he had just gotten a call from
Barrington and told Stone to climb in.

Stone balked. He had carefully planned for this moment. In the trunk of his own automobile was a duffel
bag containing heavy clothes, boots, wool socks, and a
warm jacket—the kind of stuff he would need to stay out
in the cold. "Forget it," called O'Neil as he pushed aside
his official chauffeur. The general would do his own driving today. Stone jumped in, dreading the chill he already
felt.

O'Neil clicked on the flashing police light and floored
the accelerator. Siren screeching, he sped through the
downtown streets and onto the expressway, focused on
getting to Barrington as soon as possible. It wasn't until
later that the top law enforcement officer in Rhode Island was told by his nervous passenger that he had
topped out at 115 miles per hour.

* * *

Pat Youngs was drudging through paperwork in Courtroom 2 of the big brick courthouse when someone whispered the news to him. In charge of arranging the state's calendar of prosecution, the table before him was covered in file folders representing cases awaiting disposition. The whisper jerked him upright in his chair so suddenly that his boss, Jim Ryan, realized what had happened and quietly said, "Go!"

Youngs dashed upstairs to where he was due to work on a complicated case involving a number of abortion protestors. He needed a postponement, but in the chambers of the presiding judge he pulled up short. Standing there was Mike DiLauro, one of the public defenders handling the charges against Christopher Hightower. When the judge asked why Youngs needed to be excused, Youngs said he could only tell him in private. DiLauro suspected there was only one thing that would require Youngs to say that. The bodies had been found! He left the room without protest, and Youngs received permission to postpone the abortion matter.

Youngs hurried to Barrington, not knowing the precise location of the scene. He drove around the web of roads until he found the gathering cluster of police cars. Dressed only in his go-to-court business suit, he had one consolation. He knew Mike Stone had prepared for the day by stowing away enough gear to get him through a nuclear winter, and now here they were, standing side by side, shaking in the cold, equally miserable. Stone was not amused.

But O'Neil, Youngs, and Stone were breathing easier as the well-planned operation to exhume the bodies swung into operation. The discovery had gotten them off a sharp legal hook. In only six days they had to either charge Hightower with murder or go with the minor charges for which he was being held.

While there was obscure precedent in Rhode Island to try someone for murder without a corpse as evidence, they did not want to handle the Brendel case that way.

The State would not offer Hightower any deals, but they were concerned about having to build a murder case around a garage door containing a single bloody hole the size of a pencil.

The vacant field became the busiest place in Rhode Island. Law enforcement professionals and medical and forensic specialists swarmed to the scene while a throng of media representatives was corralled on the far side of Middle Highway. TV helicopters swooped overhead until the airspace was declared off limits.

Official cars and trucks were parked several rows deep in the field, and a yellow construction backhoe and a truck, with a spiderlike appendage called a cherry picker, were maneuvered close. Men with chain saws and axes widened the working space.

Forensic specialists started their excavation inside an extraordinary security cordon. Anyone not immediately involved was expelled from the circle of workers closest to the graves, and even those inside that area had to sign in and out.

Bright lights were brought up as the gray day wore on. After a month-long search, a nearly deaf dog of uncertain heritage had done what the highly trained German shepherds and Labradors could not. Isabelle had found the bodies.

Important events sometimes turn on little things. When the tracker dogs went through the area, concern was expressed about the number of cats in the neighborhood, and all handlers were cautioned not to let their big dogs munch someone's kitty by accident. So the big dogs were leashed in the meadow and could not penetrate the tangled border. Isabelle was under no such restraint. Free to roam, the old dog turned the tables against Christopher Hightower.

At the Primrose Hill Elementary School, the telltale *wocka-wocka-wocka* of helicopters was a terrible omen.

Then someone ran in, screaming that the Brendels had been found.

Principal Betty Durfee had been through this kind of thing once before, in another state, when a woman threatened to kill everybody on a school bus. She was not about to let hysteria erupt at Primrose Hill. "Button the school down tight," she ordered. Shades were pulled. Doors were locked. Staff members telephoned a parent of every student, telling them to personally retrieve their children today. Any student who could not be picked up would be escorted home by a teacher.

Dealing with the gathering media herd was the job of Tom Connell, a big Irishman who was O'Neil's public information officer. A former radio newsman, Connell was respected as a dirty-fingernail kind of reporter who had more than paid his dues before deciding the time had come to switch sides of the microphone and get a better paycheck and some stability in his life as a state spokesman.

He knew most of the reporters by sight and promised to keep them informed. With his background, he knew when to feed the clock-watching bunch of reporters facing a deadline on a huge story.

It wasn't until he was in the field that he remembered he had scheduled a previous media event for the same time. The cops were going to recover a luxury Jaguar automobile, the color of gold, that had once belonged to a savings and loan executive who had gone down the tubes. Connell slapped his head at the oversight, since he couldn't be in two places at one time. *What the hell. Any reporter who would have gone to the Jag event is probably out here anyway.* He was right. Nobody cared about the S&L crook today.

In the holes, men and women took turns digging, following the precise instructions of the medical examiner and a forensic archeologist who had helped design just such a recovery scenario. Dirt was moved not by the shovel load, but by the spoonful, and it was all shaken through fine mesh screen and examined with a metal detector. Photographs and videotapes were made and filed. Paintbrushes dusted away the layers of soil. Everything was done in slow motion.

Steadily, transparent plastic bags were filled with the detritus and debris taken from the two graves. It would all be sent to Washington for perusal by FBI scientists.

Ernest Brendel was in one grave and Alice lay in the separate one about three feet away. Both were on their backs, legs folded. Otherwise, they would not have fit into the holes. But as the graves went deeper, there was still no sign of Emily.

Everyone at the scene was an experienced officer of the law and knew they had to keep their cop walls strong at such a time. They had to do the job without getting personally involved. The problem was that most of them already *were* emotionally caught up in the drama. They had hunted the family for weeks, gone through the Brendels' most personal belongings, read the letters and diaries, examined oil heating bills and checking accounts, and read Emily's poems. They felt they knew the Brendel family, and felt a special heart tug when they thought of eight-year-old Emily. Now they had found her mother and father. They still hoped against hope that Emily had somehow escaped the killer's hand.

Spoons and brushes, spoons and brushes. Hours passed as they went deeper into the twin pits, a quarter inch at a time. The bodies of Alice and Ernie emerged slowly from their dirt cocoons, almost as if they lay on pedestals as the workers dug alongside them. A cop with a brush felt something else under the dirt near Alice's left foot and began to work on that one area.

One layer of dirt fell away, then another, and something came into view in the stark bright floodlights as the early winter dusk began to gather and the temperature turned frigid.

Pointing up at the two dozen men and women surrounding the inner circle was the toe of a white high-topped L.A. Gear sneaker. Everyone knew the significance of the moment, for they had all memorized exactly what the child was wearing when she disappeared from the YMCA. The body of Emily Brendel had been found, buried beneath her mother.

State troopers, medical examiners, criminal lawyers, and street cops stopped for a heartbeat, their own personal worlds jarred by the sight of that single little shoe. The sudden hush surprised those gathered beyond the inner perimeter, and their tension was in turn felt by the media on the far side of the road.

O'Neil grimaced. "Hey fellas, how about a minute?" said the attorney general, staring into the grave. Ernie's decomposed body was partially exposed, Alice was in clearer view, and now their tragic search for Emily was officially over. "When we found the high-tops, we knew all hope was gone," O'Neil recalled.

Connell set up a roadside press conference, refusing to divulge anything in advance. O'Neil, State Police Captain Brian Andrews, and Chief of Police Brule left the graves for the long walk toward the microphones to make a public statement.

"Okay, Brian, I'll flip a coin with you for who has to do this," the attorney general said.

"No, you go ahead," replied the state policeman.

It was one of those perfect New England winter evenings, with a red sky promising a clear day tomorrow, and a bit of mist blowing cold against the face. The collar of his open overcoat turned up against the chill, O'Neil stepped to the rack of microphones, tried to make the best of it, and failed. His eyes glistened with tears and his voice choked. He stopped to compose himself.

The searchlights shining in the distance created an eerie glow at the news conference. O'Neil gave a brief account of what had been found and confirmed that all three bodies had been recovered.

Stone had gotten a police jacket and Pat Youngs was

wearing one of O'Neil's heavy sweaters, but both were as cold as they had ever been in their lives. That would not last long. If anything, the grim discovery of November 7 gave a new impetus to the investigation. As Schauble bluntly put it, "We were all pissed off."

23

Enter the Lynx

"God forgave me but I cannot forgive myself for being involved in the murder of an innocent child. Hightower did not kill the Brendels." Police reading the document were incredulous. In a stroke of luck, vital information concerning the Brendel murders, including details that had not been released to the public, had fallen in their laps in the form of a strange letter signed by someone calling himself the "Lynx." Since it had been passed to them by a prison informant, they knew right away that the true author was none other than Christopher Hightower.

The rambling letter was designed to portray Hightower as a helpless victim of a murder plot by members of organized crime when he stumbled upon the crime in progress. The mobsters, according to the Lynx, were furious that Ernie "stole over 2 million dollars from them" and was "executed."

The police read on, noting how the Lynx followed so closely to the statements that Hightower had given them earlier, but were fleshed out to provide excuses of why Hightower had done some specific things, such as being "sent away to pick up Emily." Lynx wrote that Ernie would not tell the four hoodlums who invaded the house where he had hidden the missing money, so they "beat him with a black crowbar," shot him several times with the crossbow, then dragged Alice into the garage to strangle her before his eyes. "Only when he was told his daughter was next did he give up the money location. Unfortunately it was too late. Once one was killed they all had to die." Therefore, Emily was also strangled and Ernie was shot in the chest and head.

"Once the entire family was killed, someone had to take the fall. Hightower slept there, his prints must have been everywhere." The Lynx had excuses for evidence found at the grave sites, told what Ernie and Alice wore, and said Hightower "did everything he was told to.

"There is a lot more to this story. If I'm not killed i plan on telling it all. They never should have killed emily. It has been eating away at me ever since it happened and I can no longer take it. I'm not one of them.

"Lynx"

If Public Defender John Hardiman expected Christopher Hightower to just sit on his butt in prison while his future was at stake, the lawyer was sadly mistaken. Hightower was just behind bars, he wasn't dead and he wasn't about to let things roll along without his guidance. The public defender had ordered Hightower not to *talk* about the case, but did not say anything about *writing*. Anyway, from what Hightower was reading in the papers, and hearing along the prison grapevine the defense attorney could use all the help he could get.

With such bizarre logic began one of the most outlandish schemes ever hatched behind prison walls. Christopher Hightower, locked away in protective custody, had plenty of time to think, and through his attorney, had access to the information being gathered by State investigators. So he created a new character. If no one would listen to him, everyone would pay attention to the Lynx!

Hightower had been in the ACI for less than a week before setting his plan in motion, befriending a bushy-haired fellow convict named Mike Giroux during interminable card games. Since Giroux was also in for murder and loved to talk, the pair of social misfits had something in common. Hightower smoothly guided the conversation.

According to Giroux, Hightower wanted to have his father-in-law, Clyde Slicker, and his sister-in-law, Kathy Slicker, killed by a hired assassin. The twisted logic was that the deaths would sufficiently frighten his wife, Sue, into returning to him, bringing along a hefty inheritance from Clyde's estate. That money would pay for his private lawyer. The murky scheme was to be unleashed in a series of anonymous letters mailed to various people, who would then mail them to lawyers and police. The notes would indicate the killers of the Brendels were threatening more harm. Hightower would have to be declared innocent, because he would still be incarcerated when the letters, bearing nonprison postmarks, were received in the outside world.

The left-handed Hightower wrote the first one in a crabby right-hand scrawl, with intentional spelling errors, only six days after he was captured. He signed it, "The Lynx." Two more followed quickly thereafter. Giroux was delighted to help. There was only one flaw in the grand plan—Hightower ignored the adage that there is no honor among thieves, much less among accused murderers. Giroux made a collect call to the Rhode Island State Police, offering to give up the Lynx.

Months later, when the wily Lynx finally became suspicious of Giroux, he found another accomplice, Frank Moniz, also in the ACI awaiting trial on a murder charge. Moniz agreed to help, and sent a Lynx letter out to his brother Raymond in East Providence. Raymond turned it over to a third Moniz brother, Richard, a detective with the Newport Police Department, who brought it over to the Hightower prosecutors.

Efforts by Hightower to enlist other prisoners in his loony scheme, including offering one $200,000 to commit murder, all ended up in a special file police created to hold the prolific correspondence being churned out by the Lynx.

As Hightower scribbled away in prison, his imagination took wing. One threat made for Sue's reading declared that the letter-writer was a "professional assassin" who had been hired to kill her boys and her sister "if you don't reconcile with your husband immediately." Another Lynx note continued that theme and added her parents to the list of probable victims if she refused to reunite with Chris. "Go to your husband now before your kids become the first to die," urged the Lynx.

While issuing anonymous threats to kill his sons, he showed the same disregard for his daughters by Ellen, having the Lynx also issue a death threat on the girls. The common thread throughout the letters was that the imprisoned Hightower was innocent.

Nobody believed him, particularly State Police Sergeant Jimmy Lynch, who stood silently watching on October 22 while FBI Agent David Wagle, a specialist in handwriting analysis, obtained writing samples by having Hightower sign his name over and over, pushing him to keep going until the prisoner's hands cramped and Hightower was too tired to disguise his writing. Those tests eventually would link Hightower to incriminating documents, including his anonymous letters from prison. The clever Lynx never knew what hit him.

There was another purpose for the police visit that day. Sergeant Mike Quinn took samples of hair and cuttings of fingernails for tests. When Quinn had Hightower drop his pants, and plucked a few pubic hairs, using long tweezers, Lynch stood by with his arms folded, thinking, *I hope it hurts.*

Events moved rapidly following the discovery of the bodies, although the autopsies left a haunting mystery. Pathologists determined Ernie died from arrow wounds to his chest and Alice was asphyxiated by a white cloth knotted around her neck so tight that the doctors had to cut it away. But the exact cause of Emily's death was inconclusive, with no signs of broken bones or other trauma. That eliminated almost every kind of death but strangulation. The uncertainty added to the fear that she may have been buried alive.

* * *

The investigation plodded toward obtaining enough circumstantial evidence to enmesh Hightower beyond question in the killings. The biggest assist for police came from the suspect himself, for Christopher Hightower seemed to have never thrown anything away, including material that would help incriminate him. Police combed through his collections with fascinated interest.

On the wall of the Barrington police station, investigators taped a long strip of butcher paper to use as a blackboard. A line representing time was drawn across the length of it and, using red ink, they listed the dates, times, and places in Hightower's statement.

Below the line, in black ink, they wrote in their own findings—sightings by people who knew the suspect, receipts from hamburger joints, grocery stores, retail outlets, and gasoline stations. The contrast was blindingly clear, and the officers believed they could prove to a jury that Hightower was lying.

The footwork seemed never to end. Gary Palumbo plundered through the trash can in the White Church to find the bits and pieces of material that Hightower had copied that Sunday. It turned out to be portions of a letter to the Commodities Future Trading Commission, a letter that was soon tracked down and recovered. The name on the business card discovered in the grass behind the Brendel house identified stockbroker Martin Parquette, who could testify Ernie Brendel was in Dedham, Massachusetts, attending a financial seminar when Hightower claimed Ernie was helping test the crossbow.

The corner of the lime bag found in Ernie's grave exactly matched the torn edge of the bag that was still in the Toyota when Hightower was arrested, and a receipt and a witness could prove Hightower had made the purchase. Such things were pure gold for the prosecution.

Some evidence resulted from glimmers of intuition. It had been assumed that the wooden rim around the back door of the house had been damaged when John Medici led the initial search. Medici had used a crowbar to pop the trunk of the Audi, so it was logical that he used the same tool to pry open the door. That would account for the pry marks on the wood trim. Throwing around ideas one morning, the investigators decided to make sure of that assumption. No, said Medici, I just kicked it in.

Suddenly the pry bar marks became significant. The damaged wood trim joined the material sent to the FBI, where scientists determined the marks exactly matched the steel pry bar found in Hightower's briefcase.

Just before the grand jury convened, Stone and Lynch played another hunch. Lynch had obtained not only long distance but also local telephone records to and from 51 Middle Highway. There was a puzzling series of Thursday night calls, however, for which they could not account.

Then they remembered the area code had recently been changed in one of the surrounding areas, and Lynch checked the mysterious telephone number with that new prefix. It was the number dialed by the automatic alarm system in the Brendel house. Although Ernie had the service disconnected, the dialing mechanism was tripped when the back door was jimmied open, and the device automatically dialed until the battery wore out. Since the alarm was off, the calls went nowhere, but were logged by the telephone company's computer as having been made.

The Hightower pry bar and the alarm system calls could prove someone tried to break into the house Thursday night.

One major point presented police with a strange assignment. The only way to investigate his claims of being pursued by members of organized crime was to actually interview a couple of people whose names have been connected to the mob. It turned out to be easy. Christopher Hightower had gotten the cops and crooks on the same wavelength.

Sergeant Doug Badger of the Rhode Island State Police, accompanied by a local officer, was invited to a sit-down at the home of John DeSistine in Narragansett. DeSistine told the officers that while he was not personally involved in criminal activities, the fathers of some friends of his youth were reputed to be linked to such things. He squashed Hightower's idea that the Mafia was behind the kidnappings of the Brendels, saying that if the trouble was with the husband, there was no way the wife and child would be involved. No way. Those freaky Colombians might do that sort of thing, but not Italians.

DeSistine said Hightower had tried to hustle business from a lawyer, James Ramano, who reportedly handled some business dealings for alleged Mafia figures. Ramano was not interested in the deal, but passed Hightower along to a couple of stockbroker friends, Jerry Molina and Rocco Caffarelli. They looked at the numbers, listened to Hightower's pitch, and took a flyer for a couple of thousand.

With Molina and Caffarelli singing praises, DeSistine and his cousin, Steve Bracchi, came up with $20,000 for Hightower to trade in early 1990. They invested with strict instructions for Hightower to close the commodities account if it dropped below $17,000. Within weeks the four men became suspicious that something was amiss. DeSistine, a man who was used to getting his way, did not like Hightower, who clicked his teeth while they talked and was a cocky bastard to boot. Bracchi checked things out through Hightower's Chicago brokerage and found out the bad news. All of the investments were in a slide, falling past the cutoff mark.

DeSistine told Badger the accounts were closed immediately, and estimated he had personally lost about $5,000. Since he had been willing to lose up to $3,000 anyway, he figured he was only down $2,000 to the con man, and that certainly was not enough for a respected citizen in his position to even threaten to kill or kidnap someone. Two thousand dollars? Chicken feed.

Then DeSistine leaned forward and told the State Police sergeant in a confidential tone that the matter was

not pursued because everyone involved figured Hightower had to be a cop trying to rip off some upstanding
citizens. "Who would lose mob money on purpose?" he
asked.

By April 1992 the prosecution was ready to take its case
before the Providence County Grand Jury. Youngs and
Stone presented a careful picture of what investigators
believed had happened at 51 Middle Highway on the awful weekend of September 20–22, 1991. Most of the same
witnesses who would later appear at the trial first told
their story to the grand jury.

The result was exactly what was sought, indicting
Christopher J. Hightower on eleven charges. There were
three charges of murder, including one for the murder of
a kidnapped child. He was also charged with kidnapping
a minor, with three felony counts of improperly disposing
of a body, one count of breaking and entering the
Brendel garage, a count of entering the house with intent to commit a felony, and two counts of forging
checks.

Most of it was window dressing. The main points were
the death of Ernie, which the state contended included
torture, and the kidnapping of Emily, an event that led
directly to her death. Each charge carried a maximum
sentence of life without parole, a sentence rarely handed
down in Rhode Island, but the strongest available in a
state that does not have a death penalty.

There was another hitch as the case inched toward a
trial date in the final months of 1992. Hightower fired
his lawyers, Hardiman and DiLauro.

Through the prison grapevine, Hightower decided he
deserved the best defense attorney available. He wrote a
moving letter to Robert A. George in Boston, a high-
profile defense specialist who loves tough cases.

Several weeks later, waiting in a small cinder-block
room of the ACI unit, Bob George was astonished when
the door opened and Hightower waddled in, clad in a

blue prison jumpsuit and shackled hand and foot. It looked as if Mr. Peepers had gone to prison.

Bob George was not easily taken aback by anything. Growing up being neither Italian nor Irish in New England, he was used to being the underdog. Unable to get work in the construction trades, he went to law school, and, upon obtaining his degree, gravitated toward the defense table. Under the Constitution, everyone is entitled to a defense, and beneath that rule is where George pitched his tent. Only thirty-eight, he already had worked through the lower rungs of the legal game and discovered he had a flair for the spotlight. The verbose and personable George became too big for firms that hired him, and opened his own law firm in 1990, specializing in providing the best defense money can buy. Bob George was the man to have at your side, but he did not work cheap. High rollers who found themselves in trouble gladly paid the price.

George was intrigued by the bespectacled, seemingly gentle man who sat before him. Of course, he was aware the man was suspected of murdering an entire family, but the literacy of the letter asking for an interview and Hightower's intelligent conversation left the lawyer intrigued. Hightower turned on the charm and somehow convinced George that money would be no problem. A family member would cover immediate expenses, and anyway, wasn't Hightower a successful commodities broker who had made fortunes for investors? Of course he could pay!

George still didn't bite right away. Other important cases demanded his attention. But he had seven other lawyers working for him now to handle such things. This Hightower was a peculiar fellow and the situation was intriguing. It did not hurt that the man could handle the fee, but the publicity the trial was certain to generate would be an invaluable advertisement for George, who was on his way to becoming New England's premier defense attorney, and that would translate down the road to even more money. And perhaps, someday when a top

Boston lawyer with an Irish surname stopped him on the street, in addition to giving congratulations on his latest case, an invitation might also follow to an Old Boy private club. That was just a dream. No matter how many dragons Bob George slew, he would remain outside the Harvard Club.

Hightower could be a win-win situation. If George somehow pulled off a victory, everybody would say he was a genius. If he lost, well, no one really expected him to win anyway. He weighed the potential time lost from his other cases against the TV and headline value of the man sitting across the table from him in the ACI.

I'll do it, he told Hightower. Now tell me exactly what happened.

Book Four

24

Trial

Courtroom 5 in the Frank Licht Judicial Complex was a cavernous square chamber with the usual trappings of a celebrity trial—an overflow crowd of spectators, a horde of reporters, a television camera, a newspaper photographer, and a thick air of expectancy. It was Monday, March 8, 1993, some eighteen months after the brutal murders of the Brendel family, and the outside world was about to get a look at Christopher Hightower.

The man walked in briskly, as if late for a business appointment, except that he was handcuffed and flanked by Marshals Alan Verdeccia, Jerry St. James, and Steve Dagliere, in their forest-green uniforms. Like the room, Hightower appeared slightly seedy. Balding, with a small trimmed beard, he wore a gray-green suit and dark blue turtleneck sweater on the advice of his attorney, who wanted the defendant to project a professorial, studious manner. As the cuffs were removed from his wrists, Hightower swept the three rows of spectator benches with his eyes, then greeted his lawyers and took the middle green padded seat at an eight-foot-long table scarred heavily from decades of court use. He folded his hands atop a yellow legal pad he aligned with the edge of an aluminum tray stacked with tiny paper cups, a water pitcher, and folded napkins.

While his lawyer, Bob George, campaigned around the room like a politician seeking election, joking with reporters, cops, and other lawyers, his client picked up a pen and began scribbling with his left hand on the pad before him, as if he were the one running the trial. George let the two young lawyers acting as his associate counsels deal with Hightower, while he concentrated on pulling the fangs almost everyone bared at his client. George's good-guy performance chipped away at the cloak of pure evil that Hightower seemed to radiate.

Four feet in front of him was the huge desk of court clerk Linda B. Parsons, and behind that, rising like a monolith, was the bench from which Judge John F. Sheehan would direct the trial, seated in a big chair between the American and Rhode Island flags. Stenographer Joann Groff sat ready to record the proceedings on her Datawriter. Four eight-bulb chandeliers cast a thick, dusty light.

At the adjacent table, reserved for the prosecution, stood the group of men who had lived with the case for months and were jittery as a bunch of racehorses at the starting gate. Pat Youngs, who would deliver the opening argument, studied his notes, while Mike Stone circled like a shark ready for a long-awaited meal. State Police Detective Sergeants Doug Badger and Jim Lynch, and Barrington Detective Sergeants Gary Palumbo and Ken Schauble, shuffled a stack of boxes jammed with evidence. They had practiced, over and over, when each of the hundreds of pieces of evidence would be introduced. The sheer volume would prove to be a logistical nightmare, so a system was worked out in which Badger, Palumbo, and Schauble would feed a piece of evidence—a cotton swab, a crossbow, a photograph, a receipt—with conveyor belt precision to the front table, where Lynch would have it ready to hand over before Stone or Youngs even sought to introduce it.

The list of witnesses was almost as hefty as the mountain of evidence. The prosecution had more than a hundred potential witnesses lined up, while George said the defense might counter with thirty-eight. Both sides trimmed their lists as the trial progressed, settling with seventy-seven testifying for the State, and only five for the defense.

The difference was more than a mere arithmetical anomaly, for the strategy of the two teams was completely different. Stone and Youngs had to prove beyond a reasonable doubt that Hightower committed the crimes and that the Brendel family deaths did not happen as the defendant had described in the strange story to which he was tenaciously clinging. Further, the prosecutors had to base their contention solely on circumstantial evidence. Even after a year and a half, Hightower was the only person who really knew what happened, and he was not about to help. George's game plan rested on the shaky ground of showing that perhaps there really was an alternative explanation for the murders. Beyond that, the defense attorney had a fallback plan—that even if his client did the horrible deed, Hightower was so mentally incompetent that he should not be held responsible. Meanwhile, Hightower would be presumed innocent unless the prosecution could prove otherwise. Without a single witness to the crime except Hightower, shaking his story would be a tough assignment for Youngs and Stone.

"Hear ye, hear ye, hear ye," called out Deputy Sheriff Joyce Mota, beginning the arcane ritual that started each trial day. "All persons having business before this Superior Court of the State of Rhode Island and Providence Plantations holden at Providence for the counties of Providence and Bristol may now draw near, give their attendance and they shall be heard. God save the State of Rhode Island and Providence Plantations."

A door at the far side of the court opened and Deputy Sheriff Joe Spiver led in the jury, a collection of sixteen men and women who were about to contribute eight weeks of their lives to the trial. Four alternates had been chosen to sit with the dozen selected as primary jurors, and at 10:07 A.M. they came in single-file to take their seats. Their route took them directly toward Christopher Hightower, who stood at the defense table like a sergeant examining a parade of troops, and several actually acknowledged him. He said hello in return and sat down, quite satisfied that he had already begun to win them over through the sheer force of his magnetic personality.

Judge Sheehan, a snow-haired jurist with a quick wit and a tongue just as quick to lash out in anger, was no stranger to major criminal matters or media hype. As a defense attorney, he once represented Newport socialite Claus von Bulow in that famous murder trial. He did not intend to let the hoopla surrounding Christopher Hightower create loopholes. Sheehan made Hightower aware that the judge's wife, Mary, worked as an assistant to Attorney General O'Neil, and obtained Hightower's approval of that potential conflict before proceeding. No one wanted a mistrial.

Youngs and Stone were happy that Bob George was on the case, as they had earlier been enthusiastic with the selection of public defenders DiLauro and Hardiman. Such lawyers, at the top of their profession, did not make legal errors that could risk opening the case to appeal.

Sheehan instructed the jury to totally ignore all printed and broadcast reports of the trial, pay attention only to what they personally saw and heard in the court, and to not even discuss the trial with their spouses around the dinner table. The judge's choice of not locking the jury away for the duration, an expensive proposition for the state, would bring the case to the brink of mistrial several times. It was nearly impossible for jurors to ignore everything that was being said about the biggest thing happening in the state. "You will remember this case for the rest of your lives," he said, and he was right.

The case began with a roll call of horror. Assistant Attorney General Pat Youngs, his dark suit coat open, adjusted his glasses and went to work. The grind of preparing for trial had already cost him a few pounds, and he was sniffling from a flu virus. "It's going to be a long road," he told the jury, outlining the police view of the heinous crime and, pointing to the defendant, said, "One man is responsible. This man right here. Christopher Hightower."

He gave a shorthand overview of the strange visit of Hightower to Connecticut, the wild story of kidnapping and ransom demands, the bloodied Toyota, the capture of the suspect and his subsequent meandering statements, the attempt to clean blood from the garage, the burial of the slaughtered family. Youngs was totally at ease as he walked the courtroom, like a professor discussing poetry. He knew the case cold, every bit of evidence, and never referred to a note. His eyes never left the jurors and his soft voice accented important passages as he lightly tapped the table with his knuckles, taps of quiet thunder to underline important points. Youngs claimed the decision of Ernie Brendel to seek revocation of Hightower's broker license was the motive for the multiple murders. "The relationship between Ernest and him wasn't of friends—they were adversaries."

Hightower, hands folded, watched Youngs's every move, and the line of policemen at the prosecution table watched Hightower's every move. George studiously avoided looking concerned at Youngs's presentation of the horrible crime, and slowly turned pages of a document, appearing to casually read it. It gave the impression that Youngs was not saying anything that he had not expected.

But Youngs was indeed saying important things, giving the jury a tour of the house on Middle Highway, telling them of the discovery of human teeth and the crossbow in the car, and how so much potential evidence had been carted away to the FBI. He pointed to discrepancies in Hightower's account of what happened and the material turned up by police, the broker's failed business dealings, and comments on the victims. "He takes her," Youngs said of the kidnapping from the YMCA. "It is the last time Emily is seen alive."

It was an early warning of the thrust of the prosecution's case. Youngs, Stone, and George all knew that the crime would not have been anywhere near as sensational and complex if Emily had not been murdered. For the next eight weeks, the prosecution attorneys would bring the name, the voice, the pictures of the little girl before the jury time and again. This trial was about Hightower choking that little girl to death, and the state intended to pound the fact into every one of the ten men and six women on the jury, almost to the exclusion of everything else. On the defense side of the table, George was also quite aware that Emily was the center of his case. Recently, an old friend had pulled him aside during a party and said that he felt personally uncomfortable that his buddy, Bob George, was representing Hightower. The friend asked, "Did he really kill that little girl?" George drew away from his friend of many years, refusing to discuss the case. But that was the very question that would hover in the minds of everyone in Courtroom 5 for weeks.

Skillfully and slowly, the soft-spoken Youngs laid down the time line as constructed by investigators, almost whispering his description of the recovery of the bodies and the distraught feelings at the gravesite when Emily's white sneaker popped into view. "All evidence points in one direction. To Christopher Hightower—he murdered Ernest Brendel, Alice Brendel, and Emily Brendel," Youngs stated with finality. After an hour and ten minutes of carefully laying out the road map the State would follow, Youngs ended his opening statement.

All eyes turned to Bob George. How in the world would he be able to counter the avalanche of damning accusations that Youngs had hurled at Christopher Hightower? George handled it by doing nothing at all, informing the court he would have no opening statement. In effect, he was challenging the prosecution, without having to reveal his own strategy. By remaining silent, the defense was sending a message to the jury:

Youngs saying that Hightower was guilty was one thing, but proving it was something else.

The State decided to play one of their big cards up front. The first witness in the trial was Christine Scriabine, the sister of Ernest Brendel and the target of Hightower's extortion attempt. The short, blocky woman in a neat gray dress marched to the witness stand with menace in her eyes, determined to do Hightower harm. When Youngs asked if Hightower was present in the courtroom, Scriabine stabbed a finger directly at the defendant, who showed not a flicker of expression.

In an unwavering voice she described how Ernie had helped her clear out their mother's condominium, taking away the wooden billy club and set of steak knives in a plastic Lord & Taylor bag. That seemingly unimportant piece of information later would become a vital piece of evidence.

Scriabine, an historian at the Museum of American Political Life in Hartford, was able to recall an extraordinary amount of detail of the hours Hightower had spent in her home. The story she told paralleled the version explained moments earlier by Pat Youngs, and jurors were impressed as the evidence wheel began to turn. Almost every time she described something she had seen or done, the cops at the prosecution table produced the piece of evidence in question: Ernie's wallet, Alice's rings, credit cards, a photo of the Brendel family that put the emotional image of Emily into the case. The jury now could put a face with the name, and knew exactly how the little girl looked.

Scriabine went through the alleged ransom demand, the condition of the Toyota, being "horrified" at the awful smell of blood, and how she became "very uncomfortable" with Hightower as he spun his incredible tale. She said she photographed him because "the story was so crazy, I wanted something to validate he was there."

Bingo! thought Bob George, sitting at the defense table. He couldn't have done it better himself! The defense attorney noted her comment on his pad, while Youngs pushed ahead with the witness. Scriabine was stern and unforgiving, detailing what she had seen and said. By the time Youngs was finished leading her through the convoluted meeting with Hightower, thirty-six pieces of evidence were already introduced.

George, in a tailored suit and with his black hair perfectly trimmed, rose to cross-examine. Betting on the witness's extraordinary recall, ignoring the physical evidence that lay heaped upon the desk of Clerk Linda Parsons, he asked how Hightower acted that evening.

"Did he try to hide from your friends . . . Did you just call it a crazy story . . . Did he ask you to do impossible things . . . How long before you realized the story wasn't piecing together right . . . Did you consider him to be telling a ridiculous story?"

A semantic battle raged, as George sought to paint Hightower's actions as those of a deranged person, while Scriabine would say only that Hightower was strange. George was going over the same ground laid out by Youngs, but presenting a different twist. Forget all that evidence, he was telling the jurors, just look at this weird duck I'm representing. Would even an amateur criminal dream up such a scheme? A kid could rob a liquor store with more precision than the supposedly intelligent Hightower displayed that night. George, almost sounding like a prosecutor, hardly challenged a single detail. It almost seemed as if he were throwing his client to the wolves.

The Mafia watching the house, armored cars, walkie-talkies, needing money and then not needing money, leaving that mountain of physical evidence, allowing his picture to be taken and dictating a statement? George planted his feet apart and put his hands on his hips as he asked Christine Scriabine, "Wasn't that the most ridiculous story you had ever heard?"

"It was farfetched," she admitted, but as an historian,

she had "probably heard more ridiculous" yarns in her time.

The first day of trial ended promptly at 4:15 P.M., with both sides having plunged to the heart of their cases. Hightower was a monster or Hightower was nuts. There would be no middle ground.

25

Evidence

The opening phase passed with the speed of a rushing locomotive. A dozen witnesses, mostly law enforcement officers, would go to the stand, and by the time the week was out 249 pieces of evidence had been presented.

On the first day of testimony, Tuesday, March 9, Sergeant Lazzaro from Barrington, FBI Special Agent Jack McGraw, and State Police Lieutenant Hurst gave detailed accounts of their interviews with Hightower, and Alex Scriabine confirmed his wife's story. The jury watched Hightower as if he were some kind of bug on display, horrified by what they heard.

And after each witness, defense attorney Bob George would rise and emphasize how wild and peculiar Christopher Hightower must have appeared to each of them. Not once did he try to punch a hole in their stories, not once did he have a piece of evidence thrown out. Nor did he vary from his obvious path of proving Hightower insane. Chris Hightower may have felt that he had added a lawyer to the prosecution team. Hightower was busy taking notes and whispering to the younger lawyers at his table, while George kept his back turned to the prisoner. Several court observers worried that George was going too far and might be fired by his client, which would throw the trial into turmoil.

As a photocopy of the $1,500 in hundred-dollar bills that Hightower was carrying when arrested was submitted, Judge Sheehan, with a smile, explained to the jury that a copy was being used because "nobody trusts anyone around here." The judge was breezy in his good mood, explaining that he liked to "inject a little humor now and then just to relax you." Defense lawyer Bob George chuckled along with the judge. So did Hightower. At the prosecution table Mike Stone wore a frown, disgusted that the jury hearing this murder case was amused. Stone's mood matched the freezing rain that was pounding Providence.

The ugly weather turned to snow overnight and dipped to frigid temperatures on Wednesday, when the jury was taken to Barrington by bus for a tour of the various sites. Hightower had a right to go along, to once again see the familiar places of his former hometown, to at least get out of prison for a while, but was told he would have to wear handcuffs and leg irons. "If I am going to be shackled, I do not wish to go," the accused murderer told Sheehan, as if his feelings were hurt. The jury, bundled against the cold, went to the Brendel home to see the damaged porch and the white garage. The only other time they left the vehicles was at the wooded gravesite behind St. Andrew's. They saw not only the burial place, but three small trees that had been planted by Barrington residents in memory of the slaughtered family. In coming months strands of English ivy and a carpet of wildflowers would bloom there.

Emily came into the courtroom on Friday.

The most dramatic moment of the trial's first week came as the jury was being deluged, almost growing bored, with evidence from the state prosecutors. But Youngs and Stone knew where they were going and had timed the drama perfectly. Item 202 was Ernie's new Panasonic combination fax and telephone answering machine that police had removed from the house. On it was a tape recording of sixteen messages that had been left between September 20, the last day the family was seen alive, and the day of Hightower's arrest on September 23.

State Police Sergeant Mike Quinn, who had supervised the police search of the house, plugged the machine into a white extension cord and placed it on the witness stand in front of him. When he turned it on, the first voice was that of Ernie Brendel, brusque and business-like: "Hello, you have reached 246-1666. We're out right now. If you wish to leave a message, please do so after the beep. You may also send a fax to this number. Thank you."

The courtroom went silent, for everyone knew that Emily had telephoned home after her class trip and left a message on the machine. The gallery was filled with somber faces awaiting the inevitable as the tape rolled.

The second message gave a preview. It was an exultant Hightower landlord, Dennis Murphy, calling at 10:30 A.M. on Friday. His message to Ernie was that the "constable and Barrington police all showed up at my office today. They were out hunting him like there's no tomorrow. Give me a call and I'll talk to you."

Then a brief message from Joe Mazza of the NFA. "You know what it's regarding." And then:

"Hi Dad, it's me." The voice was light, the chirp of a happy little girl. "I'm at the Y." There was a background mumble as she spoke to someone. "What?" She paused and continued, "It's 3:35 and you called the school for me to walk home, but I came here, cause I didn't know . . ." Relatives of the Brendels in the first row were unable to hide their emotion, and the jury sat stunned, some leaning forward. Stone and Youngs did not have to say a thing. Emily was doing the talking. The little girl was front and center in the courtroom—the focus of the trial.

While the recording was the emotional high point, the evidence cache swept up from the Brendel home and Hightower's office was actually just as important. Quinn,

Gary Palumbo, and State Police Sergeant Donald Kennedy described the treasure trove of material.

Kennedy was in charge of a six-officer team that swooped down on Maple Avenue, videotaping the office over a period of days, examining each article in it. They struck gold from the first moment, for Hightower seemed to have saved every piece of paper that had ever crossed his path. The hours he spent in the office, the little fortress that he would allow few to enter, were not used to hunt new customers, but to move meaningless pieces of paper from one place to another. Old photographs that his wives had never seen, correspondence dating back to his college days, letters and cards from his children, were all neatly filed away. The place was awash in paper. Printouts from his few accounts were in folders, copies of letters to Ernie Brendel, checkbooks and deposit slips. Little receipts in various colors from various stores, imprinted with the time, place, and sometimes even a description of item, lay stacked like little piles of leaves.

Those pieces of paper had the strength of steel, chaining Christopher Hightower to a specific moment in time. For instance, the receipt for $355.39 from Thompson's Sport Shop on September 19 for a crossbow, bolts, and points was tied to a $355.39 entry in Hightower's own checkbook. There could be no question as to who bought the deadly weapon.

Searchers found, beneath a folding table in Hightower's office, the Lord & Taylor bag containing the steak knives and police billy club that Ernie Brendel had taken from his mother's condominium. They found the Brendel electronic garage door opener. They found a small white plastic bottle of sleeping pills from the CVS drugstore, with twenty of the sixty pills missing. They found the American Tourister briefcase containing a Glock semiautomatic pistol, a length of rope, a knife, the steel pry bar, and a notepad imprinted with the name of Ernest R. Brendel. The swarm of items was so huge and unexpected that even Hightower turned, watching in amazement as Badger, Lynch, Palumbo, and Schauble ferried the material to Youngs and Stone, who laid it before the court.

Gloves, wire cutters, a piece of blue cloth, letters galore, the toolbox, a roll of garden hose, and more and more receipts. It all went in, with one big exception.

Judge Sheehan would not allow the introduction of the items inside the Hightower briefcase—particularly the pistol—because no hard evidence had been produced to show the gun was used in the crime. Viewing the Glock handgun, therefore, could sway the jury without cause. "Why don't you put a hand grenade in there? Why don't you put anything in there?" Sheehan snapped. The prosecution chose to postpone that point.

As the prosecution pitched hard and fast, defense attorney Bob George threw a couple of unexpected curve balls of his own. Instead of objecting to the office search, he loved it! George, in cross-examination of Sergeant Kennedy, actually emphasized a few things that the police had failed to mention. He pointed out part of a note from Hightower stating that "every day I go home and pray nothing has happened to my wife and kids." He read Sue's divorce affidavit that Hightower claimed to be arranging a paid assassination of her.

The jury was then given, by Hightower's own lawyer, a look at the electrifying entries on a legal pad police had found in the office, on the floor beside the desk. The prosecution had entered the pad as evidence, but not what was written upon it. George read out Hightower's handwritten list of debt, totaling $3,776. Then he read the message scrawled below the numbers, the strange statement that Hightower wrote when he daydreamed about robbing a bank, including the threat that explosives were hidden in the building.

When George had the jury's undivided attention, he served the main course, Hightower's loony poem about the world being like a circus, and the fear of falling off the Ferris wheel. By the time the lawyer resumed his seat, jurors were beginning to wonder, not whether Hightower was crazy, but just how crazy was he?

The trial would stretch over a period of two months—beginning before and ending after the much more complex trial of Los Angeles policemen accused in the senseless beating of motorist Rodney King. It almost became a mistrial on the final day of the first week. Bob George asked that the jury be polled to see if any of them had read or seen news reports claiming that Hightower had threatened his old pen pal Michael Giroux and a guard at the ACI. Sheehan agreed, saying that such reports were "wildly irresponsible" and that if any of his jurors knew of the account, he would declare the Hightower case a mistrial, if George so asked.

It was an extraordinary moment, and would not be the last such event in the trial. Sheehan had refused to sequester the jury, saying it would cost the state more than $200,000. Instead he took the risk that the panel could be tainted by the news. Hightower and the Brendels dominated the talk in bank lobbies, on bus rides, and around dinner tables. Even when jurors stood outside the courthouse awaiting rides home, they could see the big headlines of the *Journal-Bulletin* in a red box at the foot of the stairs. Going in and out of court, walking the halls, riding the elevators—all were risky actions for any juror trying to keep a neutral mind. But the judge remained adamant, telling them to close their ears and eyes to such things. His decision threatened to sink the entire operation, for while he had control of his courtroom, he did not control the First Amendment, which guarantees freedom of the press.

Bob George was ready to ask for a mistrial, although it was clear to observers that he might have bitten off more than he could chew with Hightower. The big fee he had expected was not forthcoming. One of Hightower's sisters and her husband had put up a minimal amount of money to cover trial expenses, but that would run out fast, and the chance of the rest of the family building a defense fund was nonexistent. Furthermore, Susan and the Slickers were not about to spend one more penny on Hightower, whom they wanted to stay in prison, and as far away from them as possible. It was beginning to look as if Hightower had conned one of the best defense lawyers in New England.

Sheehan spent much of Friday morning asking each juror, brought into the room separately, whether they heard that Hightower was trying to eliminate Giroux and the guard. Always wanting to keep everyone in good humor, the jurist asked each of the six women jurors if they had been the one who brought in some delicious cookies that day. Everyone chuckled. But on the serious business at hand, two jurors reported having overheard snatches of conversation about the reports, leading Sheehan to make a startling decision.

He said he was "deeply concerned." He asked Hightower to stand. In his mind, the judge said, if both jurors were dismissed, it would leave them with only fourteen in the box—or the needed twelve plus two alternates. In many states that is standard for a trial, but in Rhode Island sixteen is the desired number. It would almost take a multiple fatality automobile wreck to prevent a twelve-person jury from gathering. With a panel of sixteen, Sheehan could afford to lose four jurors and still proceed. He wanted to know if Hightower was willing to continue with only fourteen people in the box. Even Hightower was taken aback and asked permission to talk with George. After a moment he replied that he was only concerned about one of the jurors, and that he would like the trial to continue. Gratefully, Stone and Youngs, who had been sitting at the prosecution table watching their case slowly fly out the window, said they had no objection to Hightower's decision. One woman juror was dismissed and the trial continued.

Hightower was willing to proceed, but George did not want to risk a juror stumbling across a news report of the trial and once again throwing the case into possible mistrial waters. The defense lawyer asked that the jury be sequestered.

No, ruled Sheehan. Unhappy that his reach ended at the First Amendment, Sheehan sternly warned reporters that if there was a repetition of the incident, he would ban television cameras from the courtroom. Still, he would not put the jurors up in a hotel under guard for the duration of the trial.

26

Families

Susan Hightower walked into Courtroom 5 as if she owned the place. She may have been a bundle of nerves, but on the surface her composure was perfect. After she was sworn in to testify as a star witness against her husband, Christopher Hightower, he winked at her.

On Monday, March 15, the start of the second week, Kathy Slicker sat in the back row alongside her mother, Mary Lou, and some close friends. When Hightower searched the audience that morning upon entering, he saw her. "He looked at me and I looked right back at him," she said. "What we should do the next time is hiss," advised a friend.

Mary Lou Slicker, her hands busy needlepointing a piano bench cover, would attended the trial each and every day, no matter how bitter the weather outside. She was accompanied by a few church friends, many of whom also had sewing projects, and the little cluster of women on the back row became known among court regulars as the "White Church Sewing Circle." Kathy, who worked at a bank downtown, also would show up periodically, but Clyde Slicker, except for the time he testified, was never a spectator at the murder trial of his son-in-law.

Hightower's gaze also would brush over the relatives of the Brendel family. At great cost and inconvenience to their personal lives, they frequently showed up, trying to put their emotions on hold while the law sought to deal with the man accused of killing their loved ones. Alice's eldest brother, Arthur A. Bobb, Jr., and his son Fred, flew up from their home in Florida, while Donald Bobb and his wife Peggy drove over from Pennsylvania. Christine Scriabine, after her first day of testimony, was a frequent spectator, usually sitting as close as possible to Hightower, so as not to miss a single move or utterance by the man she detested. Susanne Pandich, Ernie's second sister, came in periodically from her home in Tarrytown, New York. Usually, Hightower would just glance at them before he sat down to start his court day by scribbling notes. Fred Bobb, a young, dark-haired man, once daydreamed of grabbing a policeman's gun and shooting Hightower. Christine Scriabine, unable to contain her bulldog personality one day, leaned into Hightower's face and called him a "son of a bitch." Not once throughout the long trial did a single Hightower relative come to court.

All of the families involved were well-represented on the seventh day of the trial, when Sue came in, a slight woman wearing an emerald-green suit and white silk blouse, her dark brown hair curling in just below her ears. Gold earrings that were tastefully small, a thin gold necklace, a slim wristwatch, but no wedding band. The prosecution had chosen to use her as the lead witness to shift the trial to a new stage.

The jury by now had seen the size of the case against Hightower on the evidentiary front, and the state wanted to fill in his personal background. Stone and Youngs had not been pleased with the way Bob George was deflecting the importance of the evidence, but were certain the coming personality profile was going to leave the defense lawyer with little room to maneuver. Hightower knew what was coming and clacked his jaws together nervously as Susan was sworn in. His efforts to threaten her from prison with the Lynx letters, to force her to return to him as a marriage partner, had failed miserably. Now he felt Sue would have little good to say about him. He was right.

She launched into the background of how a romance began while they worked at the Newport Creamery and how that bloomed into marriage in 1982. Sue's voice was unemotional as she recounted their married life together in the tough days back in Ohio, and how they rebounded from financial ruin to end up living with her parents in Barrington. There was no sympathy in her tone, no accusatory anger. She simply stood there and recited facts, leaving the jury uneasy, feeling like voyeurs.

The marriage had disintegrated slowly, until finally there was nothing left. She recalled September of 1991, when they argued and he threatened to have her murdered by a hired gun. "I felt intimidated by him. He stared at me in the way he often did ... He wanted to make sure I was put in my place." In the back row, Mary Lou's fingers fluttered nervously about her needlepoint project.

Susan, who had her last name changed following the finalization of the divorce in January 1992, described how her ex-husband failed miserably at being a businessman in Barrington, despite substantial financial help from her parents. She paid what rent money exchanged hands, while Hightower usually coughed up only enough money to cover his business telephones. When she spoke of him in court, it was always "Christopher Hightower," as if it were the name of a stranger.

In the intervening months between the shock of his arrest and the day she testified, Susan had effectively gone to ground to protect her privacy. As well as changing her name, she had also left her job at the White Church. But she did not leave Barrington, and would show up at normal events, such as the lighting of the outdoor Christmas tree at the Town Hall gazebo, or soccer practice, or having her hair done, chatting with old friends, determined to keep life as normal as possible for herself and her boys. The Slickers had overcome the initial shock and embarrassment too, and sought to keep disruption from their doorstep.

They were members of a polite society, and they lived

by those rules. Christopher Hightower had been a bad experience for all of them, and by the time he went on trial, Susan and her family were well on their way to re-establishing their daily routines. "It wasn't like she was wearing a veil of mourning," said one acquaintance. Townspeople had never blamed her or her family, not for a moment, and that loyalty supported her now. The trial was a major setback for everyone's recovery, but all of them knew it was something that had to be endured. Once Hightower was put away, the spotlight would move on and Barrington could return to its usual calm routine of being a rather special place in which to live.

Oddly, despite her intense battle for privacy, Susan agreed with a free-lance writer to produce a book that would describe her story, "as seen through the eyes of an oppressed and mistreated young wife."

Now, finally after dodging the spotlight for so long, she was on the witness stand. Her voice was strong and her memory clear, for she knew this was her best chance to put Chris far away from the family, forever.

She blinked when asked if she was acquainted with the victims, replying she had met Alice twice, Ernie on frequent occasions with her husband, and that Emily took an overnight trip with the Hightowers to New Hampshire in the summer of 1989.

Sue described the fear she felt the night of their final argument and how worried she became when Hightower nervously began to chomp his jaws together in an ominous nervous reflex. Then came the whiskey glass exploding against the fireplace and Hightower stalking off upstairs, telling her that no one would believe her if she reported the death threat.

The prosecution did not question why the Slickers allowed Hightower to continue living beneath their roof for a single minute after that episode, why the cops were not called instantly, how a death threat could be bandied about so casually and then familial life proceed as if nothing were wrong. But the ex-wife's recall of the series of important events surrounding her final days with

Hightower were extremely important to the case, for it allowed jurors some insights into the man's actions just before the Brendels were murdered. It became clear that when Sue filed for divorce papers and the constable threw Hightower out of 1 Jones Circle, the man was suddenly adrift on a lonely sea and, by his own words, willing to have someone killed.

When Bob George began his cross-examination, the lawyer once again turned over a few unexpected rocks. This time he referred to Hightower's reputation as an extremely intelligent man, the professorial air that he projected. To this point in the trial, almost everyone accepted the proposition that the guy holding the master's degree from Wright State University, who missed getting a Ph.D. in science by a whisker, was truly a cut above everyone else in the intelligence department. Under George's questioning, Susan noted that Hightower "didn't pass his oral and written exams in March or April of 1985." The house fires in Dayton, she confirmed, happened about the same time. Then she made the astonishing comment that during the next six years of their marriage, the two of them *never* discussed the failed exams that forced him out of college and onto a different track in life. Not once in six years was it even a topic of breakfast conversation.

In the back row Mary Lou punched in another couple of stitches of green yarn. Sue said that once she took the secretarial job at the White Church, her husband slowly got involved in volunteer work there as a youth advisor, teaching Sunday school, serving as cochairman of the Board of Christian Education. But while erecting that respectable facade, business was going badly for him—which was why she had to take the job in the first place—and that changed him. "He was failing to take financial responsibility for the family," she said. "He was not a very pleasant person to be around."

Their arguments increased after marriage counseling with the White Church pastor failed, and while Hightower never physically harmed her or the boys, Sue said

she grew afraid of him. The divorce papers filed, she saw
him briefly on Thursday evening, September 19, knowing he was still angry after their confrontation in the
church parking lot. Hightower picked up his checkbook,
car keys, and a green Army jacket he used "for dirty
work," then walked out the door without a word. It
would be the last time she would see him, face-to-face,
in the outside world. She rose early Friday morning and
went directly to work, coordinating the delivery of the
restraining order by telephone.

When Sue Hightower stepped down from the witness
stand, it would be the last time she would come to the
courthouse until the trial was complete. She had resigned from the White Church to escape the media glare
and had begun a new job in January, hoping that holding
to a normal schedule would make life easier for her and
the boys.

Now and then she would watch the trial unfold on the
television set at work, or listen to news on the radio, or
read the in-depth newspaper coverage, but mostly she
relied upon Mary Lou and Kathy to come home at night
and tell her what had happened in court during the day.
A family videotape machine recorded televised segments
for later viewing.

Her main concern was the children, still too young to
understand the crisis that had enveloped the family.
John, at seven, thought he was old enough to attend
some court sessions, and was dissuaded only when he
was told that spending a morning in court was ten times
worse than sitting in church. Bobby, five, was growing
moody and had a different outlook, for he thought that
when this thing called a "trial" was finished, his daddy
would come home. Many tender talks were needed for
both of them.

The family invited few friends to the house on Jones
Circle, and spent hours alone, talking about their lives
with Chris Hightower, trying to find some understanding
of a situation that was incomprehensible. Had he said
something that may have warned them earlier? Could

they have done something differently to ward off the tragedy? They could crack an occasional joke, but for the most part, their private conversations were an attempt to recognize their own feelings, to find a path through this terrible maze, and only another family member could understand their pain. "We held nothing back," recalled Kathy Slicker.

But throughout their ordeal, the Slicker household had received support from throughout Barrington, throughout Rhode Island and the United States. As the trial wore on, the mail became heavy with cards and letters from well-wishers. Mary Lou piled the messages into baskets around the house, and all they had to do to get a morale boost was to reach into one of the colorful heaps and pull out a card. A "Hang in there," or a "Thinking of you," written by a total stranger could supply another day of strength. Among the hundreds of messages that flooded Jones Circle, there was not a single negative note.

Later on the same trial day, Sue's father, Clyde Slicker, took the stand. The professor of education at Rhode Island College appeared to be a man whose own world was collapsing. He had genuinely liked Christopher Hightower and had helped him out spiritually and financially for years. The father of Slicker's only grandchildren was, in his opinion, a nice man. In a strata of society where most people are indeed nice, Slicker had wrongly assumed that Hightower was also decent.

Tall, wearing a neat dark suit and speaking in a loud voice, Slicker seemed pained at divulging what went on in the privacy of his home. But it was vital that Slicker corroborate the earlier testimony of his daughter. Reluctantly, he spoke of the disintegrating marriage and how his son-in-law slid from being a very active man to being a couch potato who would rather flop on the sofa and watch television than go to work.

Knowing that Sue was about to divorce Chris, Clyde Slicker still did not intervene, although the drama was unfolding before his eyes. Hightower had threatened to *kill* Sue, and still Slicker could maintain a civil attitude. While conspiring with his daughter through clandestine telephone calls on when the constable should arrive at the house, Slicker had helped Hightower repair the bent eyeglasses and laid out orange juice and granola bars as a snack.

When Hightower arrived home, dirty and disheveled after murdering Ernie Brendel, the only odd thing that Clyde reported was that he had never before seen Chris operate the washing machine.

Slicker described Hightower's surprise when confronted by police with the divorce and restraining orders. "Chris looked at me with a very cold stare that seemed to go right through me," he told the court. It was a pained Clyde Slicker who walked out of court that day, wanting to believe the best about the man he once considered his son. But in his heart Slicker realized he never really knew Christopher Hightower at all.

William McGovern was called to the witness stand to discuss the transaction at Thompson's Sport Shop, and his testimony actually placed the crossbow in the hands of the defendant. But the most important part of his testimony came when he stepped outside of the witness box to demonstrate how to cock a Devastator crossbow. With his right foot in the steel stirrup, he grabbed the top string and pulled up hard, his shoulders quivering with the effort. Several members of the jury stood to get a better view, as the steel-wound cable inched back until it clicked into place. An almost visible shudder ran through them as they imagined the incredible power such a thing would possess when hurling its arrow toward a human being.

Youngs and Stone brought forward the two men from the National Futures Association who had been dealing with Hightower's shaky business. Auditor Joseph Mazza testified that, during a 1991 audit of Hightower's books, the defendant had mentioned that he had been hooked up briefly, somehow, with organized crime, but was taking care of that situation. Both Mazza and his boss, Timothy Wigand, dealt with Hightower on the Brendel complaint. Mazza discussed the Brendel matter by telephone and was rebuffed when he tried to set up a meeting in Barrington in September of 1991. Wigand testified Hightower called him on Friday, September 20, at ten minutes before noon, and claimed Ernie Brendel had decided to drop the charges. Wigand said he told Hightower the NFA would require a letter from Brendel to that effect.

The jury was aware that at the time Hightower called Wigand, it would have been impossible for Ernie Brendel to write anything to anyone. He was already dead.

27

War Room

After each adjournment the prosecution retreated to the Handley Building, a six-floor structure of red brick at 56 Pine Street, just across from an identical building that held the office of the attorney general. Room 302-H had been rented shortly before the first of the year, when Mike Stone decided that, to prepare for the Hightower trial, the team had to consolidate. They had to get out of the daily hustle-bustle of the A.G.'s office and the Barrington P.D., away from all distractions. He found the place he wanted right next door, a plushly appointed suite with comfortable sofas, desks of polished wood, gleaming lamps, and plenty of work space. The contracts were signed, the money paid, and the deal was done. But the lawyer didn't read the fine print. When Stone opened the door the following day, he had a surprise. "The place was empty. Nothing in it. Zip," he said. Before the investigators could start work, they had to scrounge for desks, file cabinets, shelves, and chairs. Instead of a bright executive office, the place immediately took on the somewhat battered look of what it really was—a cop shop.

Stone claimed a corner room and Youngs moved into the adjacent office. The biggest room was devoted to the boxes and notebooks filled with evidence that had to be sorted and numbered, while the ebb and flow of policemen grabbed whatever seats and desks were available. It would become home away from home for Youngs, Stone, Badger, Schauble, Palumbo, and Lynch, and they affectionately dubbed it the "War Room." One plus, it was conveniently adjacent to Challenges, "the Ultimate Sports Bar."

The War Room was their sanctuary, where coats could come off, papers could be studied, arguments could be had, and cops could walk around with holstered pistols and no one noticed. The cramped place had a single purpose—everything in it was pointed toward putting away Christopher Hightower. On the wall of Stone's office they taped sheets from a yellow legal pad, end to end, until it was one piece of paper forty inches long. On it they carefully listed what they called "nails"—trial evidence they hoped spelled doom for the bearded defendant they all detested. Thirty-nine separate entries were made, gruesome reminders of the business at hand. Some, like the "Human blood on EB checkbook" and "Apex delivery," were considered nails. Others, such as the Brendel corpses being found buried in the same clothes they wore the Friday they vanished, were awarded the status of "spikes" in Hightower's coffin.

In stark contrast, defense lawyer Bob George was forced to operate at some distance from the Providence courtroom. The Hightower command center was set up in his office on Newbury Street in Boston, where he could supervise other cases being handled by his associates while he concentrated on Hightower. After a predawn start in Boston on most mornings, he would stuff the material needed for the day's work into the trunk of whatever car was ferrying him to Providence. Time was a factor for both sides, and George, with a car telephone in hand, worked his way up and down the interstate highway, planning strategy at sixty miles per hour with his co-counsel Bob Launie and paralegal Carrie Caruso at his side. He would meet with Hightower before or after court each day to assess his client's needs and mental state. Associates said he usually left those meetings with a new pile of reminders, hints, and legal advice from Hightower on how the trial should be run.

George increasingly worried about Hightower's refusal to recognize what they were up against. While the prosecution was introducing blood-soaked evidence, Hightower, at the defense table, might lean over and say something with a broad smile on his face. Such actions might not sit well with a juror.

In a related situation, Hightower almost drove Caruso, the petite, dark-haired paralegal, off the case by writing flirty little poems and asking, "Bob thinks I'm a lousy poet. What's your opinion?" She finally had George order him to leave her alone.

Bob George was also feeling the strain of the long trial and was showing a bit of temper in court, as the evidence wall grew higher each day. Even Judge Sheehan saw the mounding pile as a subject of interest. When the prosecution introduced a photo of the Brendel kitchen, with cups and dishes sitting in the sink, Sheehan cracked, "I knew you'd get to the kitchen sink before long." The line got a laugh from almost everyone in the courtroom, even Chris Hightower. Once again Mike Stone and Pat Youngs saw nothing humorous about it.

George wanted to convince the jury that the prosecution's painstaking alignment of evidence was nothing but smoke. He said Hightower never denied being in the house, or in the garage, or even in Connecticut on the deadly weekend in question. "You practically emptied the car," George stated to Mike Quinn, referring to the thorough police examination of the Brendel property. "Is it fair to say it was covered in blood?" Quinn allowed how that might be a fair assumption.

"Were you aware Christopher Hightower said he was in the barn area?"

"Yes."

"Were you aware Christopher Hightower said he picked up Emily Brendel on Friday?"

"I was not aware of that."

"Were you aware that Christopher Hightower said he was at the house when Alice was home?"

"I was not aware of that."

"Were you aware that Christopher Hightower said he used a hose to wash the garage floor?"

"I was not aware of that statement."

"Were you aware that Christopher Hightower said he was riding all over Barrington on that bicycle?"

This was how George dealt with the evidence. All the police were doing, he told the jury, was proving that Hightower was in the house and garage and picked up Emily and went to Connecticut, exactly as he had stated. So what?

But deep down Bob George had to know that the net was drawing tight around his client. It was the Chinese Water Torture School of Law. Drop by drop, water wears away rock. And George knew there were bigger drops yet to come.

On St. Patrick's Day, March 17, the prosecution presented a series of witnesses who verified Alice was at work in the Brown University library the Friday she disappeared. A bus rider testified Alice was not met at her regular bus stop, a very unusual occurrence.

Then they brought in Emily's teachers, and parents of classmates, to describe the field trip to Newport. Doing so, they managed to put into evidence photographs that had fallen into their laps. Pamela Nadol had been a parent chaperon on the Newport trip, and while the kids were at Fort Adams State Park, snapped a series of pictures. It wasn't until several months later, when the film was developed, that she noticed in a group shot that Emily Brendel sat in the center of the front row, wearing her lime-green jacket, blue jeans, and high-top white sneakers. She gave the film to investigators. When it was introduced as evidence, jurors took special notice. They had heard Emily's voice on the message tape and now were handed the color picture of a little girl looking carefree only a few hours before her terrible death.

Their eyes went to her face, then to the white sneakers that were still on her feet when her buried body was discovered.

Other witnesses described how Hightower snared Emily at the YMCA, and Pam Poirier told of sending him away at first, and releasing Emily only after Hightower produced Ernie's driver's license and a man purporting to be Ernie Brendel gave verbal permission by phone. She was almost heartbreaking in her testimony, keeping her voice crisp. Emily had been in the care of the Y until she was kidnapped by a master con man. Now all Poirier could do was testify for the prosecution to supply another bit of evidence against the man who killed the child.

Fourteen people took the stand on that Wednesday, followed by ten more on Thursday and another ten on Friday. Bank tellers pinpointed Hightower's movements when he cashed the forged checks; the mattress delivery man placed Hightower inside the Brendel house at 5:00 P.M. on Friday, and youth soccer coach Bob Pearson put Hightower at Haines Park on Saturday morning. A little girl testified that when she went over to 51 Middle Highway on Saturday afternoon to ask if Emily could come out and play, Hightower answered the door and told her Emily wasn't there. A service station attendant and one of Hightower's White Church friends saw him gassing up the Toyota on Sunday morning. Receipts put Hightower in Sears, McDonald's, and Somerville Lumber at precise moments. Hightower's footprints were traced from the time he was thrown out of 1 Jones Circle until he was arrested on Monday. Damning stuff, each and every bit.

Then the trial hit a critical moment as witness David Goyette, answering prosecution questions, explained how food was served at the McDonald's drive-through window. That accounted for a McDonald's receipt in

Hightower's possession that placed him at the restaurant although he swore he was elsewhere at the time.

Bob George rose to cross-examine, his head swimming after listening to fifty-one previous witnesses. "Mr. Mc-Donald," he began, with perfect timing to defuse the situation, blushing and stumbling to a stop, as if to catch his error. Laughter drifted through the court at the expense of the defense attorney, and even Judge Sheehan thought it was funny. "He would like to be Mr. McDonald," jibed the judge. Stone and Youngs were shocked, watching their carefully built, suspenseful case diminish as laughs swept the room. The jury was being entertained by the quick-witted defense lawyer and the judge, for whom they liked to bake cookies.

A tense situation was building. Mike Stone was on a short fuse. Stone, whose vision before the trial had been sharp enough to read a newspaper headline from across the street, was now wearing glasses to deal with the flood of papers in the case. Pat Youngs was feeling miserable, ravaged by the flu, having lost ten pounds since the first of the year and being frequently reprimanded by Judge Sheehan. Neither was in a forgiving mood.

The case was coming together as planned, each piece of material and every witness providing excellent incriminating evidence to show that Hightower had the opportunity to kill the Brendels, and the means, with the pry bar and Devastator crossbow. They were wrapping him up tight, and were infuriated that Bob George and the judge were undermining their months of work by exchanging wisecracks. That could not be allowed to continue!

For his part, George had good and bad news to consider as he went back to Boston on Friday afternoon. The good news was that he had a private detective sitting in the courtroom to evaluate the body language of the jury after a few weeks of trial. George had done his best to milk the poison from the prosecution case by selling himself as a nice guy to the jurors. In the end, it would require a unanimous verdict to convict Christopher Hightower of a crime, and while the evidence seemed to make the case a slam-dunk certainty in its outcome, all George needed was one single holdout to create a hung jury. At this point, two weeks into the trial, despite fifty-eight witnesses and 301 pieces of evidence, the central question to him was whether there was a single juror in the box who might be shaky.

His conclusion, after talking with the detective and his fellow lawyers, was there wasn't one, but *five* jurors who might not yet be convinced by the prosecution. That kind of thing can put a bounce in the step of any defense attorney.

The bad news, however, George considered, was that he was not the one on trial. He was winning the personality battle and positively loved joking with the cherubic judge, but Chris Hightower still appeared as a villain. Hightower simply was not a sympathetic character, and George knew that Youngs and Stone were readying some broadsides that could sink his little ship without a trace.

George's worst nightmare was that a juror might sidle up to him someday and whisper, "Hey, Bob. Love you. Hate your client."

28

The Joke

The third week of trial began March 22, which would have been Ernie Brendel's fifty-fifth birthday.

Christopher Hightower arrived at the courthouse wearing a blue prison jumpsuit, bringing up the rear of a threesome of criminals. At the front of the line, dressed in a well-cut business suit, was Joseph Mollicone, Jr., the former president of Heritage Loan and Investment Company, charged with embezzling millions of dollars from that institution to finance a high-rolling lifestyle and then fleeing the state to escape prosecution. Shackled between the millionaire crook and the Sunday-school-teaching mass murderer, both white men once considered pillars of their communities, was a young black man covering his face with the hood of his sweatshirt. It was as if seventeen-year-old Roderick Spears, doing two years for attempted murder, was trying to avoid being seen in such bad company.

This was the week that Youngs and Stone wanted to give the jury the third corner of their triangle of evidence. They felt they had proven the defendant possessed the opportunity and means to commit the crime, now they needed to show Hightower had a motive to kill Ernie Brendel.

S. Paul Ryan, a tall lawyer who practiced in Barrington and was a close friend of Brendel for a dozen years, gave the jury a synopsis of the Brendel-Hightower relationship since the time Ryan introduced them in his law office on a snowy day in 1987. Within a couple of years, Ryan said, Brendel put up to $40,000 with Hightower Investments—$11,000 of Ernie's own money and the rest from three acquaintances. When the investments faltered badly, Ernie accused Hightower of using "cooked" or false numbers to lure him into the investment. Ryan testified Ernie apparently got back the $29,000 his friends had invested, but not his own funds.

In June of 1991 Ryan helped Brendel file a formal complaint with the CFTC in Washington and another with the NFA in Chicago.

Ryan advised Ernie that it appeared Hightower was broke, and since it was unlikely that any money would be recovered, Brendel should drop the legal action and walk away. But Ernie was angry. He had been gypped and would not let it rest. On Thursday, September 19, Ernie told Ryan he did not want to see other people bilked out of their money by such a charlatan. Hightower had to be shut down.

That was it in a nutshell. Hightower was down to his last card, and this time, despite the lax regulation of the commodities and futures game, the Brendel complaint was almost certain to result in Hightower losing his license. That meant professional ruin, for while he could still trade a few accounts, if he had them, he would never make the big scores of his dream. Hightower would be a pariah in the professional world, humiliated among his financial peers. He could not stomach that. Combined with the personal disaster that had befallen him when Sue filed for divorce, Hightower was out of luck, out of patience, and out of time. Murder became an attractive option.

After Ryan testified, the jury heard from Jim Page, Ernie's best friend, about the mysterious telephone call from Alice on Saturday morning, September 21. A small man with tousled black hair and big glasses, Page had known Ernie for twenty years. He was Emily's godfather

and in tune with the Brendel family's ups and downs.
Page was choked up, almost tearful, as he recounted Alice's calmness that morning when she notified him that
Ernie couldn't make their planned meeting for the football game. Page had gone over the thirty-second conversation a thousand times in his mind after the murders,
wondering if there was some clue, something in the way
she spoke, something he should have picked up. But
there was nothing. It was just a quick telephone call, and
he could not take it back and make it happen again differently. "There was nothing odd in Alice's voice," he
testified.

Strangely, Chris Hightower became as animated sitting at the defense table as at any point in the trial.
There was little in Page's testimony to do injury to the
Hightower story, but Hightower was clearly agitated.
The defendant made notes, the pen in his left fist flying
over the paper, squirmed in his chair and began whispering to George and nodding toward Page. He apparently
wanted the lawyer to attack the witness. George gentled
him as one would calm a horse. Page was obviously on an
emotional edge, and any harsh grilling could backfire if
the witness started crying in front of the jury. Hightower
finally slumped back in his chair and glared at Page,
eyes full of mysterious and puzzling anger.

Gary Palumbo was witness number sixty, making his second appearance on the stand. This time, he started un-
raveling one of the mysteries inside the bigger mystery
of Chris Hightower. Palumbo said that on Monday, September 23, he had gone through the trash can beside the
photocopy machine in the White Church office. That
was where Hightower was seen by Associate Pastor Rose
Amadeo making copies the previous day, and the detective discovered the remnants of chopped and scissored
papers.

He found a letter to Vicki Evans of the CFTC, dated
September 19, and signed by Ernest Brendel, explaining
that the charges against Christopher Hightower were

being dropped. But Palumbo, digging deeper into the trash, also found a copy of the same letter, without the Brendel letterhead on it. And another copy of the letter, unsigned. He also retrieved a copy of a legal document that had the signature block cut off. And finally he came upon a piece of Ernie's stationery that had been cut with scissors.

It was a cut-and-paste forgery job that showed how Hightower sent the CFTC a letter bearing the signature of a dead man. The defendant, the prosecution claimed, took the letter typed by Alice and attached it to a copy of Ernie's signature. The prosecution, astonished to discover that Hightower left such a clear trail behind, managed to track the unopened letter to Evans's Washington office and bring it back. Amazingly, it still bore Hightower's fingerprints.

The State's lawyers then switched topics abruptly and brought on Katherine McCloy and Detective Ken Schauble to describe the discovery of the grave. Bob George made no objections as McCloy spoke, even when she mentioned things that could have been ruled inadmissible on legal technicalities. The woman found the bodies. He was supposed to argue with her?

Mike Quinn came to the stand again, to describe the careful and scientific recovery of the bodies, and over the objection of George, the prosecution showed the jury a videotape of the scene. It looked like an archeological dig. The jurors had seen worse on commercial television.

One thing that struck them hard—a zoom shot of Emily's white shoe, peeking from the dirt beneath the body of her mother.

George jumped to his feet, furious, considering even the edited version of the tape an inflammatory gut punch, enough for a basis for appeal. "It doesn't matter if it went one minute or twenty minutes. One glimpse of Emily's shoe was enough," he said after court. It was a clear setback for the defense team, and the jury went home for the night to think about what they had just seen, to think about a little white shoe, to think about Emily.

Next came the forensics folk, the scientists and doctors who oversaw the recovery process, and Mike Stone introduced the critical torn corner of the lime bag found in Ernie's grave. Exhibit 326 put the torn edge next to the ripped bag, and the jurors saw it was a perfect match. The question of how it got into the grave was almost too simple to even address. Also found in the grave was a single white candle broken in half, which gave the jury a vision of a grave being dug in dark secrecy.

If the videotape had been a punch against the defense, what came next made the stomachs of the jurors churn. The medical examiner and another doctor testified about the autopsies, and color photographs of the badly decomposed bodies were handed around. Ernie's crushed head, his arrow wounds, and Alice's swollen neck, the white cloth still tied tightly around it, were shown in detail. Medical Examiner Richard Evans said he was unable to establish the exact cause of Emily's death, but could conclude there had been a "ligature compression" of the neck, similar to the same thing that killed her mother. He said it would take only four pounds of pressure to each side of the child's neck, applied over a period of less than a minute, to result in death. The bodies of both Emily and Alice contained evidence of diphenhydramine, an antihistamine, in strong enough dosage to have put them to sleep. The prosecution wanted to show this was the very chemical contained in the sleeping pills purchased by Hightower.

Bob George protested and submitted two drugs he had purchased at a nearby store during the lunch break, Nyquil and some Dramamine antimotion pills. Diphenhydramine, he argued, was so common that it could also be found in a cold medicine and a seasick pill. Pat Youngs shot back that it had "somnambulistic properties" that were vital to this case, which meant he thought Hightower used the pills to drug Emily and Alice before killing them. George wanted to show the jury that the chemical could have gotten into the systems of the two victims in some other way, perhaps through medicine taken to cure a case of sniffles.

When George read Emily's medical reports into the record, he emphasized she had been seen by a doctor for a stomachache on August 15, 1991, and that Tylenol was prescribed. He asked Dr. John Duvally, who performed her autopsy, if diphenhydramine was found in such a medicine. Duvally said that it was. Youngs responded by having Duvally say that it was also found in sleeping pills.

The judge asked to see the bottle of pills, and by doing so, opened a Pandora's box of trouble. There was so much evidence already admitted that it was stored not in the court for easy access, but in a special vault elsewhere in the courthouse. A marshal was sent to fetch the bottle, but could not. The vault was locked and the key was missing.

Sheehan's Irish temper was something to behold that afternoon. He barked at the prosecution for not being more efficient, barked at Bob George for confusing the drug issue, barked at almost everyone in sight. Finally he calmed enough to call it a day, apologizing to the jury.

"I hope you realize that my bark is worse than my bite," he joshed. Then he recognized George for any closing comment on the matter, and the defense lawyer, knowing a straight line when he saw one, quipped, "My worry is that Your Honor's bite is worse than his bark."

The judge laughed and the tension evaporated. The marshals laughed. The jury laughed. The spectators laughed. Christopher Hightower laughed. At the end of a long and hard Tuesday spent discussing the autopsies of Emily, Alice, and Ernest Brendel, almost everyone in the place was having a good laugh.

Mike Stone detonated like a bomb.

After court was dismissed, the three lawyers and the judge gathered in Sheehan's book-lined, tiny office and

Stone angrily came to the point. His half-rim eyeglasses dangled around his neck, bouncing on his chest as he vented his frustration. An astonished Pat Youngs leaned against a wall, and Bob George stood to one side. This fight was between Stone and Sheehan.

Stone was furious, claiming the judge was throwing the prosecution's case, a *triple murder case*, open to ridicule by his lighthearted banter from the bench and George's witty responses.

Nonsense, responded the judge. We're just trying to keep things loose in the court to prevent the jury from being overwhelmed by the tragedy.

Stone was not buying that. He and the other members of the prosecution team had been on this case for a year and a half, plunging into the work at the sacrifice of their personal lives. Now their careful plans were being thwarted by jokes! Cookies! Barks and bites! Mr. McDonald! Jokes were overwhelming the evidence, and even Hightower was sitting over there, laughing and smiling, like he was in a lighthearted board room meeting!

Sheehan resented the insinuation that he was not treating the trial with all due respect. He was trying to guide the complex legal contest to a successful and fair conclusion within the law, and he did not like lawyers criticizing the way he ran his court, particularly with this long trial not even at the halfway mark.

Nothing was settled before Stone stormed out through the narrow corridor, past the empty courtroom and down the marble stairs, his dark eyes blazing as he shook his head in dismay and headed back to the War Room.

Stone, Youngs, and their cops decided during the coming hours to put this trial back on track immediately. The strategy they laid out that night would be a turning point. It was time for an attitude adjustment.

29

Here's Christopher

Spring was trying to come to Rhode Island, with temperatures rising to fifty degrees, and the frequent snow of winter grudgingly giving way to rain. Piles of dirty snow still lurked in parking lots like wet slag heaps. The mood in the courtroom was just as dirty after the previous day's showdown in the judge's chambers. When court resumed at 10:06 A.M. on Wednesday, March 24, the prosecution, defense, and judge were barely civil to each other. Bob George had made a call to Mike Stone from his car phone to apologize if his "bark-and-bite" comment was out of order. Stone said there was no problem.

Pat Youngs wasted no time in putting the jury in the politically correct frame of mind. After Danish, doughnuts, cookies and coffee, the jurors had settled into their padded chairs for trial day thirteen, unaware of the strife. Then, Youngs served notice that lightheartedness was now a thing of the past. Even before calling a witness, he introduced Exhibit Number 350—a picture of Emily Brendel after the child had been exhumed from her grave. There was not a whisper in the court as Youngs handed the picture to one juror, who winced at the awful sight. The lawyer sat down while the picture was passed, hand to hand, around the jury box, despite the angry objection of Bob George. Christopher Hightower sat at the defense table, unblinking as the jurors looked at the photo, then looked across the room at him.

Now, ladies and gentlemen of the jury, if you didn't get the idea of what was going on here, here is Exhibit 357. Youngs and Stone did not have to speak those words, for the jurors were already uncomfortable as they handed around another color photo, this one of Ernie Brendel's savaged head. Youngs then had Medical Examiner Richard Evans testify that Hightower's steel pry bar could have inflicted such extensive damage. The lawyer intentionally dropped the heavy tool on the clerk's desk, where it landed with a loud thump that reverberated in the court. He followed with still another photo of Ernie's ripped scalp, to be viewed, up close and personal, by each juror.

Bob George was outraged at the obvious assault on the jury's emotions, but could not stop it. First there had been the child's voice on the tape recording, then the glimpse of her white tennis shoe in the grave. Now this! The redundancy of the evidence was beyond question, but Stone and Youngs intended to slam hard at the jury to show the case was no laughing matter, and Judge Sheehan was apparently reluctant to interrupt the flow of gory prosecution evidence after yesterday's confrontation. George raised the occasional objection, figuring that while he could not halt this Niagara of emotion-twisting evidence, it might be good fodder for an appeal. Youngs had a whole stack of color photographs depicting close-up shots of the autopsy findings, each equally horrible in the display of torn bodies. By the mid-morning break the jury was reeling.

The tempo of the trial clearly changed. This was serious legal theater, and the trial never again veered from its purpose.

The trial had moved into a phase of scientific evidence that would bring together much of what had been introduced earlier. Over the next few days, agents from the Federal Bureau of Investigation took turns on the stand, each an expert in a specific branch of criminology and each a professionally trained witness. They addressed jurors directly, in clear voices and scientific terms that they would translate into English. They were boring, but incredibly effective.

Agent Bruce Hall placed Hightower in the Brendel garage by proving glass particles found in Hightower's jacket and jeans matched the glass from the broken window. He also matched the lime found in the graves to the lime in the bag purchased by the defendant. Agent Bob Murphy, a firearms and tools specialist, matched Hightower's wire cutters to the sliced alarm line inside the house, and said the pry bar probably caused the damage to the wooden sill around the back door. Agent Michael Weiners, a fingerprint expert, brought along large display boards to show Hightower's fingerprints were found throughout the house—on drinking glasses, a blue plastic cup, a beige telephone, the computer printer, and the letter and envelope that Hightower claimed Brendel had sent to the CFTC. Strangely, no prints at all were found on the crossbow.

On and on came the stone-faced retinue of badge-toting scientists. A computer whiz determined the date and time, 6:41 A.M. on Saturday, September 21, on a Brendel computer disk that contained the letter Hightower had forced Alice to write. In a related extraordinary find, the FBI expert and Barrington's Ken Schauble discovered that Alice, apparently trying to leave a clue, filed the letter on a computer disk she labeled with Hightower's initials, CJH. An expert on body fluids followed Mike Stone through a long checklist of swabs taken from various parts of the garage, the Toyota and Audi, file folders, Hightower's L.L. Bean jacket, the pry bar, the crossbow, the Maple Avenue office and other places, until she had identified 237 separate items, including blood, hair, and fibers. Her report was twenty-seven pages thick. A specialist in documents interpreted, using the papers Palumbo pulled from the White Church trash can, exactly how Hightower had forged the letter sent to the CFTC, then used a display of posters to prove Hightower forged Ernie's name on the two cashed checks.

Bob George was aggravated. The experts seemed to be testifying to the same thing, over and over. After listening to lengthy testimony about the check forgery, he growled, "If this is a larceny case about $4,200, then I'll pay it out of my own pocket and we can go home." On cross-examination he turned the situation back to his original point—that the defendant wasn't trying to hide his actions.

The forged signature "isn't even close" to the real thing, George observed, and the FBI man agreed. Leaning his right arm on the jury railing, winning back some of their goodwill through implied friendship, George had the witness say there had been no attempt to disguise the handwriting. Such comments reaffirmed his theory that Hightower had been acting in a very, very peculiar manner.

The prosecution's case ended after the eightieth witness. Sergeant Mike Quinn made his third appearance on Monday, March 29, testifying that a piece of a single arrow was found in the garage, and that the jugs of muriatic acid used on the garage floor had never been recovered.

Those missing items had driven investigators to distraction. Everything else seemed to have turned up, but not these few tantalizing pieces of the puzzle. Many an hour had been spent searching every roadside ditch and culvert between Barrington, Rhode Island, and Guilford, Connecticut, hoping to find them. But they never did.

Stone wrapped up the prosecution case with Exhibit 405. Standing at the jury rail, glasses perched on the end of his nose, he unfolded a green-bordered piece of paper. In an emotion-choked voice he read the details on the death certificate of Emily Anne Brendel. At 4:11 P.M. the State rested.

The prosecution team returned to the War Room, confident that the pieces tied neatly together and that

Hightower was inescapably snared in the net of circumstantial evidence. But never once in their lengthy presentation had they brought up the key issue of whether
Christopher Hightower had been in his right mind, sane
and responsible for his actions, when he murdered the
Brendels. The march of the shrinks was yet to come.

Bob George and his assistant counsel, Bob Launie, had
their usual private meeting with Christopher Hightower,
this time to decide whether Hightower should take the
witness stand. Knowing his story, the defense lawyers
felt the prisoner should skip it, so they could go straight
to the psychiatrists and the state-of-mind arguments. By
going on the stand, Hightower would play into the hands
of Mike Stone and Pat Youngs, who were hoping and
praying that Hightower would testify and thereby open
himself to cross-examination. Indeed, the prosecution
had squirreled away important evidence that could only
come before the jury under such cross-examination. If
Hightower didn't get up and talk, that vital evidence
would be suppressed.

George formally advised his client to use his constitutional right of silence. But Hightower wasn't listening.
Bob George was only the lawyer. Hightower, the defendant, would call the shots, and told his legal team that
he would testify in his own behalf. Apparently he was
still convinced of his mental superiority, and just *knew* he
would sway that jury and walk out of court a free man.
All he needed was the chance to talk his way out of it.

The next morning, reporters who had covered the
case from the start gathered in the first-floor coffee shop
to guess what would happen as the defense launched its
case. Everyone was convinced there was no way that
Christopher Hightower would pass up his moment in the
spotlight, and television stations already had laid plans
for the live broadcast of his testimony. That feeling was
bolstered when the usually friendly Bob George ducked
away from them after buying a large cup of strong, black
coffee and exchanging terse greetings. He looked

haunted. One newspaper reporter imagined that the be-leaguered attorney would introduce his client the way Ed McMahon introduced Johnny Carson. The reporter put down his chocolate doughnut and lifted his cup of coffee in mock salute. "Bob's going to have to stand up there and tell the jury, 'Hey. You think you've heard crazy stuff before? Well, *heeerre's Christopher!*' "

30

Hightower

By Tuesday, March 30, the cold and heavy rain that pelted Rhode Island lightened to a bone-chilling mist that residents considered a harbinger of spring. The harsh, lingering weather seemed intent on proving that New England has only two seasons—winter and July.

In Courtroom 5, the jury, spectators and participants—with one exception—still did not know exactly what happened at 51 Middle Highway, how Alice and Emily were held hostage, when the family was killed and buried, or the precise manner of Emily's death. The prosecution had presented a ton of evidence over the fifteen days of trial, but the question remained whether they had proven their case or had just left the jury confused. The inferences in the case were clear, but were inferences enough?

The day had been set aside for Bob George to present defense motions. He began a series of challenges to the counts facing his client. It was not a pretty sight, as Sheehan decided to nitpick, as well as rule on points of law. The judge chided George for using a big word like "inveigle" and upbraided the out-of-town lawyer for using the word "Commonwealth" to describe Rhode Island. "Let's get our terminology straight. Massachusetts is the Commonwealth, this is Rhode Island," the jurist intoned, as if promoting the tiny state to something more than a block of winter ice wedged between Connecticut and Massachusetts.

Pat Youngs, speaking for the prosecution, countered George point by point, happy that Sheehan, who seemed to enjoy criticizing Youngs in court, had made George the target for the day. Youngs needed to say little, since this was a debate between Bob George and the judge, with the outcome all but certain before the day even began.

Indeed, after hearing defense motions while the jurors were out of the courtroom, Judge Sheehan ruled that not only would all eleven charges remain in place, but predicted ominously that after hearing the evidence already presented, the jury could find Hightower "guilty of each and every one." George rubbed his left hand over his eyes during the judge's lecture and Hightower sat motionless but shaken, realizing that Sheehan thought he was guilty.

"You swear to tell the truth, the whole truth and nothing but the truth, so help you God?" Clerk Linda Parsons was wasting her breath. "I do," Christopher Hightower answered, telling the first of what would become a long line of lies, deceptions, and half-truths sprinkled with a few facts. His tale of what happened on that September weekend of 1991 would be a gripping account of dope-dealing, torture, financial skulduggery, a raccoon and a Lynx, white slavery, Mafia hoods, Chinese Tong gangsters, death threats against kids, a monster crossbow, triple murder in a New England village, extortion, lost love, and—most of all— how poor old Chris Hightower, totally innocent, was wrongly being blamed for it all.

The courtroom was jammed, and throughout Rhode Island and most of New England thousands of people missed their daytime soap operas as all three Providence television stations began their broadcasts of Hightower's testimony.

If ever a salesman was riding on a smile and a shoe

shine, it was Hightower, for he was his own star witness. He had been given access to all of the documents and evidence lists used against him and had spent much of his prison time knitting a story that would piece everything together. What the judge had said the previous day did not matter, for the judge would not be voting on the verdict. And after all, hadn't the jurors joked around on St. Joseph's Day by offering the judge some custardy Italian pastry? Hightower had taken that as a good sign. Some members of this jury were still in a good mood, they could still be had! If the balding man in the white turtleneck sweater and olive-toned suit was nervous, he hid it well. He had waited too long to blow it now. It was show time!

Bob George would pilot Hightower through the twisting story, and at times would be as surprised as anyone else, as Hightower dropped new nuggets of information that he apparently made up on the spot. George wanted to show Hightower's "state of mind" as rampaging out of control at the time of the crime, that he was suffering strange delusions that prevented him from knowing right from wrong. Later, the attorney hoped to combine those statements with evaluations from psychiatrists to effectively argue that Hightower was insane. It could spell the difference between life in prison or a sentence to a mental hospital with the possibility of eventual parole. The major flaw was that Hightower was in control. Or rather, out of control.

They started with the childhood in Florida, making sure to tiptoe around a few mine fields. Their trek did not go unnoticed by the prosecution team, which intended to fill in the blanks.

The jurors were spellbound. Until now they had sifted through *things* and listened to other people talk about this guy. They were at last getting a glimpse of the personal side of Hightower, of which they knew as little as they did of the dark side of the moon. By lunchtime on that first day, they were told that Christopher Hightower was an upstanding, clean-living man beset by hard luck

since his earliest years, who, in spite of numerous set-
backs, managed to succeed. The mild-mannered fellow
was not at all like the monster who was painted so
bleakly by the prosecutors. At least, that was the view
being provided by Chris Hightower.

He said he grew up in Winter Haven and Titusville,
Florida, and with two brothers, two sisters, his mother
and stepfather. He loved sports as a kid and got a partial
scholarship to Indian River Junior College, but did not
do well because he had to work two jobs, while at the
same time "playing basketball for the university." He
never even made the team, but who was to know?
Hightower plunged ahead with his Navy career and hospital training and the marriage to Ellen, an obstetrics
nurse, in 1973. He did not mention that she was an officer and he was a low-ranking enlisted man, unable
even twenty years afterward to admit that she might be
better than him.

As if on cue, his eyes grew large and watery, a look of
sadness fell upon him and, voice breaking with emotion,
he softly spoke of his two daughters. He admitted he had
not actually seen the girls for three years, but did not
tell the jurors that he was chronically behind in his support payments, or that he once threatened to have them
killed.

Pulling himself together, he described his happy return to academia and graduating from the University of
Rhode Island, then taking the job with Riker Labs.
Hightower modestly said that although he "excelled in
some areas," his overall performance was only average
because he was dissatisfied with the job. "I didn't like to
communicate with doctors," said the man who had spent
most of his life telling other people he wanted to be a
physician. Instead he took a job with Newport Creamery.
Then came the divorce from Ellen, which left him adrift.
He sought to pull the heartstrings of the jury, but had
barely aroused their interest, because he sounded dis-
tinctly like a loser.

Things got better for a while, he said. He met and

married Susan Slicker, and he was accepted in an elite doctoral science program at Wright State University. But hard times dogged him there too; although he became the father of two sons by Sue, he suspected his young wife was being unfaithful by the fall of 1982. Jurors did a quick review. They had only gotten married in July and a few months later she was cheating? Yes, he confirmed, he had "to keep her on a tight rein." In a reasonable tone Hightower claimed that Sue admitted the adultery, which put even more pressure on him. "I wanted to know where my wife was and what she was doing all the time," he testified.

Things were bad at home, money was tight, and his university studies were at risk, since all of the pressure caused him to fail a vital examination in the fall of 1984. Then, even more bad luck, as two fires swept his family's little home in Ohio, clearly arson, although police "never found out who did it." After that, Hightower said he felt as if he were drowning in trouble. "All I could think of doing was to keep going," he said, using a line that would reappear frequently in more vital parts of his testimony.

He was bothered by his childhood. "My father, my stepfather, had always had trouble supporting the family. And I was determined that I would provide the support for my family that I wanted them to have," the sincere man on the stand testified. "I was determined to do better."

Without mentioning the debacle of the Investors Guild, which he skinned out of $100,000 through the commodities hustle, the erstwhile Hightower described moving back to charming Barrington, Susan's hometown, where her parents supported them while he tried to get his business running. The business, however, never clicked and he never had more than a few clients. George interrupted. "How can you support a family like that?" Hightower shrugged. "You can't." The jury wondered why, if he was so determined to do better than his stepfather, he didn't simply quit snuffling around the financial trough and go get a real job, the kind of jobs the jury members themselves held.

The Hightowers and Slickers "decided to live together to keep expenses down [and] live together as a family unit." Needing a larger house, the Slickers bought the beautiful spread at 1 Jones Circle. In 1988 Hightower became very involved in White Church activities. Never once would he say he believed in any Christian principles, such as the commandment: Thou shalt not kill.

Hightower sought sympathy, tears welling in his eyes as he described how his marriage to Sue crumbled. She would not listen to his pleas, he testified, outlining one scene in which he tried to get her to discuss their problems. "I've laid here beside you for five years, and every time you wanted to talk, I did. Now you won't talk to me," he had argued. "You're killing us, you're letting our love die." She answered by leaving their bed and sleeping with the kids.

But when George lobbed a question about the business operations, Hightower bloomed like a rose, eyes steely, manner firm, bearing straight. Ah, he loved this stuff. "My approach to investment and the market is through computer analysis," he declared, and proudly announced that he had devised a system that would produce high financial returns with "low potential of risk exposure." His program for trading had one minor bug, Hightower said. He could tell when the market was about to make a move, *but not in which direction.*

The jurors were baffled. The stock market could either go up or down, right? And if you can't tell which way it's going, then the fancy program would be worthless, right? This financial wizard didn't seem to know what the hell he was talking about.

The prosecution team was ecstatic as they went to lunch, the entire group walking a few blocks to a downtown arcade. They had brown-bagged it for months, and now they meandered over to a pizza place and cheerfully discussed Hightower's rambling testimony.

When asked how he thought the star witness had done that morning, Mike Stone cracked a wry smile and said, "Well, I'm ready to drop all charges."

31

Tall Chinese Men

Chris Hightower spewed forth a porridge of strange replies and outright lies to account for everything that happened on that fatal weekend in September 1991. At almost every pause, Bob George would ask, "What was your state of mind at that time?" Hightower's answer was usually, "I was really confused, I didn't feel I had control anymore . . . and was subject to the forces around me." In other words, he was not to blame.

This was his version:

On Thursday night, September 19, Hightower hurried through dinner with Clyde, Sue, and the kids because, "through prearrangement" with Ernie Brendel, he had to buy a crossbow. Ernie was having problems with a raccoon in the garage, and a pesky groundhog that lived under the carriage house. At first Ernie asked if Chris had a small .22 caliber rifle, but Hightower said he did not, and anyway, they were concerned about the noise of a gunshot in a residential area. As an alternative, they settled on a crossbow. Hightower had a small one he had used against squawking crows around Jones Circle, but it wasn't powerful enough to take down a raccoon.

He paid for the crossbow with a personal check. Ernie had agreed to reimburse him if Chris would kill the varmints. On the way back to Middle Highway, Hightower checked his watch because he knew Ernie had some kind of appointment. It was about 6:30 P.M.

But there was a surprise waiting when Hightower drove up the long driveway. A white van was parked in front of the open garage door. Puzzled, he found Ernie. "I got the crossbow, but I need payment now," he told his friend. Ernie laid the Devastator in the garage and Hightower returned to Jones Circle, hoping to spend some quality time with his wife on her birthday. He was crushed to find that she had invited some girlfriends over instead. "I was upset that she didn't want to spend time with me, but with others," he testified.

Grabbing his old field jacket, he left and spent forty-five minutes walking back to the Brendel home in the rain. He did not drive because he was upset and "needed time to clean my head out."

About 7:30 P.M. he arrived and talked with Alice Brendel for a while. Emily was not in sight. Later, Alice unlocked the garage door with a key so he could fetch the crossbow and arrows. Then he found a spot beside the big house from which he could see the top of the garage, and settled down in the rainy darkness to "wait for the raccoon." He steeled himself for the possibility that he might be out in the ugly weather all night, but the raccoon popped into view about ten o'clock. Hightower skewered it with a magnificent shot that covered some 120 feet in the dead of night.

Ernie returned home a short time later, and Chris proudly showed him the carcass. They left it by the garage and went into the house to talk. Brendel hoped to shift Hightower's attention away from marital problems and onto their plans to do business together. To prove his solidarity, Brendel went upstairs and typed out a letter advising the CFTC that he was withdrawing his complaint. When Hightower's lawyer mentioned that an FBI computer specialist had testified that the letter was printed out on Brendel's Imagewriter at exactly 9:42 A.M. on Sunday, September 22, Hightower insisted, "No, sir. Ernie typed it on Thursday night, and it was dated September nineteenth."

Then Ernie invited Hightower to spend Thursday night on the living room couch.

Friday, he awoke rather woozy as the Brendels were getting up and about. Ernie took Emily to school and Alice to work. When they left, Chris took a shower, grabbed a cup of coffee and attempted to sort through his personal problems.

When Ernie came home, they discussed plans to convert the carriage house behind 51 Middle Highway into an office they could share. Ernie said he would be in New York the following week and would purchase supplies to get the job started when he returned. About 10:30 A.M. Hightower prepared to go home, and Ernie told him that he was welcome to use the black Raleigh bike in the garage.

Pedaling out of the driveway, however, Hightower was almost run over. A car zoomed out of the church parking lot next door, splashing mud all over him and knocking him from the bike before speeding away. "I fell off, sliced up my legs sliding on the road," he recalled. "It broke my glasses, and I was covered with mud."

In that chaotic state, he went back to Jones Circle, where Clyde Slicker offered him a snack. Hightower wanted to wear the same clothes to a pending church meeting, so he put the dirty jeans and plaid shirt into the wash. Clyde handed him the message to call the NFA, and Hightower was happy to advise them the "complaint was being dropped. Ernie Brendel and I had reached agreement."

As the clothes tumbled in the washer, Hightower answered a knock on the front door and found several uniformed men waiting. "One said he was a constable and that 'this is an ex parte restraining order. You have fifteen minutes to pack and leave.' I was totally shocked."

With the constable at his heels, the stunned Hightower rounded up a few belongings. "I didn't know what was going on," he said. "I was losing it." Carrying a bag of clothes in one arm and the briefcase in his other hand, there was no way he could ride the bike, so he set out to walk back to the Brendel house. Exhausted, he caught a ride with Susanne Henderson, who drove him to 51 Middle Highway.

"Do you know what time it was?" asked Bob George.

"No," Hightower replied. "What was time, the way things were going?"

A surprised Ernie Brendel opened the door for him. He had not expected to see Hightower again until his return from New York the next Wednesday. Hightower poured out his latest personal problems as they sat at the kitchen table. Ernie was riled that Hightower was being badly abused.

"If she's gonna do this, I'm not going to let her have the children. No way," a determined Hightower told his friend.

"Don't worry," replied Ernie. "I have friends. You're going to have money, you're going to have your children." With that, Ernie stalked away and started making telephone calls.

Until this point, things were pretty boring around the courtroom, and television viewers around Rhode Island were beginning to lose interest in Hightower's droning recitation. That was about to change.

HIGHTOWER: While he was on the telephone, some people arrived at the house and knocked on the door. I went to the foyer area, or the hallway area, and motioned to Ernie. He said let them in. So I went and opened the door and let them in.

GEORGE: Who were they?

HIGHTOWER: I don't know who they are.

GEORGE: What did they look like?

HIGHTOWER: Two of them appeared to be Chinese, and the other two appeared to be Latin American.

GEORGE: You let these four people in through the front door?

HIGHTOWER: No, through the back door.

GEORGE: What happened next?

HIGHTOWER: I went back and sat down. They went into the living room where Ernie was.

GEORGE: What happened next?

HIGHTTOWER: Shortly after that, Ernie had finished with his telephone conversations and they had a short conversation [and] they came out into the kitchen and said that there were some things that had to be done. Ernie told me not to worry about it. He said, "Just do whatever they ask you to do. Everything will be fine." And they left and went out to the garage.

GEORGE: Could you describe the heights and weights of these people?

HIGHTOWER: I thought that the two Chinese were tall for their height. They were slightly, for their, um, for being Chinese, I thought they were tall. I always thought Chinese were short. So I remember their height because they were taller than I am. And I'm five-eleven so they must have been around six-one, six-two, um, thin, and um, had dark hair. The other two Latin Americans, they were shorter, somewhat stockier. One of them was bald completely. The other one had light brown hair, I think.

Leaving him alone in the house, Hightower said, the five went out to the garage. An hour later the bald, Latin American visitor came in to tell him, in deeply accented English, that Ernie "had made arrangements for Emily to walk home and I was to go down to the crossroad and make sure she got home safely."

A peeved Judge Sheehan suddenly called the lawyers to the bench to warn Bob George to behave himself. When Hightower started talking about mysterious tall Chinese and squat Latin American visitors, George rolled his eyes. It was exactly the kind of thing Hightower should *not* say. George wanted Hightower to just shut the hell up! Mike Stone and Pat Youngs almost danced back to the prosecution table, eager to hear more from Christopher Hightower. "I'm so amazed at what I'm hearing that it's hard to take notes," Stone confided.

* * *

Hightower said he left the house at 3:00 P.M., but was told by someone he knew from the White Church that Emily had already gone to the YMCA. Back at the house, he stepped into the garage to relay the news to Ernie and apparently interrupted a business meeting. "He became a little upset," Hightower said, thrusting his car keys at Chris and telling him to go to the Y and fetch the little girl. "They wouldn't let me have her without authorization."

So he returned to the house and waited in the car until Ernie telephoned the YMCA, pulled out his wallet and handed Chris his driver's license. "You should be able to pick her up now," Brendel said. Hightower brought the girl home as instructed, and stayed downstairs while she went up to play in her room.

The clock was ticking toward 4:30 P.M. and "I was getting concerned that I hadn't made it to the bank yet." Having been once scolded, he was reluctant to "irritate" Ernie by going to the garage again.

The bald Latin American now informed Hightower that Alice Brendel would be home soon, and asked where Emily was. As Hightower said the child was watching television upstairs, there was a knock on the front door and the man, who presumably had been in the garage most of the day, stated, "Oh, that's the bedding that's coming. Mr. Brendel wants that canceled and rescheduled for Monday." Hightower relayed the message. Fine, replied the Apex deliveryman. No problem.

Ernie was still in the garage and Hightower was getting uneasy. The bank closing time was approaching and he had to clear the bounced rent check or Ray DeWall and Dennis Murphy, his landlords, would have the cops pick him up. Hightower planned to ask Ernie for a loan, as well as reimbursement for the crossbow. Then he could not only pay the back rent, but an extra month too, allowing time for he and Ernie to remodel the carriage house into office space.

When he explained the problem to the Latin man who

seemed to be babysitting him, "the gentleman said: 'Take the check and write it out.' " Hightower wrote one for $2,700, signing the name of Ernest Brendel, and logically explained to the court that "I couldn't very well sign my own" to a check that was not his.

Alice arrived about 5:30 P.M., surprised and pleased to find the Latin American man at her house. She hurried over to give him a big hug. "Raul, how good it is to see you," she called. It was the only time Hightower heard any names. But with the warm greeting from Alice, a load of worry fell from Christopher's shoulders. "It was obvious she knew him, and that alleviated my concern."

Pressing his luck, Chris telephoned Clyde Slicker to ask for the office keys and the address of his ex-wife in New York. Clyde's mention of the restraining order sent him into the dumps again.

Emily came bounding down the stairs to greet her mother, and Emily, Alice, and Raul went back upstairs. Ernie was still in the garage when Chris went out to get the car, and they talked about Hightower's trip to the banks. Brendel, who could pinch a penny tight enough to rub the beard from Abraham Lincoln, not only gave his blessing to the withdrawal of thousands of dollars from his personal bank accounts, but also gave him his Sears credit card for use in buying some new clothes, because he realized "my bills were stretched to the limit."

GEORGE: At six o'clock Friday, was Ernie Brendel a friend of yours?
HIGHTTOWER: I don't know. A benefactor.

According to Hightower's own words, in the past two days Brendel had picked up his sagging friend on several occasions, supplying him overnight lodging, food, money; withdrawing his CFTC complaint; and offering credit cards and warm, personal guidance. But Hightower did not consider him anything more than "a benefactor" at sundown on Friday.

Off he went to the bank, precisely following the instructions he had been given by Ernie—a reimbursement for the crossbow purchase, covering the bad rent check and keeping a hundred dollars in cash. "At the bank, I was doing what I was told to do," he pledged. But Hightower was uncomfortable, certain that he was being followed.

Hightower stumbled as he invented the next piece of his story. First, he would say no dinner plans were made for that evening. Then he altered it to talking with Alice about what to do for dinner, then he said Ernie talked about dinner. At any rate, Hightower stopped at a small restaurant and ordered clam chowder and fish and chips for four people, then drove back to Middle Highway, arriving shortly before eight o'clock.

Although he had already testified that Ernie was peeved about interruptions, Hightower said he drove the car straight into the garage, rolling across a carpet of papers that was "all over the floor." Police would later surmise that when Hightower spoke of the paper, he was actually referring to the blood of Ernie Brendel.

Everyone went back inside, and while the men went to the basement, the Brendels and Hightower sat around the kitchen table eating their takeout seafood. He paid no attention to the conversation. "I was thinking of my own problems, what I was getting into with Mr. Brendel, my family, what's going on in the Brendel home and how are we going to get out of it."

After eating, Ernie and two of the men went back to the garage, where "they were going through an awful lot of paperwork." One Chinese man stayed downstairs, and Raul went upstairs with Alice and Emily.

Hightower was tired and knew Saturday was going to be busy, so at 10:30 P.M. on Friday night he again curled up on the sofa and went to sleep.

He rose with the dawn Saturday and climbed the stairs to take a shower, only to find Raul banging away at the Apple computer in the hallway office. After cleaning up, Hightower told Raul he had some things to do, drank a cup of coffee and left. Ernie was back in the garage, Alice replaced Raul at the computer terminal, and Emily was still asleep.

He went out to the garage to get the bike, but realized he had left it at 1 Jones Circle the day before. He had to fetch it, but before leaving told a weary Ernie and some of the other men exactly what he was going to do that morning. They said there was no problem, and off he went.

The bewildered jurors were aware by now that, by Hightower's own story, these four men were probably going to be blamed for killing the Brendels. Yet they had allowed Hightower to repeatedly leave 51 Middle Highway, apparently trusting that he would not say anything untoward, even when they knew that one of his Saturday morning stops was going to be at the police station. The fact that he could recognize all four of them and knew one of their names was not a problem, according to Hightower. There had been no overt aggression by the men, and no foul language was used, so Hightower was not too concerned, he said. It merely seemed to him as if they were all trying to resolve some sort of issue.

About seven A.M. he walked back to Jones Circle and retrieved the bike from its hiding place, giving the house a wide berth to avoid being confronted by Sue. "I didn't want to cause any problems," he said.

His mind was still whirling when he went into the Barrington police station and dropped off the check. "I wanted to get out," he said. "I knew what we were planning on doing was illegal." Later, Hightower would explain that his reaction referred not to the people ransacking the Brendel house and garage, but to a plan that Ernie allegedly hatched to take over Hightower Investments, using Christopher as a front man for an organized crime operation.

Hightower had breakfast at the Newport Creamery, went to the Maple Avenue office and asked Ray DeWall for a new set of keys, then dropped by the post office to pick up a certified letter. He pedaled over to the soccer field. His facial muscles tightened and his voice rose as he described how he wanted to "be there" for the kids on his team.

He gathered his group around for a set of stretching and kicking exercises. "We didn't want any injuries," he said. But then Sue pulled up with his son and a short time thereafter the policeman came. Hightower told him that as the team's "primary coach," he had to be there because the kids were "dependent on me." The cop ordered him to leave.

"I looked over at my wife and son, looked at the other kids, and I left," Hightower told the court, his face turning red and his eyes weepy. Pausing between sentences, he emotionally described how he apologized to the parents present and told them how much he had enjoyed working with their "wonderful" kids, but that he "probably couldn't work with them anymore."

The humiliation was still burning a year and a half later, as he clasped both hands to the witness railing, his knuckles white, and said in a choked voice, "I really felt like I had lost it all at that point." The jury was fascinated, not about the soccer game, but about discovering the defendant had personally spoken with two policemen in a period of a few hours and said nothing about the Brendel situation.

Ernie was still in the garage, working with the visitors, who by now had been there for about twenty-four hours, when Hightower came up the driveway on the bike. As he put it in the garage, he saw the men had four big legal-size boxes stuffed with files. They told him to go into the house.

When he walked back inside, the domestic scene was one of touching normalcy. It tugged at Hightower's heartstrings, because he was losing his home and his own children to a vindictive wife and a callous legal system. Emily was playing in the kitchen, while Alice washed up some dishes.

* * *

The long day of testimony came to an end, with everyone totally exhausted. For the first time in months Bob George did not stay around to speak privately with his client, nor would he talk to Hightower the next day before court. He did not want to be accused of coaching Hightower on what to say, and had to hurry to meet with a psychotherapist who would be a key defense witness. Anyway, at that point lawyer and client had little to talk about. Christopher Hightower's nonstop soliloquy had steadily removed what little ammunition Bob George still possessed.

32

The Twilight Zone

Appropriately, Hightower's testimony resumed on April Fool's Day. A capacity crowd jammed the court and a line of spectators awaiting seats filled the corridor outside. A network morning television show carried a report on the trial nationwide, replete with pictures of the sweating, babbling defendant. Bob George looked a bit ragged after a night that afforded him little sleep, and clutched the podium with nervous hands as Chris Hightower came on for Round Two.

Hightower wasted no time before making his first stumble of the day in one of the most incredible stories ever told in a court of law. The day before, he had said Alice was washing dishes when he walked into the big white house at 51 Middle Highway on that distant Saturday. Now he said she wasn't washing the dishes, but preparing a lunch of soup and sandwiches for everyone— Chris, her family, Raul and his three pals. He noticed that the meticulous Alice, oddly, was still wearing the same clothes she had worn the previous day.

Hightower sat beside Emily in the breakfast nook, with the Brendel parents on the other side of the table, while the men loafed against various counters around the room in "kind of a hushed atmosphere," he said.

Afterward, one man took him into the living room, another went upstairs with Alice and Emily and the other two went to the basement with Ernie.

GEORGE: Were you a prisoner?

HIGHTOWER: No. One suggested that I go into the living room.

GEORGE: Did you feel there was anything wrong at this point?

HIGHTOWER: I'm not sure if I knew if anything was wrong or not. Obviously, something was being looked for ... and they were taking an awful long time to find it.

He waited patiently in the living room, with someone periodically coming in to check on him. He made no attempt to get up and walk out of the house, despite all of the strange events unfolding about him.

Ernie finally came inside and told Chris the men were trying to locate some money, then asked if they could go through the records of Hightower Investments. Hightower said they could, and accompanied by the second Latin American man, who had "brown-blondish hair," he went to 580 Maple about 3:00 P.M., where he showed the man where the records were kept and left the office.

Backtracking in his testimony, Hightower realized he had left something out. "Before leaving 51 Middle Highway, Alice said she had trouble sleeping the night before and asked me to pick up some pills," he said. So he drove to the CVS drugstore to pick up the sleeping pills, and bought the two empty gas cans.

By now the people in court and the thousands watching in televisonland were picking up the tempo of Christopher Hightower. As he droned on, one would not want to turn away from the TV set, for you never knew when he would drop a pearl of information. Persistence paid off, for Hightower now unleashed a blast that even rocked his harried lawyer, the fast-scribbling prosecution team, and the policemen who thought they had heard everything.

Hightower, speaking gently, said that when he returned to 51 Middle Highway, he found the three remaining men agitated. "They were concerned that the muriatic acid had not removed all of the residual heroin that was still left in the barn. They questioned whether gasoline should be put on the floor and set afire."

Surprise surged through the courtroom. What? Heroin? No one had heard anything about this! What the hell was he talking about?

Bob George grasped the podium even tighter, his eyes glued to the wooden surface. No use referring to notes, for Hightower was sailing in uncharted waters. George took a deep breath. "What happened then?"

Hightower explained that now a purple van was in the driveway and the men were loading it with cases of wine. He said Ernie whispered to him on *Thursday evening* that heroin was in the stock of wine, and warned, "the less you know about it, the better off you're going to be." Thursday night, Hightower now said, the men were in the garage spreading acid over the files and the wine bottles.

Judge Sheehan, trying to put this jigsaw puzzle together, questioned Hightower about the mismatched times. The defendant calmly insisted that when he arrived at 6:30 P.M. on Thursday with the crossbow, a white van was backed into the garage and the door was open. Men hurried from the garage to the house.

Hightower had not mentioned in his earlier testimony that other people were in the garage on Thursday evening, had said nothing about heroin or wine bottles, had been silent about muriatic acid in the garage, and had claimed the four mystery men arrived at 51 Middle Highway on Friday, not Thursday. Now Hightower claimed that Ernie said the acid was being spread to soak up residual heroin that may have fallen from the cases of wine.

"Ernie said he received shipments of heroin brought in via wine cases," Hightower continued, as if lecturing a class on how to smuggle drugs. The bottles were filled with heroin, then dipped in acid to erase any trace of the drug, then into a wax solution to prevent police dogs from sniffing out the contraband.

The astonished Sheehan leaned over and asked High-tower if he even remembered the earlier testimony. The defendant confidently said he did.

Ernie, he said completely out of context, intended to take control of Hightower Investments and had never re-ally intended to pursue the CFTC suit. In the courtroom an exasperated Christine Scriabine put a hand on her husband's shoulder and leaned wearily upon him.

Hightower dodged back to his Saturday drive around Barrington, adding that, not only did he go to CVS and buy the gas cans, but he also lunched at McDonald's, bought some more muriatic acid, stopped by his office and picked up the guy who had rifled through his busi-ness files. Glancing in the rearview mirror, he deter-mined he was being followed.

"What was your state of mind?" barked Bob George, his own state of mind somewhat frazzled.

"I was doing what I was told to do by people and some suggestions from Ernest Brendel," replied his client.

He said he pulled into the garage at 51 Middle High-way, but this time did not mention any van, purple or white, or the wine bottles. Instead, Ernie and the men were stacking papers in the barn.

Hightower said he went directly into the house and stayed there, while the men and Brendel continued to swarm about. Around 9:00 P.M. he was dispatched to buy garbage bags from a grocery store because there was trash to be collected. He was followed again. Returning to Middle Highway, he handed the bags to the men in the garage and went back to the house for about forty-five minutes, during which time Alice and Emily re-mained upstairs.

Bob George was pressing him, almost as if he were a policeman grilling a suspect. In reality, the lawyer was as lost as everyone else and was simply trying to figure out where Hightower was going with all of this. Certainly the witness had to realize his story was straight from the Twilight Zone. On the good side, George probably felt the performance might show Hightower had checked out of Hotel Reality.

"What happened next?" George would bark. "What happened next ... What did they look like ... What was your state of mind?" Sheehan interrupted to get George to back off. "Don't argue with your own witness," the judge said, in a rather reasonable instruction.

The courtroom audience was riveted to its seats and the home viewers to their screens as Hightower recalled the unexpected and deadly turn of events. Until then, he insisted, despite the missing money and heroin being loaded into a purple van and four burly men constantly on the scene, "there had never been any threat of danger." That came to a quick end when the men grabbed him without warning and slapped handcuffs onto his wrists. "I was incredulous. Nothing had gone wrong all weekend."

They hustled him into the garage. It looked like an abattoir, blood all over the floor and Ernie badly beaten. They were shouting at Ernie, yelling, "We want the money!"

"Mr. Brendel wouldn't tell them where the money was," Hightower said. Ernie wouldn't even talk when the men threatened to kill everyone. So they brought out Emily and Alice. One held the child, two wrestled with a distraught Alice, and one held Hightower as Ernie lay slumped against the horse stalls.

"Raul, what's going on? What's happening?" cried Alice. Without further delay "they wrapped the cloth around her neck and strangled her," he said. "I didn't believe anyone could kill someone like that. I don't believe it now."

His words were hammer blows to the Brendel relatives in the front row. Donald Bobb, Alice's brother, slumped in his seat, and his wife Peggy began to sob. Fred Bobb, Alice's nephew, leaned nervously forward, as if wanting to leap the small barrier that separated him from Hightower.

With his voice breaking, Hightower described how Ernie, even with his wife dead at his feet, still refused to tell the location of the money. Backtracking, Hightower said that the men went back into the house to fetch Emily. Only a moment ago he had stated the girl was already in the garage. His voice rising to a shrill wail, Hightower said they told the battered Ernie they were going to kill his child.

"I couldn't believe it. It's impossible. You don't kill a child!"

He said he went "crazy" and pushed the man holding him against the wall, then plowed his shoulder into the one choking Emily. The others grabbed him, kicked him in the groin, and Hightower went down on his knees as they continued to beat him.

In a macabre piece of imagination, a weepy Hightower testified the men undid the cloth they had used to strangle Alice and put it around his neck, holding his chin up, forcing him to see what was happening to Emily. "This is what is going to happen to your kids if you don't do what we tell you," Hightower testified they said. "He killed her right there."

Bob George asked, "Did you kill Emily Brendel?"

"No, I did not," replied the beet-red Hightower.

"Did you kill Alice Brendel?"

"No, I didn't kill anyone."

He went on to describe more of the nightmare scene. It was Ernie's turn to die, and the killers shot him with the crossbow, once in the chest and once in the head. As the body began to spasm, the killers turned again to Hightower and said, "You think your wife will do this when we kill her?" With that, they put a final arrow in Ernie's chest.

"I can't believe anyone would kill anyone because they wanted money, or would kill a child," Hightower testified.

"Did you kill Ernie Brendel?" asked George.

"No, I did not."

The jurors were looking at the floor, at the ceiling, anywhere but at Hightower. *These men brutally slaughtered an entire family and allowed Christopher Hightower, the lone witness, to live? Not likely.*

During a break, one police investigator summed up the morning's extraordinary testimony. "He almost lost it on the stand. He wants to confess, but he can't."

Hightower continued in the afternoon; everyone was watching him, spellbound. He said that following the murders, a pillowcase was pulled over his head, he was shoved into the Toyota and driven around aimlessly and in silence, finally ending up in some woods. He had no idea where the Brendel bodies were at the time, but the men hauled him from the car and told him to dig some graves. Hightower refused.

He was weeping on the witness stand again, tears that nobody in court believed were real. On television, close-up views of his face showed his eyes bugging out large behind his glasses and he sniveled. It was a face from a horror movie.

"We don't want to hurt his family right now," said one of his captors. "He's too valuable. So why don't we kill his sister-in-law. We know where she lives." Hightower struggled, "going crazy . . . I didn't want my family hurt." When one of the four mentioned Kathy Slicker by name, Hightower caved in to their demand, picked up the shovel and started digging. "I'll do anything you want. Just don't hurt my family," he pleaded

Just because Sue and the Slickers had disowned him didn't mean he did not still love them. As Hightower dug, the thugs warned, "We can get to them anytime. We know where the boys play soccer. We know about the home in New Hampshire." While Hightower did not know the address of his ex-wife and two daughters in New York, the killers said they did. He testified that he feared everyone he loved would be slaughtered "if I didn't do what they told me."

Another unknown person joined the group of four killers, according to Hightower, and they directed him to make the graves small and shallow so the bodies could be readily found. Then, pillowcase back on his head, he was returned to 51 Middle Highway and allowed to sleep.

Sunday morning, Hightower struck a deal with the killers. They gave him permission to see that his family was still alive, but warned they would strike if he did anything unusual.

Church was to begin at 10:00 A.M., so Hightower climbed alone into the Toyota and drove to the Newport Creamery. No. He changed his mind in mid-sentence. What happened was that he drove past the house at 1 Jones Circle and waited to see the family come out. Finally he saw Clyde, Sue, and his two boys get into the Jeep Cherokee, and he followed them to church and waited in the parking lot until the services were done. Hightower said the strangers were nearby, carefully watching him. In reality, a policeman had come to the church that day to make certain Hightower did not show up in violation of the restraining order, but Hightower did not mention seeing him.

Afterward, he went to a nearby gas station, filled up the Toyota and returned to Middle Highway. The men were waiting and told him to keep following instructions. Ernie's files were hauled from the basement and stuffed into garbage bags, and Hightower, the loyal errand boy, was told to drive over to Somerville Lumber and buy a list of items, including a bag of lime. While in the store, Hightower saw some of his watchers tagging along behind, "right there in the store with me." He left unexplained why the watchers just didn't buy the stuff themselves.

Then he returned to the garage, poured more acid onto the stained floor and scrubbed it down, cleaning the blood-spotted windows of the Toyota and sprinkling baking soda on the car seat to smother the awful smell. Returning to the house, the killers ordered him to affix Ernie's name to another letter to the CFTC concerning the Hightower-Brendel dispute.

That was why, he explained, he had to go to the White Church. Only there could he find a copying machine that would let him put the letter into the demanded form.

"Why not sign it, like you signed the check?" asked George.

Hightower's answer could not be understood. "None of this was supposed to have happened," he stammered. "I didn't feel it was wrong . . . I was concerned about the legitimacy of the signature." He was up to his neck in an alleged drug plot that had exploded into three murders, but Hightower claimed he was worried that Ernie's signature look authentic.

While at the church, completing the forgery, Hightower was nervous because other people had been unexpectedly put at risk. The church should have been empty that afternoon, but a wedding was going on in the sanctuary, and Associate Pastor Rose Amadeo entered the office while he worked. They spoke only briefly because Hightower, not wanting to jeopardize anyone else, just wanted to do his work and get out. *They* were watching.

He drove over to 580 Maple and dumped many of the things the men had stuffed into the car—including the gas cans and items Ernie had taken from his mother's condo—into the upstairs office.

After that, he was informed they still wanted money, and "the Connecticut decision was made." The men planned it down to the last item and told him exactly where to go, what to do, and what to say. "If the FBI or police showed up at the Scriabine house, they would kill my family," he told the jury.

Once in Guilford, Hightower removed the crossbow from the car trunk and placed it in the woods. "It was bad enough, what they were going to be seeing, and I didn't want them seeing it." A car was "directly behind me" all the way down.

Told by the Scriabines to come back later, Hightower swung once again by a McDonald's restaurant, and at the appointed time reappeared. He reviewed what he told Christine and Alex, including that he could raise most of the needed $200,000. Not only was that different than the figure he actually gave that night, Hightower now flipped his story while on the stand.

He said he asked the Scriabines "to provide $75,000," and only a moment later he looked directly at the jury and said, "I never asked the Scribianes to give me money." The jurors did not react when he had told the lie. It was just one of many.

Hightower said he "allowed" Christine to take his picture, but blew up when she wanted to call the FBI before the ransom deadline. "I really lost it, I turned stone-white," he testified. "There was no doubt in my mind they would do what they said they would do . . . and kill my family."

On the way out of town he stopped and picked up the hidden crossbow. Hightower stopped and considered his next words, because he was puzzled about why the FBI fingerprint specialist testified the weapon was clean. "I don't know why my prints are not on it. I handled it," he said, as if he were upset that he did not have to explain away that detail.

But he had finally accomplished something, he testified. The men were about to let him off the hook. They had killed an entire family, choking a child to death, but the hardened murderers felt sorry for Christopher Hightower. When the one following him saw him weaving "all over the road" on the way back from Connecticut, they pulled him to the side and one got into the Toyota and took the wheel.

Hightower confessed to the driver, one of the tall Chinese, that he had been unable to convince the Scriabines of the threat and that he thought they were going to call the FBI.

"That's all right. You've done what we've wanted you to do," came the reply.

By three o'clock Sunday morning he was back at 580 Maple, where he tried to get some sleep. Overnight, he felt sorry for the grieving Scriabines, so he called the next morning and told them he could raise all of the necessary funds. When he said this in court, he looked directly at Alex and Christine, sitting in the front row, and Hightower again wept. They didn't.

He left Maple Avenue and went to the post office to mail a letter and to cash the final check so he "could start running."

Judge Sheehan called time-out for lunch. It was cold and rainy outside, and everyone tried to find a nearby restaurant, not so much because of the lousy weather, but because they wanted to hurry back to Hightower. All but one. Bob George was in no hurry whatsoever. He walked back to court alone in the rain, looking weary and tired. The lawyer played his hand the best he knew how, but Hightower kept reshuffling the deck. George had no idea where this story would end up.

Hightower resumed, saying he mailed some letters to the CFTC, the NFA, and paid his American Express bill, all on instructions of the killers. Then he went by the Hospital Trust to cash the check, grabbed a bite at a doughnut shop, and returned to his office, his every move followed.

He knew he had been neatly framed for the crime. "At some point, I knew the police would be coming," he said. The men had told him after mailing the letters that he was "free to go." With him as a scapegoat, the real killers could escape. One of the men, who had been standing beside a toolshed near his office, gave one last stipulation—if Hightower spoke of what really happened within four months, his family would be slaughtered.

Hightower got into the Toyota and drove down to Newport to organize his thoughts. Despite the promised freedom, he believed they were still shadowing him. He was "totally confused" because, while he was innocent, he knew his fingerprints were all over the Brendel house. And the friction between himself and Ernie would appear in an unfavorable light, because no one knew that Ernie really had been trying to blackmail him.

He concluded that, despite the risk, he had to get help and headed toward Providence to contact the FBI. But he was arrested before he could get there.

Hightower admitted he was advised of his constitutional rights several times, and said he asked police to protect his family. But while being interviewed by Lazzaro and McGraw, it dawned on him that they thought he was guilty. He decided not to cooperate anymore when the veteran FBI agent walked to the door, leaned on it and said, "Hightower, you did it and I'm going to prove you did it." McGraw had testified differently.

"I flipped out. After that, I went back to the story I was told to tell," Hightower sobbed. "I didn't trust anybody." Beyond that first interrogation, Hightower whined that it didn't matter what he said to them anymore. "They thought I was the perpetrator."

Furthermore, he said the police denied his request for a lawyer. From the back of the courtroom, the dark eyes of John Lazzaro drilled Hightower, and the defendant felt their heat. The policeman, a friendly sort by nature, was not very friendly at the moment, as this man charged with multiple murder accused him of being unprofessional.

Hightower wasn't quite through with his lengthy court performance. He still had to explain the Lynx letters.

He said in his first week at the ACI, a deputy warden intercepted a letter from outside of the prison that warned Hightower what would befall his children if he told the truth about what happened to the Brendels.

Then along came fellow prisoner Mike Giroux, who volunteered to write threatening ransom letters to the Scriabines "to take some of the heat off me." Hightower told Giroux "he was dealing with something he knew nothing about . . . It's the Tong, and you're going to get my family killed."

Giroux apologized when he saw how frightened Hightower was. The letters that Giroux sent had been signed "Lynx," and Hightower chose to keep that pseudonym when he wrote a separate letter to reveal that the Brendels were dead.

Giroux also said that he had friends beyond the prison walls who could watch over the Hightower family, since Chris did not trust the police to shield them from the Chinese and South American mobsters. To help the surveillance, Hightower wrote out background details on Clyde and Kathy, whom he considered to be the most vulnerable because they were alone a lot.

"They said they would kill Kathy first. I was very worried about her," Hightower said, sobbing himself into a breakdown.

A tired Judge Sheehan called a recess and warned the jury that sympathy and bias had no place in his courtroom. He was telling them to ignore Hightower's histrionics. Mike Stone sat at the prosecution table, furious at Hightower. He did not know he could dislike a man so much. The man was even lying when crying. "There's not a tear in his eye. I haven't seen one yet," said Stone.

As he reached the end of his story, Hightower said Giroux gave him the bad news that his outside friends discovered that too many man-hours were needed to guard such a big family. So it would be easier just to write more threatening letters and have them intercepted by the cops, who would then take on the guard duties for Hightower's family. Chris said he wanted to call Sue and advise her what was afoot, but that after two collect calls to the White Church, that number was blocked. "I was completely shut off from communication with my family," he said, so threatening letters were his only recourse.

Hightower said he knew from the start that Giroux was in the pocket of the police, but it was fine by him because that relationship would assure that his desire to protect his family would be taken seriously. Therefore, "I became more aggressive in sending letters," he said.

Hightower said he kept the letters going until the four-month moratorium lapsed and he could once again talk about what happened to the Brendels. But even today, as he stood in the witness box, he felt the gangsters were out there somewhere, unhappy that he told his story on live television. "After my testimony today, I have grave concerns for my family," he told the jurors.

"Did you kill Emily Brendel?" Bob George asked once more.

"No sir, I did not."

"Did you kill Alice Brendel?"

"No sir, I did not."

"Did you kill Ernest Brendel?"

"No sir. I haven't killed anyone. Other people did it, one of whom was named Raul. I was present as a hostage."

Glancing at his watch, George saw it was 3:32 P.M. Hightower's direct testimony had taken two full days, and the lawyer was more than ready for it to end. He felt as if he had been through a meat grinder.

33

Forgeries

The prosecution team spent most of the night in the War Room, dovetailing their notes on Hightower's testimony and watching a videotape of his performance, hunting weaknesses. Mike Stone, who would handle the cross-examination, had hardly slept since the trial began. Still, he seemed refreshed, if edgy.

Bob George really didn't care who would be on the floor against him. He was beyond tired. The previous day he again chose not to see Hightower after court, rushing back to Massachusetts to catch up on his notes, plan strategy, and deal with the complaints from defendants who had hired him on other cases. He fell asleep watching Jay Leno's opening monologue on the *Tonight* show, but woke three hours later and spent the early morning hours working on the Hightower case. George was impeccably attired in a double-breasted suit and starched shirt when he showed up for court on Friday, but his face was lined with fatigue.

There was a new threat to the case on the final day of its fifth week because a Boston television station had broadcast its own reporter's opinion on the case, rather than sticking with fact. Bob George demanded the jury be polled to determine if anyone had seen the show. Sheehan had also called a Providence station to request they not broadcast the results of a poll on whether people believed Hightower. With so much media attention,

Sheehan knew the risk was increasing that the jury might not make it through untainted. But he pressed on, refusing to sequester them.

Hightower came into court wearing his dark blue turtleneck and the olive suit. Mike Stone waited impatiently, his half-rim glasses perched on his nose, anxious to rip into Hightower. The accused man had a minute-by-minute account of his actions, but Stone planned to ask questions out of sequence, forcing the defendant to quickly jump around in his bizarre story.

The first item on the agenda was the claim that the Barrington police, the Rhode Island State Police, and the FBI had all violated Hightower's constitutional rights. The jury *must* be certain that had not happened.

Stone, waving a red marker like a small scarlet baton, checked off items on a legal pad, getting Hightower to confirm the police had repeatedly presented him with verbal and written versions of the Miranda warnings.

Stone read each of the five rights aloud, asking Hightower if he had initialed them. The defendant said he did so without being forced.

"You wanted to help, right? You wanted to tell them your story?" asked Stone.

Yes, said Hightower.

Then came a flip-flop, as Hightower claimed he was not told by Sergeant Lazzaro that he could use the telephone. Then he testified Lazzaro offered him a phone right at the beginning of the interrogation.

"You told him that you didn't want a lawyer," Stone declared, glaring at Hightower.

The defendant balked. "A lot was going through my mind, and keeping it all organized is very difficult." That was music to the ears of the prosecutors. The cross-examination was barely under way and already Hightower could not keep things straight.

Judge Sheehan asked why Hightower did not accept the chance to call an attorney.

"It didn't matter anymore. My rights had been violated," Hightower replied.

The timing was all wrong. If Lazzaro offered a telephone call at the start of the interrogation, and McGraw's comment did not come until several hours later, how could Hightower say the FBI man's statement was the reason he did not call a lawyer?

Stone turned back to when Hightower was arrested and got out of the Toyota. He wanted to know why Hightower didn't tell police then and there about the three murders he had witnessed and the threats that had been made on his own family. Feigning disbelief and anger, Stone walked closer to him. "It wasn't, 'Now look, here's what happened . . .' Instead, you started talking about your complaint with Ernie!"

"I was not giving a narrative. I was responding to Sergeant Lazzaro." As always, someone else was at fault.

On and on they went, Hightower trying to dance and Stone pinning him to facts. The crux of the matter, according to the defendant, was Jack McGraw's statement that he was going to prove Hightower was guilty. After that, Hightower said, he felt he could no longer trust anyone in law enforcement.

"McGraw got in your face, didn't he?" Stone asked with almost a snarl.

"Yes. He leaned right over me. I was very disturbed by it." In his direct testimony, Hightower had said McGraw made the comment from the doorway, another change.

"The Barrington police trampled all over my rights," he declared, as had the FBI and the State Police detectives who interviewed him for six hours.

Stone paced the carpet, hands in his pockets. If the cops were setting Hightower up for a fall, the prosecutor queried, why go into such elaborate detail? "Why didn't you just say nothing?"

Hightower shrugged. "It just didn't matter anymore."

Stone looked surprised. "Day by day, hour by hour, you told them what you were doing. Sometimes minute by minute. And this is what the killers told you to say?"

Yes, confirmed Hightower. The whole scene, every word, had been planned by the murderers. He was just trying to obey both the police and the mobsters. A front-row juror turned and smiled at the others.

Stone detoured to Hightower's personal finances, having him admit that he was about $100,000 in debt. The man who had pledged to provide for his own family better than his stepfather probably owed his generous former in-laws, the Slickers, around $60,000.

That led to questioning of his background—growing up in Florida, his Navy career, the marriage to Ellen, and an embarrassing moment when Hightower could not recall the birthdates of his two daughters. The defendant confirmed his academic background at the University of Rhode Island, the lucrative sales career he gave up with Riker Labs, and his admission to an elite master's Ph.D. program at Wright State University.

But Hightower felt the noose tighten when Stone asked him about the zoology degree from URI. The lawyer, pacing relentlessly, asked Hightower for his grade point average.

"A 2.5, thereabouts, plus or minus a couple of points. I'm not sure."

Stone stopped dead in his tracks and seemed puzzled. "You didn't get accepted into a master's program with a 2.5 average, did you?"

"No, I did not," Hightower gulped. His face reddened. His whole facade of being a smart guy, considered brilliant by some, was about to crumble, while thousands of people watched on television.

"Why is that?" asked Stone, already knowing the answer. Early in the case, using subpoena power, the prosecution team cracked the secrecy veil that colleges erect around all students, including suspected murderers. They got his transcripts.

"Because I had contact with an individual at the University of Rhode Island and obtained a forged transcript." He knew he could not lie his way out of this one, because the prosecutors hauled out the papers documenting his college grades. Stone put the phony records into evidence.

Stone declared that when Hightower applied to Wright State, he claimed a grade point average, not of the actual 2.44, but of "a stellar 3.97," and asserted he graduated with the highest distinction. Even Intermediate German, which Hightower actually had flunked, carried a perfect A grade on the bogus transcript. His D in Invertebrate Zoology also became an A, as did General Physics, a course he had dropped. In all, forty of the forty-two subjects claimed on the transcript carried the perfect grade of A. Only a zoology seminar and General Sociology carried B's, jacked up from C's.

The forgery admission was important, but the *method* Hightower used was paramount. Bad grades were cut out of the original transcript by a sharp razor and the empty rectangular space was filled with the new, improved grades which, when photocopied, looked similar to the original. The jurors had listened only a few days earlier as an FBI scientist described the cut-and-paste job Hightower did on the CFTC letter, allegedly from Ernie Brendel. The similarity could not be missed.

Stone twisted the knife. "Without doing that, you never would have gotten into that master's program, would you?"

"I don't know," replied Hightower.

"Well, you didn't try it, did you?"

"No, I did not." Hightower flushed in humiliation at the disclosure of his cheating. When Stone revealed that Hightower had used the same forged transcripts in his applications to various medical schools, Channel 10 reporter Bob Ward, in the press row, leaned back and whispered, "He's gone."

The televised torture was not over for Hightower. Stone moved steadily along to the sales career with Riker Labs, noting that, on direct examination, Hightower claimed he was an outstanding salesman for the pharmaceutical company, ranking third in the nation in peddling one specific drug.

Stone peered over the half-rims with a smirk. "Isn't it true that rather than being an outstanding, or even an average, salesman for Riker Labs, you were a terrible salesman?"

"I don't believe so, no sir," responded a nervous Hightower.

The prosecution had also laid hands on the Riker records of employment. Sales in his assigned territory had fallen sharply when Hightower took over, Stone claimed, and added the charge that the unhappy salesman lied to his bosses about meeting clients he had not seen. Hightower, looking like a cornered animal, confirmed he filed false reports for the last three to six months he was with the company. In effect, he was admitting that lying was nothing new to him, it seemed almost second nature. And the jurors knew if he would lie about these things, then *everything* he said was suspect.

Stone hammered away at Hightower without remorse, tearing down the facade of respectability to lay bare the soul of a con artist.

He shot Hightower down on the matter of the divorce from Ellen. The defendant said he wanted the divorce, while Stone brought out the decree, which had been filed by Ellen, not her husband.

Stone zapped him on the age difference between himself and Sue when they met, and accused him of "cheating on your wife" by seducing the teenager.

"Isn't it a fact, Mr. Hightower, that the only problems with your marriage, besides the fact that you wanted to forge transcripts to go to medical school and have her pay for it, and sell the house, is the fact that you were having an affair with a younger woman?" Stone declared.

No, answered the former Sunday-school teacher, seeming indignant at the very thought of immoral behavior. He denied having an affair with Susan. It was ironic that he should leap to her defense like that, for most of the evidence Mike Stone had thrown at him that day had been found when Susan went through boxes of his personal effects. Without a second thought she had turned the papers documenting the unsavory life story of her pack-rat ex-husband over to the cops.

34

The Business

Monday was April 5, opening day of the 1993 baseball season, and the Boston Red Sox were playing at Kansas City. Pat Youngs had not missed a Red Sox home opener in the last ten years. If there was a break in the trial, he still had an outside chance to see the season's first game at Fenway Park. But for right now, the prosecution was at bat in the Hightower trial.

When court began at 10:01 A.M., one of its rare on-time starts, Judge Sheehan found a crumpled envelope waiting on the bench, and no one ever figured out exactly how it got there, lending a bit of mystery to the proceedings. It contained a *Boston Globe* article that once again put the trial at risk. The newspaper reporter claimed she had heard Bob George say he did not believe his client's testimony. In reality, George had said outside of court, to someone other than the *Globe* reporter, "Can you believe this?" in reference to a court ruling that had gone against him. Nonetheless, Sheehan blew up over the newspaper story, threatening severe action against George, including possibly excluding him from the courtroom if there was a repeat of this kind of thing. "I do not want this tried on the steps of the courthouse or in the press," he thundered. But Sheehan still would not lock the jury away.

It was an odd time for an ethics lecture from a member of the Rhode Island bench, since on that very day,

Matthew J. Smith, the state's top court administrator, whose office was just downstairs, resigned due to a pesky criminal investigation into his alleged cover-up of a theft of court funds.

After the latest Sheehan-George showdown, the trial started its sixth week. Mike Stone poured a small cup of water, while Christopher Hightower again swore to tell the truth.

The truth. Television cameras focused on the defendant, and viewers throughout New England waited for the confrontation. Stone, brimming with contempt for the man in the dock, immediately resumed the tactic of showing Hightower to be a talented liar. The lawyer introduced several typed résumés that claimed Hightower was the greatest thing since sliced bread. The résumés said he carried that astronomical 3.97 grade average at the University of Rhode Island, graduating magna cum laude; increased sales for Riker Labs by 35 percent in his assigned territory; was first in the nation among all Riker drug salesmen for several product lines; and finished three of four years in the Wright State Ph.D. program with a 3.6 grade point average. Stone asked with a smirk, "That's not true, is it?"

"That is correct," huffed Hightower.

The truth. Stone now took a chance, introducing items found in Hightower's office, letters of recommendation to Wright State signed with the names of Kerwin A. Highland, a URI professor of parasitology, and Joseph E. Callore, the district manager for Riker. The letters said the young man wanted "to resolve pain" and "open new frontiers" in disease prevention. His thirst for knowledge was "almost unquenchable," his ability to communicate was extraordinary, and few graduate students could match his zeal for learning.

Stone, in a droll tone, said there was a good reason that the letters presented a glowing recommendation of Christopher Hightower—Christopher Hightower wrote them, forging the names of Highland and Callore. Isn't that right? Hightower admitted it was his handiwork.

Doing so, he stumbled badly. For Stone had no real proof that Hightower wrote the letters. With permission from Judge Sheehan, but over George's objection, he had tricked Hightower into admitting the forgeries to help grease his path into Wright State. Again, all the defendant would have had to do is deny any knowledge of them, and the letters would have been useless to the prosecutors. Hightower always talked too much.

Having successfully painted Hightower as a liar, the prosecution now began tarring him also as a thief, by leading the jury through the defendant's convoluted business dealings. Stone said that when the going got tough in Ohio, Hightower began dealing stocks and commodities. Stone alluded briefly to the two suspicious but financially lucrative fires that struck the Hightower home in March of 1985, just when things were really bad at school and with the bank account.

Then came a discussion of how Hightower fleeced the Investors Guild of Dayton, losing all but $8,800 of the $102,000 placed in his stewardship. Stone showed a sheaf of documents that falsely reflected increased values in investments, and the prosecutor asked, "In three or four months, you basically lost it all, didn't you?"

Hightower, shifting his weight, mumbled, "Yes."

"But the valuation statements didn't show that?"

"No, they did not," he replied through clenched teeth.

When confronted by the enraged membership, Hightower testified, "I told them I hadn't stolen their money. It had been lost." Stone also pointed out that Hightower never invested any of his own money in the enterprise and had skimmed off $12,000 to repay the amount borrowed from his mother.

After turning over his house to settle a suit brought by the flummoxed investors, Hightower moved back to Barrington and set up shop to run the same commodities broker scam he had operated in Ohio.

But in Dayton he had a number of investors. In Rhode Island he would never have more than four clients at one time. Therefore, despite the thousand-dollar monthly stipend handed over by Clyde Slicker, money was tight. For his first two years in business, he didn't make a cent.

To demonstrate that while the defendant had changed locations he did not change his method of operation, Stone ran Hightower through the pitiful tale of Daniel Wagner.

Wagner, recently retired as a professor at Rhode Island College, was a friend of Clyde Slicker, who introduced him to his son-in-law, Christopher Hightower, the financial wizard. Naturally, Hightower charmed the socks off the older man, and in September 1988 wheedled a $10,000 loan from Wagner at 15 percent interest for one year, to use in buying computer equipment. When the year was up, Hightower asked for, and received, another year's extension.

By August of 1990 Hightower was able to convince Wagner that things had turned profitable and persuaded him to invest $7,000 in the get-rich-quick commodities game.

On the stand Hightower insisted that he had turned Wagner down as a client because the man was in bankruptcy, but Stone had been waiting for just such an opening, and introduced as evidence the account agreement signed by Hightower and Wagner. Hightower continued to dodge the issue, saying he never received the $7,000. Stone pounced again, bringing in documents to show a $7,000 check was sent to a brokerage, which sent it back because of the bankruptcy question. Another document showed Hightower then deposited the $7,000 in his own bank account. "I don't recall," the defendant said, shrugging.

Stone ignored him. "You continued to lead Mr. Wagner on that you were trading that $7,000, even providing statements ... to show how it was doing." Happy at his good fortune, as reflected by Hightower's numbers, Wagner added another thousand dollars to his investment account. According to Hightower Investment documents, the total of $8,000 was now worth $9,537.20.

In early 1991, Wagner realized he wasn't getting anything from his broker but a lot of talk and demanded his $18,000 back. Hightower insisted the refund demand came only after he refused to do business for a couple of Wagner's friends, whom he considered disreputable.

In February of 1991 Wagner came to Hightower's office and picked up two checks—one for the $9,150, the amount said to be in his trading account, and another for $14,183 as repayment of the original loan plus interest and penalties. "He left the office and went back down the road [to the bank]," said Stone. "By the time he got there, you had stopped payment." Hightower, eyes bulging, acknowledged that.

On March 2 Hightower gave a check for $23,367 to Clyde Slicker, who delivered it at a weekend party to his distraught friend, Dan Wagner. First thing on Monday, Wagner dashed to Citizens Bank. Too late. Hightower had already stopped payment.

Wagner, understandably outraged at what he termed "the craziness" of the situation, filed a complaint with the National Futures Association, which sent a pair of auditors on April 10 to visit Hightower Investments. Hightower told them Wagner was not an investor, but a "pathological liar" who apparently raided the Hightower office in order to forge the documents in the hands of the NFA men. "I would have done a better job forging them," Hightower told the auditors. Wagner's legal action proceeded slowly through the summer of 1991, but before a scheduled October hearing could be held, the Brendels disappeared and Hightower was arrested.

Daniel Wagner would never see a nickel of his money again.

Stone used the stories of the Investors Guild and the retired professor to illustrate that, not only could Hightower not be trusted to tell the truth, he could not be trusted with money either. Trusting Chris Hightower was hazardous to your bank account.

Having shown Hightower as both a liar and a thief, the prosecution moved to prove he was also capable of things much worse. Stone turned the spotlight to the Brendels.

In fact, Hightower had already done that, by claiming the only reason he stopped payment on Wagner's checks was because he had no choice. His bank accounts were dry because he backed out of an agreement with Ernie Brendel to publish a financial newsletter. It wasn't really his fault. It was Ernie's.

According to Hightower, Ernie's scheme was to take over Hightower Investments and publish a newsletter that could make a million dollars a year and be an easy front for laundering drug money. Hightower, being noble, said he resisted the plan, risking the dire consequences.

It began, Hightower said, with Ernie loaning him $2,000 to help set up the fancy computer system. "Consider this to be my first equity investment in the company," Brendel had told him. Hightower set up a computer in his home and one in his office so he could always be tied directly into the fast-moving marketplace around the world.

Ernie followed on May 30, 1989—five months after Hightower got the $10,000 loan from Wagner—with $15,000 for Hightower to actually *invest*. Brendel became the first and only client Hightower Investments had on the books. But Ernie was jittery when the money began to slide away, and closed the account on August 29. There were no hard feelings. Indeed, the men were becoming good friends, and the Brendels vacationed with the Hightowers in the summer of 1990 at the Slicker hideaway in Center Harbor, New Hampshire.

Hightower, with some money finally jingling in his pockets from the Brendel and Wagner loans, plus having Ernie's account on the books, was able to more effec-

tively spin tales of financial success, while beating the
bushes of Barrington for new investors. He knocked on
the doors of stockbrokers, lawyers, business executives,
and anyone that might have some cash. That included
fellow worshipers at the White Church, personal friends,
and people he bumped into on the street. "If you stood
still for five minutes, he would tell you about opportunities in pork bellies or a land deal he had working in Florida," recalled one prospect who declined Hightower's
pitches. "Put up five thousand dollars and he would triple it in ten days."

Among the doors he knocked on was the law office of
a tall Polynesian man who shooed the scam artist
away, but would stay locked in Hightower's memory to
resurface as a "tall Chinese" hoodlum. Another door
was that of James Romano, an attorney whose client
list included people alleged to be associated with organized crime. Romano turned Hightower down, but
suggested he might contact a friend who was a stockbroker.

Those meetings in late 1989 and early 1990 brought
Hightower the accounts of Molina, Bracchi, DeSistine,
and Caffarelli, which he would later transform into the
start of his troubles with the mob.

The four clients, tracking the loss of their money,
closed their accounts in March 1990. Only then did
Hightower notify the Office of the U.S. Attorney that his
former clients were linked to organized crime, and claim
he terminated the accounts when he read that Caffarelli
had mob ties.

But, Mike Stone insisted, Hightower showed Ernie
Brendel "cooked numbers" that indicated that the four
investors were still on board and turning fantastic profits. The figures claimed that Bracchi's $75,000 invest-
ment had earned $65,567 between December 13, 1990,
and April 11, 1991. Dangling the alleged 87 percent
profit as bait, Hightower successfully conned his only
friend, and on May 24, 1990, Ernie Brendel invested another $15,000 with Hightower.

That would become the motive for murder.

Stone was attempting to show the jury that Hightower was simply using Brendel as the latest in a line of pigeons. The Italian connection had cashed in their losses, so Ernie, quickly followed by Wagner, became Hightower's only customers. Stone asked if it were not true that the numbers Hightower presented to Brendel "showed your system was making big bucks, when in fact you weren't making any money at all."

"No," Hightower shot back. Hightower claimed it was Ernie who was doing a con job, not the other way around.

"Mr. Brendel was an attorney," Hightower told the incredulous court. "He knew exactly what he was doing and he set me up very well."

Ernie reinvested because he had seen that the "bugs had been worked out" of Hightower's computer program. When Hightower received Ernie's letter of May 1, 1991, claiming he had been cheated and demanding a full refund, "I realized I was being blackmailed."

Stone wanted to know why, if the system worked so well, was it losing money hand over fist? Hightower responded that the program had never really been used at all. Molina, the mob-related stock broker, was attempting to pirate the system and use it for mob purposes, so Hightower churned out inaccurate test numbers to confuse him.

Ernie, Hightower charged, had "no concern" about losing money in his personal account, claiming that extra money would be made available if losses were too great. But when the $15,000 dwindled to $3,500, Ernie suddenly "refused to put funds back in." In a familiar plea—the same as he used in explaining what happened with his Italian clients and Wagner—Hightower said that he, not Ernie Brendel, closed the account. "Now I was in trouble," Hightower moaned.

"You hated him for ruining your business!" snapped Stone.

"I was upset. Hate is a pretty strong word, sir."

"You knew Ernie Brendel didn't care about the money. He was going after your license to prevent you from doing what you did to . . . him to anyone else that might invest with you!"

Not true, insisted Hightower. Ernie did not have a trading license and needed to use Hightower as a front man, in order to create the financial newsletter. Hightower wanted the jurors to believe that Brendel, a lawyer, wasn't smart enough to obtain the same kind of CFTC-NFA license Hightower held.

Stone shifted from the strange financial subject matter to holes the prosecution had found in Hightower's rambling direct testimony. He cashed in with a series of lies and errors in fact, time, and place. "There were a lot of things I had forgotten," Hightower said of the missteps in his postarrest interviews. "After seeing three people murdered, my mind wasn't what you would say all together."

Stone unrolled the tapestry of problems:

• Hightower said Ernie was in the garage at 6:30 P.M., although another witness testified seeing Ernie in Dedham, Massachusetts, at a financial seminar fifteen minutes later. The distance between the two places made that impossible.

• Hightower had been under such pressure that time lost its relevance to him after he was thrown out of his home. But minutes later he told Susanne Henderson he was hurrying to an appointment. "Well, were you in a rush or not?" Stone demanded. "I don't recall," said the defendant.

• Hightower had said, "The cloth used to strangle Alice was wrapped around my neck" to force him to watch the death of Emily, but on cross-examination he said the thugs used one that was "similar" to the one used to kill Alice.

* * *

By the time the court day ended at 4:20 P.M., the prosecution team had punched about forty gaping holes in Hightower's crazy scenario during the afternoon session alone, and made sure the jury understood each and every one of them.

35

The Glock

There was no court on Tuesday, but when Wednesday morning came around, the twenty-first day of the trial, Christopher Hightower was still thrashing about like a hooked fish. His elaborate web of lies had become so tangled it would take a computer to keep it all straight. Hightower was heading toward a cliff, and Mike Stone delighted in pushing him closer to the edge.

"And that was a lie!" Stone would bark like a drill sergeant over some particular piece of testimony. "Another lie, right?" Each time, Hightower agreed. He had passed beyond personal mortification and could only stand there and take the beating while television broadcast his every twitch.

At mid-morning the nickel finally dropped for Judge Sheehan. He interrupted Stone's probing of why the killers let Hightower drive around Barrington in a stolen, bloody car.

"Let me ask you something, sir," intoned the judge. "Sunday morning when you went to Somerville Lumber, was it crowded there?"

"It was fairly crowded as I recall."

"And as I understand—recall I should say—that two of the men were of Chinese origin and about six-one?"

"Yes sir."

Sheehan swung his head in amazement. "Have you

ever seen a six-foot-one Chinese person in Somerville Lumber?"

"No sir."

Sheehan, satisfied, waved for Stone to continue, and the prosecutors resumed hammering Hightower. Stone would accuse, Hightower would try to dodge, Stone would land on him to expose still another inconsistency. When the tale reached Connecticut, Hightower flipped out of control again.

When he stopped to pick up the crossbow he had hidden, one of the killers was waiting in the woods beside the weapon, Hightower testified. He tripped and bumped into the mystery man, who dropped a walkie-talkie, which hit a rock and broke. "He was furious and threw it into the woods," said the witness. Bob George almost groaned in dismay.

Hightower was so worried about his family that he followed the killers' directions to the letter, correct? asked Stone. When Hightower confirmed that, the prosecutor asked why he changed his story about how much ransom was wanted. He had asked the Scriabines for only $75,000 when he had been ordered to get either $200,000 or $300,000, depending on which version of the story was being examined. Hightower admitted disobeying the orders. Sheehan interrupted again. This business of the Chinese men—first mentioned eight days previously—still itched.

"Let me ask you a question, Mr. Hightower. How long prior to September 1991 have you lived in Barrington?"

"Since 1986, sir."

"Since 1986 to September 1991 in the town of Barrington, have you ever seen one or two six-foot-one Chinese people?"

"Yes sir."

"You have?"

"Yes sir." Actually, there was one rather tall Asian man in Barrington, a college professor. When combined with the tall Polynesian lawyer who refused to get involved with Hightower Investments, the witness had

come up with two tall Chinese men. There was no explanation for the pair of swarthy Latin Americans.

Stone resumed, and Hightower spent several more
hours trying to keep track of his story, failing at almost
every turn. The prosecutor brought up the Hightower
claim that Ernie wanted to take over the business so he
could create a financial newsletter, which Hightower testified he opposed. From the police bag of tricks, Stone
dredged up Hightower's business plan, written long before he had even met Brendel. It stated that once the
business had a successful track record, Hightower would
"then produce and promote an advisory newsletter for
the public."

Mike Stone then let a confused and weary Hightower
walk into still another trap. A vital piece of evidence had
been barred from the trial when Sheehan ruled the pistol in the briefcase could not be introduced until it was
shown to be relevant. At this point the jury did not know
the gun existed.

Stone questioned, in an unusually reasonable tone,
why Hightower did not resist the hoodlums. Hightower
explained that all four of the men carried pistols in their
belts. Continuing his habit of saying more than he
should, he went a sentence too far. Hightower testified
he could not tell the difference between a .45 caliber pistol, a nine-millimeter, or a .25 caliber.

That answer sprung open the briefcase and let out the
devil.

"What is a Glock?" asked Stone.

"A semiautomatic pistol, nine millimeter," Hightower
replied instantly.

"Do you own such a pistol?"

"Yes. I bought it in the spring of 1990."

"Was the Glock in your briefcase?"

"Yes."

Stone, the infantry officer who had been wounded in
combat, picked up the black pistol, mean and lethal,
from the table and held it in his right palm. Reaching

over with his left hand, he pulled back the slide to cock the empty pistol and the loud *clack-clack* of metal sliding on metal thundered in the courtroom, startling jurors. A crossbow might be rather abstract, but they all understood big pistols. Stone had Hightower confirm that two full clips of ammunition, a total of thirty-eight bullets, were also in the briefcase that was always in his possession.

"You were so concerned about the safety of your wife and your children, your father-in-law, your mother-in-law, your ex-wife in Long Island, your children in Long Island, and your children [in Barrington], yet you never once, having full access to a nine-millimeter handgun with what may be thirty-eight rounds of ammunition in it, took any action on your own to protect them?"

It was a knockout blow, as big a piece of evidence as Emily's white tennis shoe or the little girl's voice on the tape recording. Bob George leaped from his chair to shout, "Objection!"

"Overruled," said Sheehan. The briefcase would remain open, the Glock finally exposed.

Hightower waffled. "My mind was not in the state that I was thinking—"

"Please just answer the question. Yes or no?" snapped Stone.

"No sir. No sir."

As bad as it was, things could have been worse. The court officers had been concerned that Pat Youngs might be doing the floor work when the pistol came into evidence, and that frightened one and all. For while Youngs is a brilliant attorney, he is a klutz with weapons. He once broke open a shotgun for a jury, to demonstrate how to snap it apart with one hand, only to bang himself so hard on the knee that he almost fell over. Another time he handed a large knife to a man on the witness stand being tried for using that very weapon in a murder. In still another trial, slamming down a knife for emphasis, he almost impaled a court reporter. So everyone was just as happy that Youngs sat this one out.

The jury realized that Hightower easily had the means to make Emily and Alice obey until he murdered them. None thought for a moment that a normal man under such conditions would not have used the big Glock 17 to save his own family.

There would be a few more moments of high drama in court that afternoon, as Stone whipped Hightower with the Lynx letters. It seemed as if every time the defendant opened his mouth, he made it that much harder for jurors to believe him.

At one point Hightower recounted how one Lynx letter instructed him to tell everything. Hightower testified that he "perceived it to be just the reverse. If I told, harm would come to my family. I thought it was a subliminal message, telling me just the opposite." That was too much for one juror, who shifted in his seat and turned away to avoid laughing aloud.

Hightower had insisted there was no ransom demand, but Stone made him read the Lynx letter saying a ransom of $200,000 was required for the Brendels' safe return. The manic writings left Hightower wobbling on the stand, his eyes bugging wide behind the glasses and sweat draining down his face.

So many messages from the Lynx, some giving details of the crime that only the person who committed it would have known. Messages to Sue: "I am a professional assassin. If you don't reconcile with your husband immediately, the cops can't protect you forever." Details of Kathy Slicker's car and where Clyde Slicker played tennis. A message for Mary Lou Slicker, threatening that someone could easily drown in the lake at their New Hampshire property.

Finally, Stone brought out a plainly sadistic letter Christopher Hightower had written, claiming that the bodies of Ernie and Alice Brendel had been cut up, burned, and buried in the Vermont mountains, while Emily had been sold into slavery in South America for $50,000.

The letter bore the date of November 6, 1991—the day before the slain Brendels were discovered in a pair of shallow graves only a few blocks from their home.

The drumbeat continued on Hightower's final day of testimony, Thursday, April 8. He was in so deep now that his strategy was simply to deny almost everything.

Before court opened for the day, Christine Scriabine commented on how ridiculous it was to hear Hightower's earlier testimony that he planned to write books for children while he was in prison. "What is he going to call his first one, 'Emily, Girl Slave in Caracas'?" she asked a reporter.

The prosecution strategy had been from the first day to prove every charge a dozen times. But Stone was finally ready to bring it to a close with a few more notes from the Lynx.

For Mary Lou Slicker, a letter claimed that if Hightower talked, "no one is safe" and that "someone could even drown in that lovely secluded pond this summer."

For Sue, there was a telephone call that equated divorce with death and added, "Enjoy your last Christmas."

For one of his convict buddies, a plan: "You will revel in its madness and beauty . . ." And a final one concerning an unintelligible "parable of life" that concluded, "You can bet your ass I'm not writing anything." They all ended up in the files of the State Police.

Stone paced the carpet before the bench as he made his summary, trying to put together the points that had come out on cross-examination, so the jury could pick some truth from the vast field of material. In a preview of his closing argument, he charged that Hightower went to violent extremes because Ernie Brendel would not drop the complaint. He tried to break into the Brendel house with the pry bar, hid in the woods when the alarm went off, and spent the night in the garage. The next morning, he murdered Ernie and rode the victim's three-speed bike to 1 Jones Circle, where "the unexpected happened" and the constable showed up while Hightower was washing clothes. Getting back to 51 Middle Highway, he forged two checks when he couldn't find enough cash in the house, then kidnapped the unsuspecting Emily and Alice. He "secured them somewhere in the house, probably the cellar," forced Alice to call Jim Page the next morning, then killed them both and disposed of all three bodies in the shallow graves. He got greedy and went to the Scriabine residence with an extortion demand, which blew up in his face when they called the FBI.

"Isn't it a fact, Mr. Hightower, that you lied to the Scriabines, you lied to the police, and now you lied to this jury!" snapped Mike Stone, glaring at Christopher Hightower.

The defendant said that just wasn't true. "I did what I was told. Since I've been here, to the best of my recollection, I have told the jury the truth on what has happened."

Like a soldier emerging from the safety of a foxhole to discover that the earth all around him has been bombed, Bob George rose and straightened his suit. He had warned Hightower not to testify, but the man insisted, and now George had to clean up the mess.

He managed to toss a few softball questions that let Hightower insist his forged documents were only an attempt to provide a better life for his family, that the Investors Guild lost their money in the marketplace, that Ernie was going to create the newsletter in order to launder drug money, that he did indeed sell a lot of drugs for Riker Labs, that he told police about having the Glock 17 pistol, and that he could have continued his business even if the CFTC had taken his license. The bottom line, Hightower said, was that "I had nothing to do with the deaths of the Brendel family."

After only nineteen minutes of questioning Stone's exhaustive cross-examination, Bob George sat down. There was nothing else to say. "Greatest witness since Oliver

North," an observer cracked to a rueful George as they went to lunch.

The defense put on its handful of witnesses that bright spring afternoon, and went nowhere fast. To George, it didn't really matter because the only chance his client had now was for a psychiatrist to convince the jury that his client was nuts.

David Carriere of Bristol was brought to the stand in hopes of testifying that Hightower and Ernie were quite friendly. Instead he ended up saying he had only met Brendel once and the only talk he ever heard about a newsletter had come from an enthusiastic Chris Hightower. Carriere was a strange choice for a character witness, since he had known the Slicker family for seventeen years and Hightower owed him $800.

Next came John Borsey, who was on the stand for thirteen minutes, testifying he was driving a landscape truck by the house on Middle Highway on Monday, September 23, when a white van bolted out of the driveway and cut him off. Hightower had testified that the killers arrived in a white van. The description that Borsey gave of the driver, however, matched Hightower, not a tall Chinese man nor a squat Latin American.

Finally, Elizabeth Kojian, who works at the Brown library, said she saw Alice get into a small, light-colored car about 2:30 P.M. on Friday, September 20. Her testimony, in the face of conflicting reports that Alice was still at work that afternoon and rode home on the bus, proved nothing.

But for the moment nothing was all that Bob George had. All he could think about, as the final nonprofessional witness stepped down was, Thank God it's Friday.

36

Mind Field

Dr. Walter Eric Penk, a clinical psychologist with the Massachusetts Department of Mental Health, spent a dozen hours testing Christopher Hightower, reviewed records for another fifteen hours, and watched videotape of Hightower on the witness stand. Penk, with thirty-one years in the field, would be the heart of George's case, and on a drizzly Monday morning, the tall, angular psychologist took the stand. Over the Easter weekend, Bob George bought his kids a brown bunny, which they named Lucky. He could have used Lucky and all four of the rabbit's feet with him this day, as he tried to convince the jury that Hightower was a paranoid schizophrenic, who lived in a fantasy world, gripped by a mental illness that prevented him from knowing the difference between right and wrong. That would mean the "delusional" Hightower was not legally responsible for the deaths of the Brendel family. But the jury had fallen in love with Emily Brendel and was not going to let Hightower escape prison just because Penk thought the man accused of killing her was not playing with a full deck. It was going to be uphill all the way.

The spectators and jury would get a look inside the brain of the accused murderer. The battle lines were drawn on the issue of criminal responsibility, because prosecution experts would argue that Hightower was not mentally ill, but just a run-of-the-mill con man and murderer who was not very good at anything he did.

Penk would spend more than four and a half hours testifying over a two-day period as Hightower's last, best chance. The irony was strong, because, according to Mary Lou Slicker, Hightower "hated everything having to do with psychiatry."

Penk's presentation was flawed almost from the start, for the scholarly witness had an extremely soft voice, excellent in dealing with a patient, but lousy in a courtroom. Despite the efforts of Judge Sheehan and Bob George, Penk's entire testimony would be given in tones just above a mumble, thereby severely damaging his argument. But it was extraordinary that the worried Penk was on the witness stand at all, since his wife was extremely ill and about to undergo surgery.

In his professional opinion, Penk said, Hightower "was in a residual phase of paranoid schizophrenia" at the time of the crisis because of "a past serious psychiatric break." Penk said throughout his long examination, Hightower never once referred to the killings of the Brendels. Likewise, Penk sidestepped talking about the multiple murders, saying that Hightower's peculiar behavior resulted from "having witnessed some horrible deeds."

Meanwhile, at the defense table, Christopher Hightower leaned back, forced to listen to his own expert witness say, in big words, that he was crazy. For the man who had prized the facade of respectability, it was the ultimate embarrassment, and he blushed as Penk's testimony unrolled. At the prosecution table, detectives Palumbo, Schauble, and Badger shifted in their seats, worried that the jittery Hightower, being viciously insulted, might explode and have to be wrestled down.

Penk defined a delusion as a fixed belief that the afflicted person will "do or say anything" to maintain. That differed from an outright lie, which is when a person "is deliberately trying to deceive" someone. The schizophrenia that Hightower suffered was a deteriorating illness in which "a person increasingly loses touch with reality."

Those definitions fit George's defense pattern perfectly. Hightower, in that scenario, did not try to deceive people, because he had left so many obvious clues behind, from eyewitnesses, such as bank tellers and the Scriabines, to hard evidence, like the paper trail of receipts and poorly forged checks. Out of touch with reality, according to Penk, the man would just go freewheeling along, giving no thought to the right or wrong of a particular situation, until he was brought to a forced halt by the authorities.

The key to Hightower's ability to function somewhat normally was that he landed in situations that afforded structure and support, propping him up when he would have otherwise fallen flat. Penk's examples of such systems included the Navy, academia, his marriages, the support of his in-laws and the community, and the loans and leeway given by friends and clients who put up with his schemes. "He couldn't meet the ordinary demands of work and life, and people tried to encourage him," Penk surmised. By doing so, they only prolonged the inevitable crisis. It was a neat way of shifting the responsibility from Hightower to those who tried to help.

The psychologist said the demons that beset Hightower dated back to elementary school, when Hightower learned he was a bastard and never knew his real father. Complicating that, his stepfather was a failure and could not provide for his family, launching Hightower's devotion to making money.

While growing up in structured settings, Hightower could hide his illness behind "a mask of sanity," even while maintaining grandiose illusions, such as his belief that he could become a physician. The problem with that dream was simply that Hightower was not smart enough to pull it off. The IQ test administered by Penk showed Hightower ranked at exactly 100, precisely average and at a level Penk said was incapable of even doing basic college work.

A person's IQ, or intelligence quotient, is an arithmetical figure derived by dividing the subject's mental age, as determined by psychological tests, by the age in years, and multiplying by 100. For example, to determine the IQ of a nine-year-old child who tests at a twelve-year-old mental level, divide the 12 by the 9 to get 1.33 and multiply that figure by 100 to erase the decimal. The result would be 133, which would be considered exceptional.

A person whose tested mental age was totally consistent with his or her chronological age would rate at exactly 100, as did Christopher Hightower. His intelligence was about as average as average could be. An IQ over 130 is considered to be very superior, in the top 2 percent of everyone who has taken the tests. The Mensa Society, an organization of the highly intelligent, requires a minimum IQ of 132 for membership. At the other end of the spectrum, an IQ of 69 denotes someone who is considered to be mentally deficient. From 90 to 109 is considered average. In the opinion of Penk, Hightower's IQ and other tests indicated his intelligence might still be average, but it seemed to be diminishing.

Hightower's failure in his first marriage, his studies at Wright State, and his botched Investors Guild scheme did not prevent him from chasing his illusions of grandeur in Barrington, disguised behind the "trappings of normalcy," according to Penk. It was only when many of the required support systems were yanked away simultaneously—the divorce action by Sue, being thrown out of his house, losing his children and the support of Clyde Slicker, the trading business going down the tubes, his computers being repossessed, and Ernie Brendel's federal complaint—that Hightower could no longer cope. The developments "worked together to remove all shreds of adjustment," and "completely overwhelmed" Hightower, who then acted "at the whim of his emotions" with no ability to appreciate what he did. Such behavior as his "aimless wandering" by driving around in a bloody car simply "don't make any sense," Penk stated.

In a Rorschach inkblot test, Hightower described one

image as "a seething caldron," reflecting how he felt inside, while appearing quite normal on the outside.

"Mr. Hightower is able to see life very simply in black and white, in absolutes of right or wrong: people are either for you [or] against you," declared Penk. "He is unable to accept criticisms from others."

Hightower had difficulty controlling feelings of anger and outrage, but any positive feelings were suppressed. "He is completely devoid of the ability to self-criticize, lacking the ability to regard himself as an agent in whatever goes wrong in his life, always holding everything and everyone else responsible for his troubles."

As far as delusional thinking, the Lynx letters were perfect examples of "getting caught up in fantasies."

Pat Youngs had a reprieve. The Red Sox home opener had been rained out, giving him a final chance to see the opening home game tomorrow, when no court was scheduled. He was in a good mood when he stood to deal with the technical cross-examination of Penk.

He struck pay dirt immediately by pestering Penk with questions on whether Hightower was "delusional" when it came to making money and murdering Emily Brendel to cover the tracks of an earlier murder. "He was in a delusional state where he did not understand the rightfulness or wrongfulness of his act," Penk replied.

It was the exact answer the prosecution wanted to hear, one that Bob George had skillfully sidestepped during the direct examination of the psychologist. It opened the whole range of decision-making to question, and Judge Sheehan immediately told the jury it was up to them, not to the doctors, to decide the mental condition of the defendant.

Youngs countered the alleged delusional thought process by introducing specific items, such as Hightower ordering cheeseburgers and forging transcripts, saying, "That's a *fact*, right? To keep the delusion intact, he would lie?"

"He would certainly deceive," Penk responded.

Youngs also brought out that Penk gave Hightower a list of 560 true-false questions in a personality test, and the results were devastating. To the question, "I believe most people lie to get ahead," Hightower answered, "True." Asked, "When I am cornered, I tell that portion of the truth that is not likely to hurt me," he also answered, "True."

Bob George would respond later with questions from the same test, such as "I sometimes feel I'm going to pieces" and "I feel anxiety ... almost all of the time," both of which Hightower answered as true. Scores on various other tests fell within normal limits, leaving the entire process open to interpretation. It could be read either way.

The prosecution also attacked the idea that Hightower was wandering aimlessly over the weekend. "Was going to Thompson's sporting goods to buy a crossbow aimless wandering? Was going to Sears to buy Reeboks?" asked Youngs. "What is aimless about going somewhere with a purpose?" Penk wrote it off to disorganization.

Round and round they went, talking about whether the murders were fantasies, whether it was disorganized thinking to buy a bag of lime, how Hightower was said by many witnesses to be totally calm, whether he was delusional or simply "trying to cover up a crime."

When Penk's testimony concluded, the defense team was certain they had laid a foundation for the argument that Hightower was crazed when he murdered the Brendels. The prosecution felt just as strongly they had shown Hightower was thinking clearly at the time of the slaughter and was only a crook trying to cover up his crimes with a lunacy plea.

Naturally, State prosecutors were ready for the psychiatric ploy, which had been expected from before the trial began. Since George had introduced Hightower's state of mind as an issue by bringing in Penk, the prosecution was allowed to argue the point with their own witnesses. So in order to rebut the Penk analysis of Hightower's mental condition, they brought on not one, but three experts. Unfortunately, to prepare for their testimony, baseball fan Pat Youngs spent the court's day off in the War Room, missing the first Red Sox home game of the season. His television set played videotapes of Hightower, not baseball.

The following day, Thomas Guilmette, director of neuropsychology at Rhode Island Hospital, testified Hightower was a self-serving sociopath who thought "lying, cheating, and stealing" was appropriate behavior. He said the defendant's actions appeared to be planned and systematic. Guilmette said the tests administered by Penk reflected not schizophrenia, but an "antisocial personality." Hightower was a sociopath in the opinion of Guilmette.

That was a vital issue as far as Youngs and Stone were concerned. Under Rhode Island law, a sociopath views people as objects, knows right from wrong and is not insane. That conclusion was buttressed by testimony from Alan Feinstein, the clinical psychologist at the ACI, and Eileen McNamara, a professor at Brown University.

Feinstein said he had met Hightower about fifty times in prison, and not once had the inmate shown any sign of paranoid schizophrenia. Feinstein had even told Hightower that he was shocked to learn Bob George was planning an insanity defense. Hightower, he testified, laughed, and said, "That was my lawyer's idea to throw the prosecution off balance."

The haughty McNamara, who had watched Hightower testify, said the only times he laughed during his six days on the witness stand were when relating how he worked some deception. "He truly takes pleasure in hoodwinking other people and feeling superior to them," she said. He knows right from wrong, she stated, he just chooses to disregard it.

To the jury, the legal, medical, and psychiatric jargon came down to a simple conclusion. Three out of four head shrinkers thought Hightower wasn't crazy enough to slip through the law's insanity loophole.

37

End Game

On trial day twenty-five, Monday, April 19, courtroom seats were at a premium for the closing arguments in the trial that had grabbed Rhode Island by the throat. As Christopher Hightower was brought in by the marshals, he almost bumped into James Romano, the attorney who had declined to invest with Hightower but referred him to a couple of Italian friends and thus helped create Hightower's mob scenario. They did not speak. When the jurors filed in that morning, they also did not speak or nod as they passed the defendant, who stood politely.

Bob George lined up his legal pads at the podium. He had spent five hours polishing his final comments on Sunday, then tried to get some rest for the coming ordeal. Now he had to make his closing statement and wrap up a case that had been mortally damaged by the wild, meandering story that Christopher Hightower had spent days telling a stunned courtroom.

In his most reasonable tone, George told the jury the State wanted them to believe that Hightower, a man who had no history of violence, slaughtered an entire family over a measly $11,236.

The jurors must remember, George argued, that the State had to prove beyond a reasonable doubt that Hightower—with premeditation and malice aforethought—committed the crimes. "I suggest to you that there is no evidence in this case that indicates the defendant is capable of that kind of intent, and the fact that the crime is so horrendous doesn't make it so," George declared. Several jurors gawked at the assertion of Hightower's innocence. It was exactly the reaction George wanted.

Yes, Hightower was a poor provider, he had done things wrong in his past, he had forged checks and failed as a financial consultant. But "where is the evidence of a monster who kills whole families, including eight-year-old children? There is none, members of the jury. There's no evidence of that whatsoever."

The defense lawyer was saying that the mountain of evidence introduced over the past eight weeks was not high enough. "Hey," George declared, spreading his hands wide, "even if you find that he forged the checks, does that make him a murderer?"

Then he astonished them again, asking them to actually "believe Mr. Hightower's story"—the Chinese Tong, Ernie's secret life, heroin in wine bottles, the whole nine yards.

Because, George proposed, the Christopher Hightower who might have done the strange things described during his six days on the witness stand was not the same man who had lived quietly in a suburban community for years prior to the horrible weekend.

To counter the prosecution psychiatrists, George told the jurors that when they heard a story as bizarre as the one told by his client, "you don't even need doctors to tell you that someone is delusional."

Going to the Barrington police station to pay the back rent "like life was going to go on"? Lying in the rain with a crossbow for five hours waiting for a raccoon? The Mafia? Armored cars? Driving around in a "nightmare-filled car?" Writing letters about selling Emily into slavery? These were not the acts of a normal person, George said, and the jurors certainly had to agree with him.

Because of the sudden removal of all of his support systems, Hightower had become someone else. "The soccer coach, the Cub Scout leader, the family man. He wasn't them anymore . . . Mr. Hightower was a walking shell of what he had been for years."

Without saying so, George was giving up the fight to prove that Hightower may not have committed the crimes with which he was charged. The physical evidence against the prisoner was simply too overwhelming. Whatever chance the defense still had was centered solely on persuading the jury to believe that Hightower was insane, therefore innocent, because he didn't know what he was doing. "He was a delusional paranoid schizophrenic during September of 1991," the defense attorney declared.

George also had to deal with the sympathy that jurors felt for the murdered family. "I don't want you to think I have forgotten the Brendels died in this case, because I haven't," he said. "Ernest Brendel will never get to see his daughter go to college and Emily will never get married. I understand all that."

But he asked the jury to put aside their passion and look at the case in a neutral light, emphasizing they should consider "everything," meaning giving credence to Dr. Penk's conclusion of the defendant's "delusional behavior."

With the strange story they had heard from Hightower's lips, they might conclude he really had mentally snapped. The Christopher Hightower who had spent a lifetime as a meek, nonviolent man "was incapable of harboring the kind of thoughts that are necessary to commit crimes of this nature," George said. Therefore, Hightower and the merciless killer who slaughtered the Brendel family could not have been the same man. In other words, George concluded, Christopher Hightower was insane and therefore not legally responsible.

Mike Stone had spent the weekend in the War Room, not getting home until eleven Sunday night. Less than a dozen hours later he moved to the podium. Bob George leaned over and whispered to Hightower, probably tell-

ing him that at some point in the State's closing argument, Stone would get right in Hightower's face. It was
a standard tactic straight out of the prosecutors' man-
ual, something jurors loved to see in a particularly heinous case, and George would have been obligated to
warn his client to expect such a confrontation and not
react.

Stone wasted little time raising the image of Emily.
"We don't know how she died. Was she strangled? Was
she choked, as Mr. Hightower says? Was she put in that
grave still alive, with her mother's body on top of her,
suffocated in the grave? We don't know." Several jurors
visibly winced.

Then he launched into an account of the case, from
the bloodstained steel pry bar to the clothes the Brendel
bodies wore being the same as they had on the Friday
they vanished. Mike Stone had lived with the evidence
for a year and a half and could recite it backward. He
had no need for notes.

When Hightower was first arrested, he never impli-
cated himself in a single criminal act, but police did not
believe his story. Stone, his mouth in a tight, mirthless
smile, strolled over to the defense table, leaned on it and
glared at Hightower from a distance of only six inches as
he gleefully quoted what Hightower said the FBI's
McGraw told him: "I don't believe you. You killed them
and I'm going to prove it." Despite George's apparent
warning, Hightower blinked, and his nervous jaw once
again tightened.

Stone then told the jury Hightower spent a lifetime
treating other people as mere objects, because "nothing
in his life is more important than him." That tunnel vision was his downfall when he faced simultaneous as-
saults on his professional and personal lives.

Ernie Brendel was outraged to discover Hightower
defrauded him, and, being a lawyer, "knew how to take
action . . . that would result in the end of Hightower Investments." Once the NFA learned of the cooked figures,
they would shut it down.

And on the home front, Hightower's wife told him the marriage was over. "There goes the meal ticket," Stone declared. Now, if he lost the business, "he is back to being what he was before all of this." Stone glanced at Hightower and sneered the next word. "Nothing."

Therefore, Hightower was driven to remove Brendel's complaint against his little company and find enough money to stay afloat, Stone said.

Stone carefully threaded the case together, demolishing what he said were "lies peppered with a few little truths." He charged that Hightower bought a "silent, deadly" crossbow and stalked Brendel. "Since Ernie won't drop the complaint, Ernie has to die."

But then, out of the blue, a constable served the divorce papers and Hightower's plan "gets flawed like he never expected." In a panic, he suddenly has to deal with Emily and Alice too. The next day, after forcing Alice to call Jim Page, "Alice Brendel and Emily Brendel were of no further use to Christopher Hightower," so they were drugged and murdered.

Stone carefully attacked the discrepancies in the times Hightower claimed to be in one place when a person or document proved him to be elsewhere. "You can't be two places at once. This is not *Star Trek*. You can't beam me over there, Scotty."

Stone described in detail one "fatal mistake" Hightower made when recounting the murders. The defendant claimed the murderers took the cloth they had used to choke Alice and put it around his own neck. "We know that's not true," Stone said, because the medical examiner testified the cloth was wrapped so tightly it had to be sliced off with a scalpel.

Hightower had known his elaborate tale was being destroyed by evidence, so he created the bizarre tale of the Mafia kidnappers, "while sitting out at the ACI trying to figure out a better lie to tell." Stone brought forward the Lynx letters, which he said contained "many details that only someone involved in the killings would know about."

As far as Hightower being delusional, Stone belittled

the idea. "What you are dealing with here is a person
who has a full adult history of treating people like nothing more than objects, who is capable of doing anything
to achieve his ends. And that, my friends, includes even
the murder of an eight-year-old girl."

Stone stretched his hands flat on the jury box rail,
swept his dark eyes across each of them and reminded
them of the Lynx letter that said a forgiving God already
had pardoned the Lynx. "Maybe God forgave him. That
doesn't mean we have to forgive him," Stone said. "Let
God judge him later on. You judge him now."

The case then went to Judge Sheehan, who spent the
rest of the afternoon delivering his charge to the jury,
telling them they could return three possible verdicts—
guilty, not guilty, or not criminally responsible, due to a
mental disease or defect. Then deliberations started. But
no verdict was reached that afternoon, and everyone
went home to read and watch the big news, not about
the Hightower trial, but about the horrible fires that
had engulfed the Waco, Texas, compound of self-styled
messiah David Koresh and his Branch Davidian follow-
ers.

Tuesday, April 20, was the twenty-sixth day of trial,
and the jury went back to work, munching chocolate
chip swirl cookies that one member had baked.

Under Rhode Island's peculiar justice system, everyone involved in a case must stick close to the courtroom
until the jury reaches a verdict. So for five hours and
forty minutes over those two days, the lawyers, the spectators, cops, and family members paced the marble hall-
ways, found snacks in the coffee shop, smoked cigarettes
in a little garden, and wondered why the jury was taking
so long. Hightower waited in a special lockup room.
Speculation ranged from the case being too complex for
a jury to handle swiftly, to the possibility of a holdout
forcing a potential hung jury.

Fred Bobb, the nephew of Ernie and Alice, was betting

that his Libra horoscope for the day was correct when it said, "Legal obstacle removed."

Deputy Sheriff Joe Spiver came into the hallway at 3:16 P.M., tapping a buff envelope on his fingers. After five hours and forty minutes of deliberations, the jury had reached a verdict.

Courtroom 5 quickly filled, and a large group of marshals was scattered throughout the room when Hightower was brought forward. The spectators seemed as nervous as the defendant. "My heart is beating really fast," whispered Fred Bobb. Mary Lou Slicker unconsciously twisted her fingers into a knot.

As usual, Hightower politely stood as the jury filed into the courtroom, but now they did not meet his eyes. His jaw was clenched tight by the time he resumed his seat.

Sheehan called the court to order and instructed Clerk Linda Parsons to ask if the jury had reached its decisions. Foreman Donne Nochomowitz answered, "We have."

Parsons slowly read each charge, and every time, Nochomowitz answered, "Guilty." Hightower began to redden in anger and embarrassment—*They had not believed him!*—and leaned close to whisper to Bob George while the guilty verdicts continued to roll in.

George nodded at Hightower's request, and when the roll call was done, he requested the individual jurors be polled. Parsons then asked each juror for his or her decision on each count. Each time, a juror would stand up and pronounce the word "Guilty." Mike Stone buried his face in steepled fingers and Pat Youngs wrote some notes as the guilty verdicts droned on and on. Bob George, his duty done, nibbled at the nail on his left index finger. Detectives Palumbo, Badger, Schauble, and Quinn kept their eyes on Hightower. Just in case. Just in case. When the polling was over, Hightower, who had listened to the verdicts without further emotion, had been pronounced guilty 133 times.

A wave of relief swept through the courtroom, eddying

around and over the seated Christopher Hightower. Suddenly, he was ignored, as if he were not even there. Marshals stepped forward with the steel manacles for his wrists, treating him as nothing more than a common criminal.

Family members embraced, and Christine Scriabine looked over her right shoulder and exchanged smiles with Mary Lou Slicker. Short Mike Stone put a bear hug on tall Pat Youngs as their police teammates grinned like kids and pumped each other's hands. Spectators who had come throughout the trial exchanged excited comments and turned to watch as the stunned Hightower was led away.

Outside the courtroom the temperature was in the low sixties and sunshine filled the sky. Radio and television reporters flashed the news around the state, and a motorist driving by the courthouse yelled from his window that "justice has been served!"

Still, the job was not finished. The jury would deliberate the next day on whether Hightower's crimes met the stringent conditions of recommending a life-without-parole sentence.

On arriving in court, the newly convicted Hightower might have found comfort in the results of a television poll. The survey, taken early during his testimony but held back at the request of the judge, indicated 42 percent of viewers believed Hightower. Maybe so, but one hundred percent of the jury did not believe him.

On April 21, the twenty-seventh day of trial, the jury had to decide whether Emily died as a direct result of being kidnapped, and whether Ernie was tortured prior to his death.

George frankly had not expected to have to argue his case still again, and spoke extemporaneously. He argued that Emily probably died the day *after* she was kidnapped, so the two events were not related. Ernie's head wounds probably were not torture, because he was already dead when they were inflicted. The jurors listened politely as he urged them not to be motivated "by passion or revenge."

Pat Youngs was glad to lay out the State's case once again, and in a soft voice walked through the events one last time. He picked up the crossbow for emphasis and laid it on a rail before the jurors. Ernie, he said, endured "sheer torture and sheer agony" in that garage. That was enough for one sentence of life without parole, he said. And as for the other, well, could anyone doubt that Emily died as a direct result of her kidnapping? "Hightower stalked her," Youngs said. "And when he didn't need her anymore, he killed her." But for the kidnapping, Emily would not have died.

The jury went out at 10:44 A.M., and they decided the kidnap-murder issue "within five seconds," one juror said later. Hightower was guilty, they decided, but they could not announce that verdict until they decided the other, more ambiguous matter of torture.

They returned to the jury box to have Sheehan carefully explain that torture only had to last a few seconds, and did not mean that someone had to be put "on the rack." When they resumed deliberations, they took the ugly crossbow and an arrow into the room with them. Still, they could not come to a unanimous verdict. After almost eight weeks of trial and hours of deliberations, they appeared to be stuck.

Lunch was called, but no one wanted to eat. Cops and lawyers and spectators simply wanted to know what was taking so long in that little room. What could be the holdup? Could Hightower really escape one of the maximum sentences? He had been looking at the awesome prospect of back-to-back life terms, a much heavier sentence than a single life verdict. Actually, most of the people in the hall would have preferred to see him swinging at the end of a rope, or lashed into an electric chair, or taking a whiff of lethal gas, than serving a life sentence, but they would take what they could get.

Sheehan used the break to chastise Youngs lightheartedly for handling the crossbow in court. The judge ordered a detective not to let the lawyer touch the weapon again. Everyone had a laugh, but humor was tinged with tension.

It took three and a half hours for the jurors to reach agreement that the assault with the crossbow and pry bar had left Ernie Brendel wounded and in agony, and thereby met the torture test. One person had been holding out, but was eventually convinced that torture did not have to last more than a millisecond to qualify for the ultimate penalty.

Again Hightower listened stonelike to the verdicts, asked for a poll of the jury, and had the bad news repeated. When Sheehan adjourned court until a sentencing date could be set, both Hightower and Bob George seemed to vanish in a blink. Hightower went back to prison. George just wanted to escape Courtroom 5 and be alone for a while.

Afterward, the jurors were unanimous in their criticism of Hightower. "I think he hung himself as soon as he took the stand. He tried to make us look like fools with his story," said Edwin Andrade. Juror Victor Trindade said "the icing on the cake was when he said the Brendels were drug dealers. That was just totally ridiculous. These were very quiet people who kept to themselves, who went to church. It was insulting."

The prosecution team had spent most of its emotion on the verdicts yesterday, but there was still some residual joy for them, as evidenced by Doug Badger of the State Police strolling down the hall, jauntily wearing a golf hat that bore the word, "Lynx."

The final act came several months later, on June 8, when Hightower was brought into court again to hear Sheehan's sentence. Seated in the audience for the first time was Susan Slicker Hightower, who by now was carrying another name. She sat with her family in the middle row of benches, neat in a silk blouse of blue, white, and purple flowers and a knee-length blue skirt. Since the fall of 1991 she had wanted closure on this matter, wanted to make sure that her violent and menacing ex-husband who had committed a triple murder would no longer present a threat to her own family. She wanted Christopher Hightower out of her life once and for all.

Also ready for the last chapter were the Brendel relatives, who were ushered to seats in the jury box for the proceedings from the jury box. They would be able to watch Hightower's face as the harshest sentence the state could impose was ordered. Some were angry, some shed tears, but all were glad that the awful ordeal was about over.

The prisoner sat without so much as a twitch on his face throughout a one-hour session in which Bob George acknowledged the futility of further argument. "When you are in this deep a hole, it's hard to argue," George told Judge Sheehan. Still, he asked for the judge to be lenient and not make the life sentences consecutive. Hightower, wearing his trademark white turtleneck and olive suit, showed no sign of remorse. He was sticking with his story to the last.

Before pronouncing his sentence, Sheehan gave each of the victims' relatives an opportunity to address the court, and their comments showed not a shred of sympathy for the convicted man who sat at a table about fifteen feet away from them and not only avoided their eyes, but seemed to shut out their words. Indeed, he seemed almost to be somewhere else.

"Christopher Hightower will always haunt my sleep and the dark corners of empty rooms," Christine Scriabine said. "I know now that I have met evil eye-to-eye. It hides under the cover of banality and covers its trail with deceit. Auschwitz, Cambodia, Bosnia, and the gulag are no longer mysteries. Christopher Hightower deserves no mercy."

Susanne Pandich, Ernie's other sister, described how her daughter, the same age of her good pal Emily, "has lost her innocence and learned there is unspeakable evil in the world." Hightower ignored her when she turned from the podium to stare at him, tears brimming in her eyes. "He's poisoned my life with hate. I have never hated anyone the way I hate this man," she declared.

Donald Bobb, Alice's brother, said he mourns her death every day, and particularly "the cruel and horrible circumstances under which she died." Bobb described Emily as "a precious child" and said, "Nothing has so affected my family as Emily's cruel death.

"To say that Hightower is evil and depraved understates the case. His personal culpability is obvious, and he manifestly deserves permanent separation from civilized society."

Fred Bobb was back from Florida for the final day, still recalling the launch of the space shuttle *Discovery* the previous night, when it carved its fiery way into orbit. The launch had reminded him of Titusville, Titusville had reminded him of Hightower, Hightower had reminded him of Emily. Fred Bobb glared at Hightower with undisguised contempt, hoping the murderer would look at him. But the bully was a coward and kept his eyes glued to the table. Bobb taunted him: "Mr. Hightower, I want to use your words. How can anybody kill a child?"

The judge gave them all the time they needed, and when they were through, he allowed Hightower an opportunity to speak. The convicted murderer rose, as if to address a class of particularly awkward students, buttoned his suit coat and folded his hands before him. His remarks were addressed directly to Sheehan.

"I also experience the nightmares of the deaths of these people every single night. Their deaths are certainly a tragedy," he said. But he still stuck by his story, adding that the real tragedy was the four Mafia killers were "running free," and he predicted, "At some point, these people are going to kill again."

Sheehan adjusted his glasses and the sleeves of his black robe, then leaned forward to address the defendant, saying that his task today was simple. He loosed his Irish wrath upon Hightower, whom he said had not indicated "one iota of remorse" during the long trial.

"To hold those two women in that house while their father was dead, and causing the mother to make that phone call to cover up, was the most basic evil I have seen in my career, and I hope never to see it again," the judge barked.

"I have never in my entire career seen such abhorrent evil as this. You deserve life without parole, and I intend to give you life without parole."

It marked only the seventh time that the maximum sentence had been handed down in Rhode Island. Not only did Sheehan make good on his words, he ignored George's plea for leniency and ordered that the two life terms without parole would run consecutively.

As five marshals formed a circle around Hightower and took him out of the courtroom, starting his journey back to a lonely prison cell, Hightower did not look over at Susan. Had he done so, he would have seen his ex-wife break into a grin and happily give her mother a big hug.

Afterward, Susan finally broke her silence. Appearing before a television camera, she calmly spoke the only public words she had issued in months. "This has been a very, very difficult two years for me, and for the family, for the town," she said.

Asked about the severity of the sentence, she told a reporter, "It was the only sentence there was" under current law to fit the crime.

"I came here because I needed to see the closing so I can heal, and so I can tell my children I was there when they ask."

Epilogue

There was not so much an end as a final turning point in this complex story. The horrible events unleashed by Christopher Hightower left indelible marks upon everyone who came in contact with him. They seemed to have a dual need to see Hightower behind prison walls for the rest of his life and to return to normalcy. The second could not be realized until the first was accomplished.

The entire state of Rhode Island seemed to breathe a sigh of relief when Judge Sheehan pronounced the final sentencing, appropriately just as the first touches of a beautiful spring chased away the snow and cold of winter. All those who had been glued to their television sets and gobbled up newspaper accounts of the long trial could now dismiss the cruel Hightower to the prison system and get on with their own lives. Despite his protests that the killers of the Brendel family were still on the loose, few people could believe him.

The end of the trial brought at least a temporary end to the turmoil that had engulfed the picturesque village of Barrington. Families could gather again and talk of other things, and children were not so morbidly fascinated by the big, empty house at 51 Middle Highway, which sat empty, the white paint peeling away in great shreds. Even so, the place had assumed a haunted quality.

Several renters went through brief leases there, including an FBI agent who was ordered by his superiors to find other lodging. Others who tried living there decided to move because of the continual traffic of gawkers and people yelling wisecracks from passing cars. The Brendel house and property was appraised at $185,000, but because of its reputation, an asking price of only $165,000 was posted. The estate received an offer of $160,000 from an out-of-state family, who withdrew after visiting Barrington and learning of the bleak history of the home. The property was eventually sold at a substantial financial loss.

Susan Slicker and her children, with new last names to rid themselves of Hightower, remained with her parents at 1 Jones Circle, slowly putting their lives back together. "She was determined that she was not going to sacrifice her entire life for this," a friend observed after meeting Sue in a beauty salon, where she read a magazine, had her hair done, and talked with old friends. The boys continued their classes at Nyatt Elementary, near their home, and each passing day put them further away from the nightmare that their father had visited upon them. Too young to understand the full enormity of the crime, they have begun asking more questions. The primary goal of their mother and grandparents is to keep the children's lives as normal as possible.

The key to the family's passage has been the extraordinary support by the community of Barrington and their friends at the White Church. They were accepted without reservation during the long months before the justice system finally put Hightower out of their midst forever. The Slickers and their daughters, Susan and Kathy, are true residents of Barrington, and that lifetime membership in the community provided a comforting shield.

Hightower was taken from court to prison, where he began serving some hard time for threatening his Lynxletter pal, Mike Giroux, and a prison guard. Even when that punishment tour was done, he was confined to a solitary cell for twenty-three hours of every day.

Detective Sergeant Jim Lynch of the Rhode Island State Police had commented before the trial was over that Hightower "was going to have a rough time. The prisoners hate him, the guards hate him." Lynch was correct. Shortly after Hightower was sentenced, while playing chess in the prison dayroom during the one hour a day that he was out of his cell, fellow convict Stanley Ostrowski, doing fourteen years for robbery, swatted Hightower in the back of the head with a broom handle. Hightower was taken to the infirmary for stitches and Ostrowski was given an extra thirty days at the end of his own sentence, a mild punishment for what might have been considered attempted murder in the outside world.

Hightower said that he feared for his life at the Adult Correctional Institutions, and asked to be transferred to a prison in Oklahoma, where his sister and her husband live. Rhode Island authorities eventually traded him to Illinois for one of that state's violent felons, and Hightower was sent to the notorious prison in Joliet, Illinois.

Bob George has distanced himself from his former client, without so much as a telephone conversation with him since the end of the trial. Hightower obviously could not afford an attorney to represent him, and private attorneys, knowing the history of the case, did not volunteer for the long and costly appeals process. The court needed almost a year to persuade a public defender to take the job. Even so, Hightower may well become his own lawyer, scratching out his appeals from law books in the prison library. In prison he spends his few free hours playing basketball, working out with weights, and being frustrated that he, a fanatic about being clean, cannot shower when he wants.

If a poll were taken among the relatives of Alice, Ernie, and Emily Brendel, there would be a unanimous verdict that the death penalty should be restored in Rhode Island and Hightower should be executed. That will not happen, but the feeling was expressed repeatedly not only by family members, but by dozens of people interviewed for this book. Hightower, to them, was the classic villain, and his ability to threaten people while incarcerated was frightening. The relatives had been on an emotional roller coaster for so long that, with the final sentencing, there was a sense of relief that they too could start putting their lives back together.

One interesting point was that although Barrington went to great lengths to provide psychologists and psychiatrists to help the kids and townspeople through the Hightower trauma, there was a general sense that most of that professional help was neither needed nor wanted. The village had an inner strength, born of ancient ties to the land and a strong heritage of stubborn determination that helped its residents ride out the storm, depending on themselves, their friends, and their neighbors for support. In the end, as horrible as he is, Christopher Hightower will be nothing more than a footnote in Barrington's library files.

The prosecution team and the myriad people who supported them during the investigation and trial forged a bond of friendship that has outlasted the actual days they spent together. Gary Palumbo described it as a "sort of magnetic force" that welds them together, with Hightower the common link. There is a sense of mutual admiration and pride that they put away such a vicious person, and that, at least in this case, the system worked. As the post-trial months passed, they all watched in dismay as their beloved Boston Red Sox went into the usual swoon by the end of the baseball season, but delighted in a new game being played by those closely involved with the case—Hightower Trivia, in which a name is tossed out and the players have to guess who the person is and their role in the case. The betting is usually on Mike Stone to be the winner.

To have gained the trust of so many people involved in this tragic case was a total surprise for this author. It seemed as though the sources *wanted* and *needed* to speak of what happened to verbally sort it out, to solve the puzzle and get beyond it.

Nobody walked away from this case unchanged either by Hightower's calculated evil or the innocence of Emily Brendel and her parents. We all now carry a little touch of Emily with us, probably forever, and that is not a bad thing.

The murders never should have happened, but there was absolutely nothing anyone could have done to stop them. In retrospect, everyone understands that and, correctly, no one blames themselves for a step not taken, for doing something that might have changed things. Once events began to unroll, there was nothing that could be done to stop Hightower. As the saying goes, sometimes bad things happen to good people.

Perhaps things have come full circle. Peace has been restored to Barrington, the Brendels are at rest with a proper burial, Hightower will spend the rest of his life in prison, and time will work its healing magic on the relatives of both families.

A final footnote provides the ultimate symbolism of both stability and change. Susan Slicker has become a Sunday-school teacher at the White Church.